HENRY ROTH

The Man And His Work

by

BONNIE LYONS

NEW YORK

COOPER SQUARE PUBLISHERS, INC.

1976

Published 1976 by Cooper Square Publishers, Inc.
59 Fourth Avenue, New York, N. Y. 10003

Library of Congress Cataloging in Publication Data

Lyons, Bonnie.
Henry Roth, the man and his work.
Bibliography: p.
Includes index.
1. Roth, Henry—Criticism and interpretation.
I. Title.
PS3535.0783Z78 813'.5'2 76-29874
ISBN 0-8154-0516-2

Printed in the United States of America
by Sentry Press, Inc., New York, N. Y. 10013

INTRODUCTION

To criticise is to appreciate, to appropriate, to take intellectual possession, to establish in fine a relation with the criticised thing and make it one's own.

—Henry James

Walter Allen described Henry Roth's novel *Call It Sleep* as one of "the great achievements in American writing this century."[1] This book grew out of my belief that Allen's judgment is accurate. *Call It Sleep* is an elaborate, densely-wrought novel which demands the close scrutiny usually given to poetry: the organic symbolic structure, complex interweaving of motifs, wide variety of narrative techniques, and subtle exploitation of language and dialect all deserve careful critical attention.

Call It Sleep has yet to receive this close study for two reasons. First, much interest has focused on the fascinating publishing history of *Call It Sleep* and on Roth's life itself. Published in 1934, the novel received generally excellent reviews and sold well considering the times. But then the novel—and Henry Roth—disappeared from view. Reissued twenty-six years later in 1960, *Call It Sleep* reawakened critical notice and almost one million copies of a paperback edition have been sold. The neglect and obscurity followed by critical acclaim and wide readership suggest a literary Cinderella story.

Likewise, Roth's life—including his unusual careers as precision tool grinder, state hospital attendant, and poultry farmer—is certainly striking. What happened to Henry Roth after *Call It Sleep?* Why did he never finish and publish another novel? The multiple causes of Roth's relative silence after the publication of *Call It Sleep* in 1934 include complex personal circumstances, especially a ten-year affair with Eda Lou Walton, as well as his reaction to the atmosphere of the Thirties.

[1] Walter Allen, *The Modern Novel in Britain and the United States* (New York: Dutton, 1965), p. 175.

Actually, the attention to Roth's life is not without usefulness as an approach to his work, because from his earliest essay in 1925 until his most recent published story in 1969, Roth has drawn upon his own experiences and reflections as the raw material for his fiction. In fact, his abandonment of an autobiographical focus in his second novel is one reason for his failure to complete it. Moreover, certain life-long preoccupations—his highly-charged relationship to his father and to Judaism—are dominant themes in his work.

The second reason *Call It Sleep* has yet to receive the critical attention—and acclaim—it deserves is the limiting nature of some of the criticism written about the novel. By calling the novel a great "proletarian," "Joycean," "immigrant," or "Jewish" novel, critics have denied *Call It Sleep* the *sine qua non* of great literature: universality. As my remarks thus far suggest, I believe *Call It Sleep* transcends all limiting categories and is, first and foremost, a great work of art. This is not to say that *Call It Sleep* does not lend itself to a variety of interpretations and classifications, just that it is not subsumed under these categories. *Call It Sleep* is a Joycean novel: Roth took what he learned from *Ulysses* about stream of consciousness and the handling of symbols and motifs and applied this knowledge to his own quite different fictional aims. Likewise, *Call It Sleep* is a profoundly Jewish novel in its language and allusions. Indeed, the Isaiah story and Passover celebration are basic narrative materials which Roth manipulates to describe David Schearl's mystical search.

The little-known extant fragment of Roth's never-completed second novel and his seven published short stories have dual literary interest: they reveal Roth's mastery of the short story form and are thematically closely related to his life and to *Call It Sleep*. Still, *Call It Sleep* is clearly Roth's masterpiece. My contention is that its beauty and intricacy have never been adequately revealed—or appreciated.

I wish to express my thanks to Henry and Muriel Roth, to David Greenhood, and to Howard B. Gotlieb for their cooperation and enthusiasm for my project. I originally offered a version of this book as a dissertation at Tulane University. My dissertation committee members, Professors Richard P. Adams and Donald Pizer, were extremely helpful. I am grateful to my dissertation director, Professor Dale Edmonds, for his unstinting assistance and guidance. Grants from the Tulane University Graduate Student Support Fund and the Woodrow Wilson Foundation helped considerably in the early stages of this work.

ACKNOWLEDGMENTS

Parts of this book were published in somewhat different form in the following journals to whose editors grateful acknowledgment is made.

American Literature: "After *Call It Sleep*" (January, 1974). Copyright 1974 by the Duke University Press.

Contemporary Literature: "The Symbolic Structure of Henry Roth's *Call It Sleep*" (Spring, 1972.

The Explicator: "Roth's *Call It Sleep*" (October, 1974).

Shenandoah: "An Interview with Henry Roth" (Fall, 1973). Copyright 1973 by *Shenandoah,* reprinted from *Shenandoah:* The Washington and Lee University Review with the permission of the Editor.

Studies in Short Fiction: " 'Broker': An Overlooked Story by Henry Roth" (Winter, 1973).

TABLE OF CONTENTS

PUBLISHER'S ERRATA

page 33:
footnote 3—p. 175.
4—p. 159.
9—p. 172.
12—p. 168.
13—p. 168.
15—p. 169.
16—p. 169.
17—p. 168.
20—p. 161.
21—p. 160.
22—p. 160.

page 34:
footnote 27—p. 161.
30—p. 165.
31—p. 160.
32—p. 166.
33—p. 166.
34—p. 162.
36—p. 167.
37—p. 167.
38—p. 167.
39—p. 167.
40—p. 167.
41—pp. 166-167.
43—p. 165.
44—p. 165.
45—p. 165.
46—p. 164.
47—p. 161.
48—p. 161.
49—p. 163.
62—p. 163.
63—p. 166.
65—p. 172.
66—p. 173.
67—p. 173.

page 35:
footnote 69—p. 160.
70—p. 164.
71—p. 172.
75—p. 162.
76—p. 173.
80—p. 163.
81—p. 162.
82—p. 164.
84—p. 175.
100—p. 160.
101—p. 175.

page 36:
footnote 118—p. 175.
120—p. 176.
122—p. 172.
123—p. 176.
124—p. 176.
125—p. 176.

page 64:
footnote 1—p. 169.
6—pp. 169-170.

page 114:
footnote 3—p. 171.
5—p. 169.

page 124:
footnote 3—p. 168.
6—p. 175.
9—p. 168.
10—p. 169.

page 134:
footnote 9—p. 169.
28—p. 174.
29—p. 169.

page 156:
footnote 5—p. 175.
7—p. 168.
19—p. 176.
21—p. 175.

Page 178: Disregard both references listed above: "Other Works consulted.
On page 180, insert under Lyons in the bibliography:

"After *Call It Sleep*." *American Literature,* 45 (Jan. 1974), 610-612.

" 'Broker': An Overlooked Story by Henry Roth." *SSF,* 10 (Winter 1973), 97-98.

"An Interview with Henry Roth." *Shenandoah,* 25 (Fall 1973), 48-71.

"Roth's *Call It Sleep*." *The Explicator,* 33 (Oct. 1974), item 10.

"The Symbolic Structure of Henry Roth's *Call It Sleep*." *Contemporary Literature,* 13 (Spring 1972), 186-203.

PART I

LIFE AND LITERARY CAREER

Henry Roth was born on February 8, 1906, in Tysmenitsa near Lemberg, Galicia (then an Austrian Crownland), to Herman and Leah Roth.[1] Eighteen months later, his mother brought him to this country. Although physically she carried little other than the child, her "mental baggage" was heavy. In this instance, Roth's "real" life is clearly reflected in his art; the familial tension so subtly portrayed in the prologue to *Call It Sleep* parallels the "facts" of his and his mother's arrival in America. Roth's father had gone to America before his wife and child and earned money for their passage to New York. But their arrival was no bright beginning for Herman Roth. As Albert Schearl, the father in *Call It Sleep* bitterly muses over his wife's failure to recognize him: " 'A fine taste of what lies before me!' "[2] so Roth's father already saw the tarnished brassiness of his life in the Golden Land. Before the mother and child arrived, Herman and Leah Roth were already emotionally estranged, for Henry's birth date and paternity were in question, as is that of David Schearl, the novel's protagonist. The seeds of familial discord were already sown; the fruit was to be a deep bitterness between Roth's parents. Their marital relationship deteriorated as the years passed and probably was the precipitating factor in Leah Roth's nervous breakdown.

The parental strife, of course, affected all the family relationships. Leah Roth drew her son ever closer to her, while Herman favored their daughter, Rose, who was born in America two years after Henry's birth.

In addition to the emotional strain of this Oedipal situation, Herman and Leah Roth suffered the more general immigrant problem of adapting to the New World. For Eastern European Jews like Roth's parents, the move to New York meant a move in time as well as place: they left a secure, if stagnant, pastoral village for the chaos, tumult, and anonymity of a modern city.

Unlike Albert Schearl in *Call It Sleep,* Herman Roth was a diminutive man in physical stature, but, at least in his son's eyes, he exuded the ever-impending rage and barely suppressed violence of the fictional figure.

According to Henry Roth, his father was "a most unadmirable little guy" even "a despicable guy"—and the father-son relationship was "never resolved." [3]

Just as Roth increased his father's physical dimensions in *Call It Sleep* to give a sense of the child's fear of his parent's unpredictability and power, he depicted his mother in an artful and not simply biographical way. In *Call It Sleep,* Genya, the mother, is aloof, contemplative, almost regal, while her sister Bertha is talkative, vulgar, and extroverted. Leah Roth possessed both sets of traits and was the source of both fictional characters. Of his use of his mother in the novel, Roth says, "All I had to do was remember Mom in her contemplative moments and she was Genya; in her irritations, anxieties, and angers she was Bertha." [4]

With his immediate family polarized—father and daughter on one side and mother and son on the other—it is not surprising that much of Henry Roth's security derived from the community in which he grew up rather than from his family. The Roth family (like the Schearls) settled down in Brownsville at first, but two years later, in 1910, moved to Ninth Street on the Lower East Side of Manhattan.[5]

Despite poverty, over-crowding, and poor sanitary conditions, the Lower East Side was, in those days, an emotionally satisfying place to live. By this I do not mean to gloss over the appalling physical conditions with false sentimentality, but only to indicate how the Lower East Side differed from the usual ghetto. In *The Other America,* Michael Harrington brilliantly pinpointed the essence of poverty as a mental not physical condition, a state of mind rather than purely a state of physical deprivation:

> If a group has internal vitality, a will—if it has aspiration—it may live in dilapidated housing, it may eat an inadequate diet, and it may suffer poverty, but it is not impoverished. So it was in those ethnic slums of the immigrants that played such a dramatic role in the unfolding of the American dream. The people found themselves in slums, but they were not slum dwellers.[6]

The largely immigrant Jewish population of the Lower East Side was a group such as Harrington described, dwelling in physically substandard conditions, but possessing "internal vitality" and "aspiration."

The characters in *Call It Sleep* also aspire hopefully for a better life. Genya and Luter (Albert's friend and foreman and Genya's secret suitor) discuss the possibility of David's becoming a doctor (p. 41), and Aunt

Bertha and her husband Nathan confidently plan to open a candy store, save money, and then move to a home with "stimm hitt" and modern bathroom facilities (p. 185). Before his break with Luter, even Albert talks of opening a printing shop with his friend: " 'Who knows? A little money. In time I might even suggest to him that we try—Well! In time! In time!' " (p. 32).

The Lower East Side offered the young Henry Roth a sense of belonging, of community. In his own words, he felt "surrounded by a homogeneous environment and . . . completely identified with it." The Jewishness of the Lower East Side was pervasive, and "In that atmosphere of devoutness and orthodoxy it would not have occurred to anyone to question the dietary regulations or the observance of holiday rituals." The Lower East Side, with its sense of communality and shared experience, provided an emotional haven for Roth in his youth, especially since his parental home never provided that protection. When Roth's family left the Lower East Side in 1914, this departure caused a deep anxiety in him and as he says, "produced a shock from which . . . I never recovered." [7]

The reason for the move was that Roth's maternal grandparents as well as four uncles and aunts arrived in America immediately before the outbreak of World War I and settled in Harlem. Leah Roth wanted to be near her family; so in the summer of 1914, she and Herman and their children left the Lower East Side.

Torn from a homogeneous and tightly-knit community, the eight-year-old Henry Roth found himself in a much more cosmopolitan and threatening environment. The Roths "settled at 108 East 119th Street, near the trestle of the New York-New Haven Railroad. This part of the neighborhood, squeezed in between Little Italy to the east and the more prosperous and predominately Jewish area to the west, was considered the poorer part of Harlem. It was a mixture of Irish, Italians, and Jews, and a rough mixture." [8]

The abrupt physical move was also crucial to Roth because his sense of Jewishness and of Jewish identity was severely shaken. At the time his family left the Lower East Side, Roth had not yet reached the stage of translation, or *chumish,* in religious school. Like David Schearl in *Call It Sleep,* he had at this point learned only to pronounce the Hebrew words without understanding their meaning. Thus the move to Harlem was particularly disturbing, for it took Roth from the *cheder* at what he calls "this very sensitive hinge place" or transition period in his religious studies. Translation would have opened up the deeper religious aspects of Judaism to him and, in Roth's words, "would have riveted me to Judaism much more strongly." But Roth felt trapped in an alien, threatening environment in Harlem and "wanted to adapt to this gentile Irish neighborhood in the shortest time possible; and one of the conditions for adapting was to get away from Judaism." [9] Roth's ambivalence about his Jewishness, his feeling of being an outsider in a gentile society, and his fear of rejection by non-Jews are all evoked in his story "Petey and Yotsee and Mario" (*The New Yorker,* July 14, 1956). The narrator of this story tells how he was afraid that the non-Jewish boys who had saved him from drowning would reject his mother's "reward"—a Jewish-style cake.

The religious faith of Roth's parents had never been deeply felt. Partly in reaction to the fanatical orthodoxy of her father, Leah Roth was somewhat "tongue-in-cheek" in her faith. Likewise, although Herman Roth observed some of the more prominent Jewish holidays such as Yom Kippur and Passover, as Roth says, "at the core true devoutness no longer existed." [10] Although nominally observant, Roth's parents did not reinforce their religion at home enough to help their son withstand the anti-Jewish, external pressures he felt impinging on him from outside. At his parents' insistence Roth celebrated his Bar Mitzvah, but the following year, at the age of fourteen, insisted he was an atheist.

The move from the Lower East Side to Harlem, with its dual loss of sense of community and Jewish identification apparently caused serious changes in Roth's personality and development. Before the move, he had been a good student in both public and religious school and enjoyed physical activity and the friendship of other children. But after leaving the secure environment of the Lower East Side, Roth, in reaction, clung to his mother for protection and stayed indoors to avoid hostile contact. He grew fat from lack of activity, earning the nickname "Fatty"—a biographical detail which is reflected in "Petey and Yotsee and Mario" (the first person narrator recalls how the neighborhood children called him "Fat"). Roth's grades in school worsened. After a brief aggressive period in which he fought at school, he simply withdrew into himself. In his own words, as reported by Bronsen, "I retreated into myself and stayed out of other people's way." [11]

One source of pleasure and interest for him during these tense Harlem years was reading. Always attracted to literature with a strong narrative—"any damn yarn"—Roth read "uncritically but voluminously." [12] At about the age of ten, he began to read a sequence of fairy tales which were collected in books with covers of different colors—blue, purple, yellow, etc.

Roth's story "Somebody Always Grabs the Purple" (*The New Yorker,* March 23, 1940) reflects this deep childhood affection for fairy tales. In the story, Sammy Farber (like the author himself, one presumes) persists in his search for a particularly desirable volume in a purple cover despite his mother's sarcasm about the childishness of fairy tales and the librarian's "helpful" suggestions about adventure stories and fiction.

Roth says that fairy tales "had as much influence on my literary style and novelistic structure as anything."[13] The influence of fairy tales on Roth's work is apparent in two ways. First, the gripping narrative line of the fairy tale is apparent in the narrative strength of *Call It Sleep.* Second, fairy tales often embody certain archetypal patterns of initiation, as does *Call It Sleep.* Discussing fairy tales in *Rites and Symbols of Initiation,* Mircea Eliade pointed out that

> the ordeals and adventures of their [fairy tales'] heroes and heroines are almost always translatable into initiatory terms. Now this to me seems of the utmost importance: from the time—which it is so difficult to determine—when fairy tales took shape as such, men both primitive and civilized alike, have listened to them with a pleasure susceptible of indefinite repetition. This amounts to saying that initiatory scenarios—even camouflaged, as they are in fairy tales—are the expression of a psychodrama that answers a deep need in the human being. Every man wants to experience certain perilous situations, to confront exceptional ordeals, to make his way into the Other World—and he experiences all this, on the level of his imaginative life, by hearing or reading fairy tales, or, on the level of his dream life, by dreaming.[14]

The fact that David Schearl's quest in *Call It Sleep* recapitulates archetypal initiation patterns, especially in the climactic chapter, may be partly attributable to Roth's early and deep interest in fairy tales.

Asked about his knowledge of mythology at the time he wrote *Call It Sleep,* Roth observed, "Mythology itself I read as part of the whole fairy tale sequence."[15] Although Roth had read *The Waste Land* and Frazer's *The Golden Bough* by the time he began to write *Call It Sleep,* his primary source of contact with mythological and archetypal materials was his first literary love—the fairy tales themselves.[16]

Over the years, Roth's reading "went all the way from fairy tales to people like Twain and Jack London, to playwrights and Hugo, all the way to Eliot and Joyce."[17]

After graduating from DeWitt Clinton High School in Manhattan in 1924, Roth enrolled in City College of New York. His goal at the time was to become a biology teacher or zoologist. Two events occurred during his freshman year which were to deflect him from his original aim and, indeed, to shape his entire future: his first publication appeared, and he met Eda Lou Walton.

Told by his freshman English teacher to write an expository essay on an experiment or "how to construct something," Roth chose to write a piece about how to install plumbing pipes. The previous summer, before entering college, Roth had been employed as a plumber's helper in the Bronx, installing pipes in newly-constructed two-story wooden buildings. Although the assignment was to write an expository theme, Roth's essay "suddenly . . . turned into an impressionistic piece." At the end of the semester, the instructor returned the class themes and said that one of them "was so good that he would recommend it for publication in the City College *Lavender.*" In Roth's words, "When he mentioned my name, I almost died—and yet again I wasn't *too* surprised." Roth's essay appeared in *The Lavender of* May, 1925. It was for Roth his "first intimation that [he] had something special." [18]

"Impressions of a Plumber" is hardly a major piece. The essay has the special disadvantage of being the product of conflicting aims; in it, Roth attempts to fulfill the instructor's assignment to write an expository essay, while the writer's budding interest in the human, "fictional" elements emerges willy-nilly. Under the pressure of his assignment, Roth dutifully explains the intricacies of "roughing," "corking," and "threading" pipes. But the essay also contains several of Roth's special touches and reveals some of his life-long interests: a firm sense of structure, a clever use of dialogue, and a good "ear" for dialect and speech patterns. Despite the limitations of his assignment, Roth effectively organizes the piece. He describes one day in the life of a plumber's helper, beginning with his reluctant awakening and closing with the wry 5:00 o'clock farewell of Hymie, the master plumber: " 'S'long, kid; anudda day, anudda dollar.' " [19]

In several places in the essay Roth's keen psychological insight is suggested, but the words he uses to embody these thoughts are stilted and the phrasing is awkward. For example, describing how he is unlike the other workmen on the subway, Roth writes: "Grim Toil has graven on their faces his trademark; he hasn't touched me. With them it's all work and one Sunday; with me it's an experiment. They must earn their bread to live, while I think with selfish satisfaction of my father's apparent good health"

(p. 5). The ideas implicit here far outdistance their expression; the wordiness and stilted language ("Grim Toil") reveal the author's youth.

Despite an occasional heavy touch ("the vernacular of my uncouth mentor") and coy spelling ("altho" and "thru"), the piece has certain strengths characteristic of Roth's work in general. He offers first evidence of what might be called his "onomatopoeic touch": he suggests the actual sound of the lunch whistle: "Tooooooot!" Also, Roth records the colloquialisms and rough humor of Hymie, the master plumber, with surprising ease. Hymie's ethnic joke about a Negro workman is both well-told in itself and reveals the personality of the teller. In this joke a Negro worker, who had accidently dropped his coat into a sewer ditch, asks for a wire to retrieve it. Hymie remarks: " 'Wot de H--l d'ya want de coat fer . . . its 'n ole coat anyhow, ain't it?' " The Negro replies: " 'Aw . . . I don't give a d--n fer de coat, I got my lunch in it' " (p. 8).

Without pressing too hard, one can see a developing class consciousness in Roth's reflections about the boss who shows up to check on the plumber and his helpers.

> Soon I see the boss' foot reaching down for the next rung. He has never spoken a word of disapproval to me, yet I hope he misses the rung. Why? It's hard to define. He is the boss; I am the laborer. He gets fat contracts, and does nothing but ride around in his Ford, and call down his men, no matter how hard they work. I get 28 dollars a week, which represents the sweat of my body pressed into a solid form. (p. 9)

"Impressions of a Plumber," a minor but interesting piece of juvenilia, did more than give Roth his first intimation that he "had something special." It gave him a D in the course—for whatever else the essay is, it is not a successful piece of exposition.

Roth's college career was, in his words, "full of these incredible seesaws."[20] While he received a D in English his first semester, he received an A the next. He was not outstanding academically in general; his transcript shows 3 A's, 8 B's, 36 C's, 9 D's, and 1 G—for dropping a math course.

Besides his first publication, Roth's freshman year brought him into contact with Eda Lou Walton, a New York University professor and poet. This contact proved crucial to both his personal life and his literary career. Roth met Eda Lou Walton through Lester Winter, an old friend from

DeWitt Clinton days, who was then attending NYU. In Roth's estimation, his friend "was a very, very handsome middle-class boy—polished, worldly, well-groomed—why he latched on to *me* is still a bit of a mystery."[21] Miss Walton, who was Lester Winter's freshman English instructor at NYU, formed a club for aspiring writers; Roth met her at one of these club meetings. Lester Winter was secretary of the club and also Miss Walton's lover. Roth reminisces: "During their relationship, I would tag along. I would be invited—and while they spooned, I read. God, I felt just like a toad!"[22] By 1928 when Roth graduated from CCNY, *he* was living with Eda Lou Walton.

Eda Lou Walton's background could hardly be more different from Roth's. Born in Deming, New Mexico, on January 19, 1894, she was twelve years Roth's senior. Her father, William Bell Walton, a man of Pennsylvania Quaker stock, was one of four Democrats in the Territorial legislature and one of the few in the first New Mexico State Senate. Her mother was the daughter of a prominent Territorial lawyer. While Henry Roth spent his youth in marginal areas of New York City where his father worked as a milkman and waiter, Miss Walton grew up in Silver City, where her father edited a newspaper and served as the president of the Board of Regents of the New Mexico Normal School.[23]

During the years she was studying for her Ph.D. in anthropology at the University of California at Berkeley, Eda Lou also studied poetry under Witter Bynner, who had formed a verse-writing class in the spring of 1919. Bynner described Miss Walton as his "most promising student."[24] In 1919 she won the university's chief honor for student poetry, the Emily Chamberlain Cook Prize. The following year, she completed her doctorate. "Navajo Traditional Poetry, Its Content and Form," the title of her dissertation, reflects her two principal interests—anthropology and poetry.

After teaching for several years in California, Miss Walton moved to New York City to take a job at NYU. During her early years in New York, Miss Walton, according to David Greenhood, "along with several other poets, including Léonie Adams, Louise Bogan, and Genevieve Taggard, carried on a lively association with anthropologists, Ruth Benedict, Margaret Mead, and Edward Sapir, who were earnestly interested in poetry and wrote poems for publication."[25]

In addition to pursuing her studies and translations of Navajo poetry and writing poetry herself, Miss Walton seems to have been an exceptional teacher. According to Roth, she was the only academic in New York at that time who "was really tackling the modern temperament and the modern dilemma." Actively writing poetry herself and friendly with other writers, she invited these poets to read their work at the club she formed. Thus, the atmosphere, unlike that of many collegiate clubs, was "very exciting," and "the students had a chance to see people who had published—in the flesh, so to speak." [26]

When Roth began living with Eda Lou Walton in 1928, he was already emotionally estranged from his family. The fact that he was living with a non-Jewish woman twelve years older than himself perhaps deepened but did not *cause* any breach with his family. Roth reflects that by this time (the beginning of his affair with Eda Lou) "like so many first generation American Jewish youth, I had already come to dissociate from family, Judaism, the whole thing—and to embrace the American scene, the new American attitudes." Moreover, his mother knew of their relationship and, in Roth's ironic words, "I think she approved. She wanted *somebody* to take care of me!" [27]

Eda Lou Walton seems to have been, by nature, someone well-fitted—perhaps driven—"to take care of" other people. In the article from which I have quoted, David Greenhood, her long-time friend, stressed her continuous "current of out-giving." [28] Elsewhere Greenhood observed that although "a frail, little thing" and "a not healthy person," she "mothered everyone including her own mother"; in addition to helping Roth, she "encouraged the meagerest, slimmest sprouting of talent" in others.[29] In Roth's words, she "mothered, initiated, and otherwise befriended young writers, poets, and artists. You might say that she would take on these people who needed strong maternal affection, because she herself had a strong maternal urge." [30]

The compulsive side of her need to mother is perhaps reflected in her unstable sexual life and in her poor health. According to Roth, her affair with Lester Winter "says something about this woman: she was thirty and an instructor and he was a freshman of eighteen—what her insecurity and neuroses were I found out in time in terms of my living with her." [31] Throughout the ten year period that Roth lived with her, Miss Walton suffered from "increasing pain, discomfort from her whole intestinal tract." As her intestinal problems worsened over the years, "she consumed more and more alcohol." [32] As Roth notes, "Maybe again this was counteractive to the neuroticism which expressed itself in her extreme intestinal discomfort."[33]

Although Eda Lou and Roth moved in an active intellectual circle, which included anthropologists such as Constance Rourke and Ruth Benedict and poets such as Hart Crane and Léonie Adams, Roth felt basically isolated as a man and as an artist. The world of his childhood and that of his present life were too disparate, too unconnected for him to feel at ease in the present milieu: "I couldn't bridge my background. I was able to speak glibly enough at the cocktail party level, but as far as *digesting* what was going on, especially in the literary world, it just didn't sink in. My whole orientation was to try to understand my own childhood, my own background." [34]

In the summer of 1930, Eda Lou Walton was invited to Peterborough, an art colony; Roth accompanied her and stayed at a nearby inn, where he began to write *Call It Sleep*.[35] The only real writing he had done before he began the novel was "Impressions of a Plumber," and the leap from that slight, boyish essay to the full-blown achievement of *Call It Sleep* is one of the most extraordinary facts of Roth's literary career.

As with "Impressions of a Plumber," Roth began writing the novel in the first person, as a straight autobiography, and "slavishly kept to the facts for about 75 pages." But just as the more literary and impressionistic aspects of "Impressions" emerged in spite of his "assignment," here the impulse to fiction and significant form became insistent. That is, while Roth diligently pursued the "facts" of his life "other fancies, ideas, and notions were taking hold" of him which "weren't true." [36] The inevitable conflict between fiction and autobiography, between form and fact, became extremely intense, and he stopped writing.

His "fabricating side" eventually conquered his original autobiographical impulses, and Roth spent the next two weeks outlining furiously. Writing in pencil in little blue examination booklets which were readily available in Eda Lou's apartment, he not only outlined the events of various chapters, but also consciously decided to focus the novel more sharply by transforming real life figures into literary characters. In his words, "That's when I split Mama into two people and Pa had to take on much greater magnitude." [37]

As time went on, Roth modified this original outline and continued to add to it, each time writing "in between" his original notes; thus, in the end, the outline "was some sort of graphology" for he had "written in every conceivable place." While some of these additions and variations pertained to the plot, others indicated places where he "just wanted to replace one word with another." [38]

The fact that the ending of *Call It Sleep* with its deep sense of artistic inevitability was not part of the original plan shows how far Roth moved from what promised to be a loose chronicle to an unusually well-constructed novel. Roth himself says, "I never dreamed I was going to finish still in the childhood of the character." Roth's original plan was to bring the protagonist, David Schearl, at least to adolescence. The triumphant climax of the novel, Roth claims, "came as sort of an artistic accession or assumption into artistry. The whole process of development of the writer took place in *Call It Sleep*—starting from just a straight autobiography"[39] and ending with a highly-structured, consciously shaped work of art.

Although the first major steps—Roth's abandoning the original 75 pages of the novel, then outlining for two weeks—were rapid, the novel developed slowly over a period of three and one-half years. Like the much revised outline, the novel itself was handwritten in pencil in blue books which, Roth remarks, "were good because after you finish one of those eight page jobs, you have a feeling of accomplishment."[40]

Call It Sleep was "actually the product of its own process"[41]—Roth learned how to write a novel by (and while) writing one. As Roth himself became more self-conscious as an artist, more aware of formal problems, he continued to revise and rearrange his material. Financially and emotionally supported by Eda Lou Walton, he spent these years working in a strikingly hermitic way—showing his work to no one. Part of the time he worked in her apartment, part of the time he worked in a studio which she paid for, and he spent one memorable and productive period in Norridgewock, Maine.

Roth went to Maine in the summer of 1932, planning to stay with friends. When this plan fell through, he located a farmhouse, owned by a widow in her seventies, which had a vacant room. During the school year the widow rented the room to a local school teacher, but, since it was summer, she agreed to accept Roth as a boarder. He arrived in June; although he expected to leave by Labor Day, he stayed on through November. For $7.00 a week, he received an excellent room and "the most stupendous meals you can imagine." In addition to working on the novel, Roth did some minor farm chores for exercise. He got along so well with the widow that by the time he left the farm he was "near to adoption,"[42] and the widow told him not to feel that he had to pay—although he did anyhow.

Besides being happy, these months were extremely productive, and Roth returned to New York "about two-thirds of the way through [the novel]."[43] Back in the city, he continued to work steadily, and by late

1933 had his first presentable draft. Early in 1934, he sent *Call It Sleep* to several publishers, including Harcourt, Brace, who turned it down on the grounds that material of this type would not have much market in depression-locked America.

One seemingly minor incident which occurred during the months he spent in Maine might be interpreted as a foreshadowing of some of Roth's problems after *Call It Sleep*. While in Maine, Roth received a letter from Eda Lou telling him that she had met an interesting man in New York. Roth wrote back that "if she had finally found an adult who would take care of her, she ought to go ahead and marry him." Although at the time Roth believed his reply to be an act of self-abnegation, he subsequently recognized that what he was doing was "blindly trying to rescue"[44] himself from a psychologically dangerous situation: his extreme emotional and financial dependence on Eda Lou was keeping him from developing fully as an adult. Although they did not separate at this time, emotional problems which became pressing a few years later were already apparent.

The emotional atmosphere surrounding Roth during the years he was writing *Call It Sleep* and underlying the circumstances of its publication were complex and sometimes most ironic. The circumstances of the publication of *Call It Sleep* by Robert O. Ballou Publishing Company are a case in point. David Mandel, who later was to marry Eda Lou Walton, was her lover during part of the time Roth was living with her. Roth knew about the situation, and in his words, "It became a kind of *ménage à trois*. This probably didn't help my ego either even though I said 'What can I do?' at the moment. It also seems to me an indication of a moral breakdown—not in the sense of puritanism—but of moral fiber."[45] On the one hand, Mandel's liaison with Eda Lou Walton was emotionally disturbing to Roth; on the other hand, Mandel was instrumental in having Roth's novel published. Mandel was a partner in Ballou, and Eda Lou pressured him to publish *Call It Sleep*.

Similarly, Roth's financial dependence on Eda Lou was both essential to the production of *Call It Sleep* and emotionally taxing to its author. Most of the novel was written during the Depression years when, as Roth puts it, "there were breadlines without end, souplines, people living in hovels, shacks made out of tin and cardboard, and literally scrounging out an existence from garbage cans." Coming from a poor family himself, Roth would not have been able to spend these years completely absorbed in writing his novel without Eda Lou's assistance: he acknowledges that he "could not have written *Call It Sleep* without her generosity." On the other hand, this financial cushioning was psychologically detrimental. It filled him with intense guilt feelings about the poverty around him and kept him from feeling self-sufficient. Although he did not live luxuriously during these Depression years, Roth was comfortable, "even to the extent of having a studio and having all the time at [his] disposal for writing, rewriting, experimenting, wiping out experiments." [46]

One way Roth's guilt expressed itself was that in 1933 he joined the Communist Party. Although she herself became politically active several years later, Eda Lou Walton opposed what she thought was Roth's "premature politicalization," and "thought it was [his] finish as a writer." [47] Roth himself observes that his joining the Party was both "sentimental" and "Procrustean, trying to force life into this class polarity" [48] which he himself did not truly accept. His membership in the Community Party temporarily assuaged his guilt about living comfortably in the midst of poverty and filled the tremendous gap (loss of sense of community and of Jewish identification) that had been left in Roth's life when his family moved from the Lower East Side nineteen years earlier. Like many other Jews who had lost their religious faith and thus "lacked the larger thing with which to identify," Roth in these years saw Communism as an opportunity for "a re-entry into the people as a whole." [49]

When *Call It Sleep* appeared in December, 1934, the critical reception was, in general, extremely favorable, especially for a first novel. And, considering the times, the novel sold well, going through a first edition of 1,500 copies and a second of 2,500. One example of the acclaim the novel received is a review entitled "A Great Novel about Manhattan Boyhood" which appeared in *New York Herald Tribune Books*. In this appraisal, Fred T. Marsh commented: "I believe it [the novel] to be the most compelling and moving, the most accurate and profound study of an American slum childhood that has yet appeared." Marsh called the novel "a work of superior craftsmanship, more than that a work of significance, authority and depth"; and he praised the "detachment and universality of the artist." Marsh said he hoped the novel would win the Pulitzer Prize and predicted —alas, wrongly—that *Call It Sleep* would be "remembered for some time to come" for "its profound intensity, its rare virtuousity, its sensitive realism, its sheer weight, its power, circumference, and depth." [50]

Particularly impressed by Roth's remarkable handling of language in the novel, Horace Gregory commented in *The Nation* that *Call It Sleep* is a "first novel of extraordinary character," and added that, although "it will not fall readily into the classification of 'proletarian' novel," it reveals "more of the actual conditions of living in New York's East Side than any other book I have ever read." Gregory concluded that reading *Call It Sleep* is "an experience which few readers of contemporary fiction can afford to ignore."[51] In a similar vein, Paul Wren in *The New Republic* remarked on the novel's "palpable truth and balanced density,"[52] and Lewis Gannett thought *Call It Sleep* suggestive of "the great Russians."[53]

The only adverse criticism which the novel received was for its frank language and sexual descriptions. Even Fred T. Marsh, who praised the novel so highly, felt compelled to defend its language and frankness in dealing with sex: "Neither the language nor the license in physical, including sexual, details are dragged in for the sake of virtuosity." Anticipating an outcry against the cursing and alleged "obscenity" in the novel, Marsh perhaps sought to disarm the sanctimonious by observing: "Expressions used here will shock only because they appear in print. If one had never heard of them he would not know what they meant."[54]

H. W. Boynton began his review of the novel in *The New York Times* by commenting that "we are spared nothing of what he [David Schearl] hears and sees" and that "the book lays all possible stress on the nastiness of the human animal." Boynton bemoaned the fact that such sordidness was "the fashion" and that he and his readers "must make the best of a spectacle of a fine book deliberately and as it were doggedly smeared with verbal filthiness." But after questioning whether the world had "arrived once more at the phase of decadence . . . which makes a cult of the excremental," Boynton was forced to concede that *Call It Sleep,* because of its sheer art, survived his indictments; ironically he closed the review with grudging praise by saying that the climactic chapter is "so strongly colored and firmly woven that you find yourself conceding against all qualms the rightness as well as (you would have said) unspeakable grossness of its human ingredients."[55]

On the whole, the liberal press gave *Call It Sleep* remarkably laudatory reviews; what is especially noteworthy is the wide variety of things the critics found to praise, including its realism, vision, use of language, characterization, and plot. But the novel received quite a different reception in the Communist press. In an unsigned, one paragraph review in the *New Masses, Call It Sleep* was attacked, among other things, for being too long "by at least two hundred pages," for displaying a sensibility which "often degenerates into impressionism on the rampage," for the "vile" spelling of the dialects, and for over-emphasizing "the sex phobias of this six year old Proust." The anonymous reviewer haughtily concluded: "It is a pity that so many young writers drawn from the proletariat can make no better use of their working class experience than as material for introspective and febrile novels."[56]

This supercilious dismissal of the novel did not go unanswered by other left-wing sympathizers. But even more significant than the pro-Roth outcry that the *New Masses* review caused is the fact that each of the advocates of the novel felt called upon to defend the novel in *political* terms. The *sine qua non* of each review was Roth's or the novel's political acceptability. One week after the original review, the *New Masses* printed a letter by David Greenhood criticizing the anonymous review and defending the novel for its literary merit: "*Call It Sleep* . . . has perhaps fewer first-novel defects than any early-life studies which have been offered in quite a blue moon. This book gets under the skin as no other East Side novel I've ever read does and the reason is that Roth instinctively works deep." However, the real basis of Greenhood's claims for the novel's worthiness is political: "*Call It Sleep* is about the working-class bottom, written by one of its own naturals who became articulate long before he wrote the novel, and who while he wrote it was engaged, as he has never ceased to be, in the one struggle that counts."[57] That is, in Greenhood's view, the novel deserved better treatment because of Roth's political views and the novel's working-class milieu.

The following week, the *New Masses* printed two more letters in defense of *Call It Sleep*. In one, Kenneth Burke observed that he thought "Roth caught with considerable sympathy and humor, the 'pre-political' thinking of childhood, the stage of development wherein we follow much the same patterns of magic as Frazer outlines in *The Golden Bough*." He concluded that,

> insofar as the propaganda of Communists is an attempt to give the people new meanings, I think that Communist critics should show special concern for such a book as Roth's, which deals fluently with the psychological phenomena of orientation and "rebirth." And insofar as children *are* pre-political savages, living in a world of symbolism and magic, I question whether any realistic philosophy could properly condemn a writer for reviving such a picture of childhood.[58]

In the other letter, Alvah C. Brothers suggested that the *New Masses* publish another review of the novel in light of its "lengthy treatment in the bourgeois journals." Apparently suspicious of these favorable reviews in bourgeois magazines, he wondered "why this work by a proletarian author who is so closely associated with the revolutionary movement has been so generously welcomed by the bourgeois critics." [59]

Finally on March 5, the *New Masses* printed an essay, "Caesar or Nothing," in which Edwin Seaver not only defended the novel but asserted that the original negative review of *Call It Sleep* was symptomatic and indicative of the weaknesses of leftist criticism in general. He caustically observed that, "from this infantile disorder of leftism, this romantic demand for Caesar or nothing, derives that schematism whose alternative names are dogmatism and sterility." Seaver commented that such thinking caused Communist critics to deduce truths which were not in the literary works themselves and (as the case of *Call It Sleep*) to attack books for failing to bring out certain desired truths. Ironically, Seaver himself then went on to defend Roth's novel on the grounds that it dealt with a "pre-political period of our history"—much as Burke defended it as dealing with a "pre-political" stage of individual human life:

> What better use could Roth have made of his working-class experience as a child than to have shown honestly and greatly exactly what that experience consisted of? Should little David Schearl have joined the Young Pioneers, a non-existent organization? Should David's working-class father have been a Socialist when he was not? Should the author himself have played Jehovah and moved history to satisfy his critics?

Seaver concluded: "When we close the book we honestly feel that such a childhood can mature into a revolutionary manhood." [60]

Ironically, even Eda Lou Walton apparently saw *Call It Sleep* in sociological or "proletarian" terms. In an essay printed in 1936 (by which time she was politically active), Miss Walton asserted that Roth, along with Farrell, Dahlberg, Halper, Conroy, Cantwell, and Caldwell, were "definitely attacking our economic set-up" in their writing. While this judgment seems incorrect in its analysis of *Call It Sleep,* Miss Walton's article is noteworthy for its revelations about the seeming inevitability of politicalization in the Thirties. As she described the contemporary scene,

> No one escaped making some decision. Talk was everywhere. Crowds in movie houses, [sic] jeered or clapped political figures. The terror and need of decision became general. Publishers, at the business end of literature, therefore catered to it. Writers tried to direct it. Critics

> spent their time analyzing it. All in all, we are a very long ways removed from the literary activities of 1929.[61]

Besides discovering "a new perspective, a new range of experience" and "a new class of characters," the contemporary novelist, according to Miss Walton, "has returned to describing action." In her words, "The retreat into the study of states of mind, the studies of static pictures of various static states of mind is no longer interesting to us." This last comment does much to explain the *New Masses* reviewer's objection to *Call It Sleep* as being "introspective and febrile."

As Miss Walton's remarks suggest, the literary atmosphere in the Thirties, especially in New York, was intensely political. Even though Roth believed that "the proletarian revolution was the necessary step for establishing a just society,"[62] he never accepted the prevailing Communist slogan of "art as a weapon." In his words, "Life never illuminated itself to me in terms of class struggle. It was just some sort of blob that went in all directions at once. *Call It Sleep* did not illuminate or reflect the massive class struggle that was going on at the time. If the novel exalted anything, it exalted human beings, not the proletariat."[63]

But while Roth did not succumb to the slogans of the period, the prevailing political atmosphere made itself felt in his work in a more subtle way: the fact that Roth chose to focus his second novel on a midwestern American worker who becomes a Communist after being injured in an industrial accident certainly reflects the political preoccupations of the times. Through the Communist Party Roth met a man he planned to use as a model for the protagonist of this second novel:

> The man was a tough, second-generation German-American who had been raised on the streets of Cincinnati and relied on his fists and his physical stamina to cope with life. Being an illiterate, he had acquired almost everything he knew through his own experience. I was attracted to him because he always took pride in being able to defend himself, no matter what happened. . . . Then suddenly this man who had fought and brawled his way through life lost his right hand in an industrial accident. With that came the terrible shock and realization that he was no longer able to fight the world alone. His personal tragedy and the knowledge that he would have to turn to others for help were terrifying blows that hit him at the depth of the Depression and changed his whole outlook on life.[64]

Roth began this second novel in 1935 "after the trauma of *Call It Sleep* had worn off," and he had begun "to get the itch to write again."[65] He carefully gathered material about his character's life, wrote 100-125 pages, and submitted them to Scribner's, which had bought the rights to his second novel from Robert O. Ballou when the latter folded. Maxwell Perkins was extremely impressed with the material submitted, and everything seemed to be going well for Roth. But, as Roth reflects, "This is the irony: as soon as they accepted the first section, I didn't want to write any more."[66] In 1936 a twenty-page opening section of this second novel was published in *Signatures: Work in Progress* (Autumn 1936) under the title "If We Had Bacon." But Roth never completed the novel, and, except for "If We Had Bacon," destroyed all he had written of it several years later.

A highly complex combination of situations contributed to Roth's failure to complete this second novel—a failure which, he says, was crucial. According to him, "My will was gone, broken by this first failure."[67] First, Roth probably should have finished the novel before showing it to anyone. This had been his procedure with *Call It Sleep*, on which he worked for three and one-half years without showing it to anyone except Eda Lou, to whom the novel was dedicated. In fact, David Greenhood, a close friend of Roth's at that time (and now), says that, when *Call It Sleep* was published, he was "astonished by the writing in it," since he, literally, had never seen anything Roth had written before.[68] Roth's showing the fragment to Perkins and publishing "If We Had Bacon"—while seemingly signs of literary progress and success—ironically signaled disaster.

Other aspects of Roth's life in the mid-Thirties probably contributed even more to his failure to complete the second novel. *Call It Sleep* is an autobiographical novel in which Roth used memories and impressions of his own childhood. Roth himself observes, "At the time I wrote *Call It Sleep* I thought I was honestly portraying my childhood. I think this is one of the things which gives the novel its strength."[69] But while the autobiographical veracity does give *Call It Sleep* a special convincingness, a special sense of reality, it also is the basis of an artistic problem: how to go on to write another, presumably less subjective, novel.

This quite common "second novel" problem was compounded for Roth by the fact that, in his own analysis, "I apparently belong to that category of writer who has to write about the stages of his own development and then when he does it, he is ready to go on to the next stage."[70] By not writing about the next stage in his life, the adolescent years, and, instead, trying to write about a midwestern worker who becomes a Communist, Roth abandoned his own natural bent, apparently under the influence of the current *Weltanschauung*. Roth remarks:

> Now here is where the Party must have had its influence—because I now felt that I wanted to break away from an extension of the immigrant East Side Jewish child and do somebody from the American middle west. Now if I hadn't known anything about the Party—I probably would have done the adolescent years, perhaps taking it as far as meeting Eda Lou or consciousness of artistic abilities. Instead I broke away and was going to do the proletariat, right out of the American scene.[71]

Still other facets of Roth's personality and life contributed to his literary problems after *Call It Sleep*. Describing the period during which he wrote *Call It Sleep,* Roth says:

> I finished it when I was 27, and for the three and one-half years up till then I was in a sort of general mystical state. I had a sense about the unifying force of some power I neither knew nor had to bother to know. It was part of having been an Orthodox Jew. I wasn't formally religious anymore, but still the Hebrew uprightness of that orthodoxy was diffused in me. I could see a gleam wherever I looked.[72]

The "mystical state" and "gleam" he saw wherever he looked are deeply present in the novel, and, no doubt, are the underlying source of the extreme potency of the novel. As Roth wrote *Call It Sleep,* he was what may be called a "possessed" artist." In Robert Heilman's view, the "symptoms" of the "possessed artist" are "The sense of largeness that somehow bursts out of the evident construction, the fertility that borders on the excessive and frenzied, the intensity that is not a surrogate for magnanimity, and finally an apprehension of reality so vivid that it seems to slide over into madness."[73] While the works of such writers are probably the deepest and most moving ever written, the cost to the artists is extreme. It is more than coincidental that Malcolm Lowry—the subject of Heilman's article —was, like Roth, essentially a one-novel author.

Because in *Call It Sleep* Roth looked inward and back in time toward his childhood, he was able to live in his own emotionally self-sustaining world. In his words, "Most writers have to rely on their environments to feed them. I didn't then. Something inside fed me."[74] After *Call It Sleep,* Roth was more dependent on his environment to feed him—and he found himself unable to finish his second novel. Roth explains his psychological state after *Call It Sleep:*

> The main reason I think I didn't go on was that I didn't mature. In *Call It Sleep* I stuck with the child, so I didn't have to mature. And I was being supported by Eda Lou, so I didn't have to mature. I think I just failed at maturity, at adulthood.[75]

Even Eda Lou's financial support worked against Roth psychologically: there was no pressing financial need for him to finish the second novel. Of this fact Roth remarks ironically, "If I had been a poor guy and they said, 'Finish another section and you get another $1000' [Scribner's had paid such a sum for the first section], I probably would have knuckled down. But with no necessity, I just fooled around."[76]

Deciding that he had made a mistake in focusing his second novel on a midwestern Communist, Roth abandoned this project and began to write another novel which was to deal with his own adolescence: "This work was to be far more ambitious and of greater scope; in it I would deal with the Jewish intellectual embracing many more elements of the social world."[77]

But, in the wake of his inability to finish the second novel, Roth found himself floundering emotionally and artistically:

> "I wasn't sure of anything anymore. All of a sudden I realized I was capable of loving things I'd always thought I hated. I found I could sympathize with Indians on the warpath as readily as with white settlers, antebellum slave owners with pretty belles on their arms as easily as Negro slaves. I could even imagine myself as a German Nazi, filled with ideals about Deutscher brotherhood, just as easily as an old rabbi with curling sideburns. I no longer had a point of view."[78]

Roth's failure with the second novel proved crucial; he was unable to mold the subsequent novel about his adolescence to his own satisfaction. In his words, "I struggled with both the style and content, getting only so far before again running up against immobility and total frustration."[79] While his faith in his literary ability was collapsing, so was his relationship with Eda Lou. He felt inadequate in both his personal life and his career. "They were very intimately linked: my literary frustration and this feeling of just rotting away in dependency upon her."[80]

During the summer of 1938 Roth went to Yaddo, the artists' colony at Saratoga Springs. While there, he met Muriel Parker, a young composer. As Roth describes their relationship, "It was hardly a romantic love affair. I feel that Muriel just retrieved me in time. I don't think I would have lived long; I just didn't feel like it." [81] After Roth's return to New York City, he and Eda Lou separated. Although he says he "went back for clothes and things like that," as well as to "try to explain," [82] the break was permanent.

The following year Roth and Muriel married and settled in New York, supported largely by WPA and relief. During the next two years Roth tried half-heartedly to write short stories for a living. "Broker" appeared in *The New Yorker* of November 18, 1939; "Somebody Always Grabs the Purple" a year later. When Roth notified the relief agency that he had received $300 for the publication of "Somebody," he was "reclassified as being no longer indigent, and promptly removed from the rolls." [83] Roth now believes that he "probably could have made it as a short story writer if [he] had just persisted." [84] Both of these stories are related to actual incidents in Roth's life. "Broker," which is about a Negro truckdriver with a seemingly accursed truck, developed out of an incident which Roth witnessed and was able to "spin out, embroider." The second published story, "Somebody," has a young protagonist who, like Roth himself as a child, has a passion for fairy tales. Despite this "proof" that he was still able to write and have his work published, Roth recognized that "this particular creative force that had been efficient in *Call It Sleep* was no longer operating to anywhere near the same extent." [85] Writing short stories was for Roth "awfully hard work without that particular feeling and inspiration." Without the inspiration, "writing became just a task," and he told himself "that there might be tasks which would appeal to [him] more." Giving up the attempt to support himself by writing, and even more importantly, giving up the *idea* of himself as a writer, Roth found the possibility of pursuing any semi-literary job distasteful: "Anything remotely touching on my former interest—and that included advertising as well as clerical and office work—was repulsive to me." [86]

Obtaining a steady job as a substitute teacher at Theodore Roosevelt High School in the Bronx, Roth taught until 1940. By that time the world was involved in World War II. Roth learned that additional skilled craftsmen were needed to keep up with the increased volume of war materials and decided to apply his interest in mathematics and become a precision grinder. Exulting that "the pieces of metal were pure abstraction," Roth liked the high precision finishing work.[87]

Although he was pleased by the slow, demanding exactness required for precision grinding, Roth's feeling of intense dissatisfaction with himself for having failed as a writer was transferred to the *scene* of his failure and he "developed a distaste for New York."[88] In 1945 he and his family moved to Cambridge, Massachusetts, and Roth worked in Boston for one and a half years at the same type of job he had done in New York. But while he was economically a member of the working-class, Roth's background and personality kept him an alien in the lower-class environment. By 1945, the Roths had two sons, Jeremy (or Jeb) and Hugh, ages three and one respectively. The older boy developed a stammer, and a doctor suggested a change of environment. As Roth describes the situation,

> "You see, our neighbors were a little different from us. They threw their garbage in the streets and we dumped ours in a can. The men and women drank heavily and we were sober. In addition, the husbands beat their wives regularly and the doctor told us that our son was disturbed by the fact that his parents were different. So we decided to move."[89]

A move to the country seemed like a good idea for his sons; in addition, Roth "wanted to get away from a world [he] had completely failed in." Thus the move represented a further retreat, and escape from his sense of a "terrific failure, a terrific frustration." Looking around for a place to settle, Roth discovered that Maine real estate was extremely cheap. Moreover, memories of the happy and productive months he had spent in Maine in 1932 while writing *Call It Sleep* made it seem a desirable place to settle. With the move Roth was convinced that his whole literary career was over. Feeling that his literary past "no longer had any bearing" on him, he destroyed the fragmentary second and third novels; it seemed to him that saving these manuscripts was "just carrying around a lot of baggage."[90]

Roth sent his family to Montville, Maine, on Memorial Day 1946, the farm having been purchased the previous winter; he joined them on Labor Day. Roth's 110 acre farm, which he bought for $1200, was actually "a ribbon a couple of hundred yards wide and a mile long."[91] During the next few years Roth was busy trying to make a living and rear his sons. For one year he taught in a one-room school house and "nearly went mad before the term was over."[92] All eight grades of the school were jammed into one room, and while Roth tried to teach one grade level, the others would become rowdy, making him feel like "a juggler trying to keep up an illusion of perpetual motion."[93]

At first Roth worked as a psychiatric aide at the Augusta State Hospital, earning $26.70 a week including room and board. Six months later, he was promoted to acting assistant supervisor. He soon asked to be relieved of this position because the increase in pay was not commensurate with the increase in responsibility, and more importantly, because he found himself in sympathy with his underpaid and overworked subordinates.

After leaving the hospital in 1953 (because he saw no real future for himself there,) Roth decided to try to raise waterfowl. Since a brook ran behind his house, he believed that his farm would be a suitable site. With the help of his sons, he began to raise and dress ducks and geese; he "used to winter forty breeders each of ducks and geese in order to have fertile eggs in the spring."[95] Then he would "incubate the eggs and peddle the ducklings and goslings." In addition, he slaughtered geese and ducks for other farmers as well, receiving 50 cents for plucking a goose and $2.00 a pound for goose feathers.

The ingenuity with which Roth developed his waterfowl farming is strikingly revealed in a short article entitled "Equipment for Pennies" that he wrote for *The Magazine of Ducks and Geese* in Fall, 1954. He begins: "If you know what you're after, the local junk yard is one of the most fertile sources of dressing equipment"; he goes on to explain how discarded articles like broken washing machines can be adapted as scalding and waxing equipment.[96]

For Roth the best part of these years was the closeness to his sons that developed during their work together. Describing these Maine years to a friend, Roth comments: "It has been a wonderful place to live and bring up a couple of hardy kids. The only trouble with Maine is that there are only two seasons: winter and the Fourth of July."[97]

The family closeness was especially important to Roth because he had cut himself off from his past in New York and because he felt no real involvement with his neighbors in Maine: "The neighbors are wonderful, practical people, but with them we just talk around the edges of things. For them things don't reverberate."[98] The reverberations Roth continued to feel led him to try to write about his years in Harlem, and "somewhere between 1953 and 1955"[99] he tried to organize this material into a book. "Petey and Yotsee and Mario" was written during this period, but in general Roth felt dissatisfied with his output.

In "Petey," the narrator recalls how in his youth he was saved from drowning by three gentile neighborhood boys. Subsequently the narrator's mother gives the boys a cake as a gesture of thanks, despite her son's fear that they will spurn the Jewish-style baking. The three boys in the story are similar to the three boys in *Call It Sleep* who force David Schearl to push a "sword" into the trolley tracks. There is a striking difference, however. The three boys in the novel are anti-Semitic; those in the story are not. This difference reflects a profound shift in Roth's ideas about himself and his own past. At the time he wrote the novel in 1934, he thought he was "honestly portraying" his childhood. Years later, he decided that "the child is much too innocent, almost completely victimized, passive. It was simply an idealization based on the notion that I was a much finer sensibility than what was around me—so fine that I was being persecuted and victimized."[100] By the time he wrote "Petey" in the mid-Fifties Roth had changed his view of himself as a child:

> I had lots wrong with me to justify antagonism, if not anti-Semitism—kids like everybody else just look for the first handle they can grab. The attitude that I changed—and this was the most difficult one to transform—was from the feeling of being victimized to one where I saw that I was as much to blame, as much an active agent as a passive agent.[101]

In 1956, when Roth turned fifty, he experienced a profound depression: this chronological milestone underlined his failure in his own eyes. The depression he felt was alleviated to some degree in 1957 when he rediscovered his interest in mathematics and began to tutor some of the boys in the neighborhood. Over the next few years, Roth pursued this interest, taking correspondence courses in calculus from the University of Maine and exchanging letters with Professor G. B. Thomas, Jr., a mathematics professor at MIT, whose book Roth was studying. As in all his pursuits—from writing to precision tool-grinding to waterfowl farming—Roth's assiduousness and tenacity in his study of mathematics are apparent. Professor Thomas's letters to Roth include such comments as "Thank you for your suggestion," "I am pleased to have it and will be glad to include it in the next revision," "as usual you are right," and "as usual I am grateful to you for telling me."[102]

While 1956 was a psychologically depressing "milestone" in Roth's life, ironically it also marked the beginning of the rebirth of *Call It Sleep*. Although the novel had not been totally forgotten over the years, 1956 was clearly an important year in its resurrection. That year *The American Scholar* published a special feature entitled "The Most Neglected Books of the Past 25 Years" and invited outstanding scholars and critics to suggest which book of the last quarter of a century they believed was "the most undeservedly neglected." *Call It Sleep* was the only book mentioned more than once.

In describing the virtues of Roth's novel, Alfred Kazin said,

> If you can imagine the patient sensibility of Wordsworth and the unselfconscious honesty of Dreiser brought to the shock of this environment [the Lower East Side] upon the senses, you may have some inkling of the slowness, the patience and the strange inner serenity of this book—as of something won, very far deep within, against the conventional cruelties of modern city life.[103]

Leslie Fiedler, the other critic who chose *Call It Sleep* as his "most neglected book," commented,

> For sheer virtuousity, *Call It Sleep* is hard to best; no one has ever distilled such poetry and wit from the counterpoint between maimed English and the subtle Yiddish of the immigrant. No one has reproduced so sensitively the terror of family life in the imagination of a child caught between two cultures.[104]

In closing, Fiedler asserted that "to let another year go by without reprinting it would be unforgivable." After going virtually unmentioned in literary histories for over twenty years, in 1956 (the same year the Kazin and Fiedler articles appeared in the *The American Scholar*) *Call It Sleep* was acclaimed "the most distinguished single proletarian novel" by Walter B. Rideout in *The Radical Novel in the United States*.[105]

While critics continued to praise the novel highly, the next major event in its strange saga was the serendipitous meeting two years later of the novelist Charles Angoff and Roth's sister, Rose Broder, which Angoff described in *The Rise of American Jewish Literature*:

> In a lecture at the Jewish Community Center in Queens, New York, in 1958, I, as usual when discussing American Jewish writing, spoke

> of *Call It Sleep* and added that its author had not been heard of since and seemed to have vanished. At the end of the lecture a woman approached and told me she was Roth's sister. She gave me his address. I wrote at once, and told others, and thus began one of the strangest revivals in American literary history.[106]

Angoff passed along the information about Roth's whereabouts to Harold U. Ribalow, a critic and anthologist of American Jewish writing, who began corresponding with Roth and visited him in Maine in the summer of 1959. Discussing the possibility of republication of *Call It Sleep,* Ribalow pointed out that Roth's copyright on the novel was about to expire. In Roth's own words, "My obliviousness to the fact shows how divorced I was from literature and writing." [107]

Roth's extraordinary rediscovery by the literary world resulted in an interest in the author as well as his work. Of special interest, naturally, was the question of what happened after *Call It Sleep*—why did Roth never publish another novel? In two short parables which appeared in *Commentary* ("At Times in Flight," July, 1959, and "The Dun Dakotas," August, 1960) Roth addressed himself obliquely to these questions. In "At Times" Roth deals with the summer of 1938, which he spent at Yaddo. The Roth character sees a horse that while warming up for a race seems "at times in flight," destroyed when the race becomes "real." So, too, one might interpret, was Roth's art destroyed by the reality of life. In the second parable, "The Dun Dakotas," Roth considers the problem of his artistic collapse in less personal terms—in relation to the atmosphere of the Thirties. This parable closes on a note of muted hope; an Indian chief who for twenty-five years had stopped an expedition party trying to cross a "waste land," now "motioned them the way of their journey." This hopeful tone, suggesting a reawakening in the author after years at an impasse, parallels chronologically the rebirth of the novel in the same year: Ribalow's efforts on behalf of *Call It Sleep* resulted in its republication in hardback form in 1960 by Cooper Square Publishers.

This edition includes a history of the novel by Ribalow, a critical introduction by Maxwell Geismar, and a personal appreciation by Meyer Levin. Although a beautiful edition, the book did not really receive much notice from the general reading public or from critics until its issuance as a paperback in 1964, thirty years after its original publication.

With its publication in paperback, the novel achieved astonishing popular and critical success. On October 25, 1964, *The New York Times*

Book Review printed a front-page review of the novel by Irving Howe—the first time a paperback reprint had ever been given such coverage. In this extraordinarily laudatory review, Howe asserted that *Call It Sleep* was "a splendid book, one of the few genuinely distinguished novels written by a 20th-century American."[108] Howe closed his review by saying that "at the end of a novel like *Call It Sleep,* one has lived through a completeness of rendered life, and all one need do is silently acknowledge its truth."[109]

The original 1934 edition of the novel went through two editions totaling 4,000 copies; the paperback edition represented a publishing bonanza: a first edition of 25,000 copies, a second of 50,000, a third of 75,000, and a fourth of 100,000, all sold out in the first three weeks. On November 8, 1964, *Call It Sleep* was listed as the best-selling paperback in the country—with Irving Shulman's *Harlow* as number two![110] The incredible success of the paperback astonished not only Roth but his publishers as well. Frank Taylor and Peter Mayer of Avon Books said they brought the paperback out "mostly as a labor of love." Mayer observed: " 'We didn't even think there'd be much profit in it . . . much less that five weeks after it appeared we'd be ordering a sixth printing—nor that after so long we could help make Henry Roth a rich man.' "[111]

The extraordinary publishing history of *Call It Sleep* (for which its title seems so strangely fitting) was the basis of an article entitled "The Belated Success of Henry Roth" published in *Life* on January 8, 1965. With a snowball effect, this article, in turn, increased the novel's sales by bringing it to the attention of a mass audience. The novel is now in its twenty-third printing, and more than one million copies have been sold.

Roth's reaction to this incredible rags to riches saga was, predictably, mixed. In the *Life* article in 1965, he observed: " 'I don't have the kind of temperament that expects to win sweepstakes. . . . Now that it has happened, I don't know what I'll do. It kind of scares me.' "[112] In January 1965, he wrote his father: "Had enough of fame? I have."[113]

Besides completely shaking up his quiet private life, the success undermined Roth's tenuous sense of identity. Interviewed by the local radio station in Maine, he said "You have to re-examine everything you've been in the last thirty years," and added that he felt "almost pushed into a corner."[114] Similarly, in the *Life* article, he commented that he worried that his neighbors might treat him differently and he might "lose the identity it's taken . . . all this time to rebuild."[115]

On March 3, 1965, Roth received a grant for $2,500 from the National Institute of Arts and Letters "in recognition for [his] creative work in literature." His letter of acceptance, written seventeen days later, is worth quoting in detail because it provides insight into Roth's mixed feelings about the re-emergence of *Call It Sleep*—and about himself:

> The grant does two things: it seals off a way of life I have known and been more or less content with for the past nineteen years, longer, twenty-five, from the last time I seriously tried to write. It seals it off simply because, together with the reappearance of *Call It Sleep,* it annuls the necessity and even the internal consistency of that way of life. At the same time it sets a seal of confidence on my resumption of a new way of life based on a performance anteceding the old. Understandably I welcome that confidence, but equally understandably I don't welcome the change. I failed on the ground for which the grant is given. But whether I welcome the one and not the other is immaterial: I can no longer continue to do what I was doing. And that brings me to some indication of what I plan to do: It is, since I know it so well, to examine the literary potential of exactly that situation, that frame of mind, the precarious equilibrium between the welcome and the loath, to see what resolution springs therefrom.[116]

While Roth greeted his success with no small amount of apprehension, he recognized that the money resulting from it brought the freedom and time to write, and the critical acclaim and popularity prodded him to do so. Asked what he intended to do with his royalties, Roth told the Maine radio interviewer in 1965 that he would probably use some of the money for travel. He explained that he "wouldn't be traveling merely to see places," but rather "to attempt to try to document something that was beginning to take shape."[117] Since that time Roth and his wife have traveled extensively in Mexico, Europe, and Israel.

However, Roth's development since 1965 has not followed a path he had foreseen; in his words, "This is interesting—how peculiarly, how concealed, how obscure the individual's drives are from himself."[118] In 1965, when he was in Seville, Roth "felt this strong urge to do something about the Inquisition." His interest in the Spanish persecution of the Jews centuries ago came as a surprise to Roth himself. Since childhood he had not identified himself with Judaism. A comment he made in *Midstream* in 1963 reveals his estrangement from Judaism. He stated that he rejected the Orthodox upbringing he had been given as a child and suggested that American Jews pursue a general cultural ideal, "orienting themselves toward ceasing to be Jews." Although he later repudiated that position in 1963 Roth "thought that assimilation was the only way out for the Jews."[119]

Although Roth never completed the work he was contemplating about the Inquisition, he did publish a story "The Surveyor" *(The New Yorker,* August 6, 1966) in which the central figures are an American couple, very much like Roth and his wife, who try to discover the long-forgotten location of the *quemadero* (where heretics were burned during the Inquisition) and to place a wreath on the spot. Thematically the story explores the Roth-like character's ambiguous, contradictory attitudes toward religious faith and disbelief. In Roth's words, "What I was interested in, as I look back on it now, was trying to find my way back into something related to Judaism. It's like a blind force looking for an outlet."[129]

Roth found the outlet he was seeking two years later, in June, 1967, when the Six-Day War broke out in the Middle East. Living in Guadalajara, Mexico, at the time, he followed the daily events of the war "with great avidity" and found himself "identifying intensely with the Israelis and their military feats."[121] Roth no longer believes in assimilation, although he still does not have any great attachment to Diaspora Judaism.[122] His real Jewish identification is with Israel. In his words, "I don't think of myself as a Zionist exactly—but I think of myself as a partisan of a country. It's like a regeneration process when a person like me can think of patriotism and valor."

The Roths left their Maine farm permanently in 1968, after nineteen years. In the summer of that year, Roth was named the eleventh D. H. Lawrence Fellow at the University of New Mexico. The fellowship paid for a summer at the secluded Lawrence ranch near Taos, which was deeded to the university by Lawrence's widow, Frieda. Apparently delighted with the Southwest, the Roths stayed on in Albuquerque after the fellowship expired. Of his new home, Roth comments: "I just wish I'd come sooner—you can get out more and it's cheerier. In New England, those long, long winters really aid and abet depression. You know the New Englander and his dour ways."[123] In the summer of 1972 the Roths moved to a large two-bedroom mobile home in an old and green section of Albuquerque, where they live with their dog Shiksa (Yiddish for a gentile female—whom the neighbors calle Trixie. Their fourteen foot wide trailer—which does not at all seem like a trailer—contains a Steinway piano and stereo equipment, but no television set. Outside, Roth has built a tool shed from two piano crates, which he calls "Steinway Hall."

The "regeneration process" Roth felt because of his new identification with Israel in 1967 prompted a growing desire to pursue his writing. He began to keep a "continuum" journal of "reminiscences and observations" about his surroundings. For the last three years, however, he has been writing something more formal; he is currently engaged in writing a novel about "the entrance of the young man into consciousness of a literary impulse, a desire to create great art." Not surprisingly, this novel, like all of Roth's work, uses autobiographical materials:

> It brings to bear the peculiar, separate, and yet distinctly related world of the Jews in Harlem—that's the parental, Jewish world—and the world of Greenwich Village and the literary intellectuals. The individual about whom I'm writing is a young man who slowly becomes conscious of his literary tendencies. He is the nexus between the two worlds that never meet. He simply carries it back and forth like a shuttle.[124]

The current work-in-progress, like *Call It Sleep,* like almost all of Roth's work since the first published essay, is an autobiographical knot—one period of his life viewed in the transforming perspective of a later period. Like the earlier works it will undoubtedly have some influence on how Roth views his present life and on the direction he gives his life in the future. A recent comment by Roth on his latest work and on his plans in general is characteristically ironic, self-deprecatory—and open-ended: "I shall finish this particular draft and then go back to it. And God knows what will happen."[125]

NOTES

[1] A duplicate birth certificate Roth recently obtained gives his birthdate as February 8, 1906. In his childhood, confusion arose because his mother used her marriage date, January 10, 1905, as his birthdate, in order to enroll him in school earlier than his age warranted.

[2] Henry Roth, *Call It Sleep* (New York: Avon Books, 1964), p. 14. Subsequent page references to this edition will appear parenthetically in the text.

[3] I interviewed Henry Roth in Albuquerque on October 17 and 18, 1972. An edited version of a transcription of this interview is included as an appendix to this book. Subsequent quotations from the appendix are footnoted as "Appendix," followed by the page number. For the quotation in question, see Appendix, p. 307.

[4] Appendix, p. 276.

[5] David Bronsen, "A Conversation With Henry Roth," *Partisan Review,* 36 (1969), 265.

[6] Michael Harrington, *The Other America: Poverty in the United States* (Baltimore, Maryland: Penguin Books, 1963), p. 17.

[7] All quotations in this paragraph are from Bronsen, pp. 265-266.

[8] Bronsen, p. 266.

[9] All quotations in this paragraph are from the Appendix, pp. 300-301.

[10] Bronsen, p. 264.

[11] All information in this paragraph is from Bronsen, p. 266.

[12] Appendix, p. 293.

[13] Appendix, p. 293.

[14] Mircea Eliade, *Rites and Symbols of Initiation: The Mysteries of Birth and Rebirth,* trans. Willard R. Trask (New York: Harper & Row, 1965), p. 126.

[15] Appendix, p. 295.

[16] Appendix, p. 295.

[17] Appendix, p. 293.

[18] All quotations in this paragraph are from the Appendix, pp. 278-279.

[19] *The Lavender,* p. 9. Subsequent references to "Impressions of a Plumber" are documented in the text by page number.

[20] Appendix, p. 279.

[21] Appendix, p. 278.

[22] Appendix, p. 278.

[23] All information in this paragraph pertaining to Eda Lou Walton's background comes from David Greenhood, "Eda Lou Walton's Use of Her Native Scene," *New Mexico Quarterly,* 33 (1963), 253.

[24] Greenhood, p. 256.

[25] Greenhood, pp. 258-259.

[26] During the interview conducted on October 17 and 18, 1972, Roth made these comments to me; however, they are not included in the edited version, the Appendix.

Hereafter I shall document such material as follows: Interview, October 17 and 18, 1972. Not in Appendix.

[27] Appendix, p. 280.

[28] Greenhood, p. 256.

[29] Greenhood made these comments to me during an interview held on October 18, 1972 in Santa Fe.

[30] Appendix, p. 288.

[31] Appendix, p. 278.

[32] Appendix, p. 289.

[33] Appendix, p. 289.

[34] Appendix, p. 281.

[35] A letter from Roth dated February 18, 1975, corrects his earlier statements that he began *Call It Sleep* in 1929.

[36] All quotations in this paragraph are from the Appendix, p. 291.

[37] Appendix, p. 291.

[38] Appendix, pp. 291-292.

[39] Appendix, p. 292.

[40] Appendix, p. 291.

[41] Appendix, p. 290.

[42] Interview, October 17 and 18, 1972. Not in Appendix.

[43] Appendix, p. 288.

[44] Appendix, p. 288.

[45] Appendix, p. 288.

[46] Appendix, pp. 286-287.

[47] Appendix, p. 280.

[48] Appendix, p. 280.

[49] Appendix, p. 283.

[50] Fred T. Marsh, "A Great Novel about Manhattan Boyhood," *New York Herald Tribune Books,* 17 Feb. 1935, p. 6.

[51] Horace Gregory, "East Side World," *The Nation,* 140 (27 Feb. 1935), 255.

[52] Paul Wren, "Boy in the Ghetto," *The New Republic,* 82 (27 Feb. 1935), 82.

[53] Lewish Gannett, "East Side Boy," *New York Herald Tribune,* 16 February 1935, p. 9.

[54] Marsh, p. 6.

[55] H. W. Boynton, "The Story of a Ghetto Childhood," *The New York Times,* 17 Feb. 1935, p. 7.

[56] "Brief Review," *New Masses,* 14 (12 Feb. 1935), 27.

[57] David Greenhood, "Another View of 'Call It Sleep,'" *New Masses,* 14 (19 Feb. 1935), 21.

[58] Kenneth Burke, "More About Roth's Call It Sleep," *New Masses,* 14 (26 Feb. 1935), 21.

[59] Alvah C. Brothers, "Bourgeois-Critical Exploitation," *New Masses,* 14 (26 Feb. 1935), 21.

[60] Edwin Seaver, "Caesar or Nothing," *New Masses,* 14 (5 March 1935), 20.

[61] Eda Lou Walton, "The Scene in Books Today," *Signatures: Work in Progress,* 1 (1936), n. pag.

[62] Appendix, p. 281.

[63] Appendix, p. 290.

[64] Bronsen, p. 271.

[65] Appendix, p. 302.

[66] Appendix, p. 302.

[67] Appendix, p. 303.

[68] Greenhood made this comment to me during our interview on October 18, 1972.

[69] Appendix, p. 277.

[70] Appendix, p. 285.

[71] Appendix, p. 302.

[72] Jane Howard, "The Belated Success of Henry Roth," *Life,* 53 (8 Jan. 1965), 76.

[73] Robert B. Heilman, "The Possessed Artist and the Ailing Soul," *Canadian Literature,* No. 8 (Spring 1961), p. 8.

[74] Howard, p. 76.

[75] Appendix, p. 282.

[76] Appendix, pp. 302-303.

[77] Bronsen, p. 272.

[78] Howard, p. 76.

[79] Bronsen, p. 273.

[80] Appendix, p. 284.

[81] Appendix, p. 286.

[82] Appendix, p. 282.

[83] Bronsen, p. 275.

[84] Appendix, p. 306.

[85] Roth made these remarks during an interview conducted by radio station WFAU in Augusta, Maine, on January 8, 1965. A tape recording of the interview is part of the Henry Roth Collection at the Boston University Mugar Memorial Library. Further references to this interview are footnoted "WFAU interview."

[86] Bronsen, p. 276.

[87] Howard, p. 75.

[88] Bronsen, p. 276.

[89] Ribalow, p. xxvi.

[90] All the quotations in this paragraph are from the Appendix, p. 303.

[91] Bronsen, p. 276.

[92] Ribalow, p. xxvi.

[93] Bronsen, p. 277.

[94] Bronsen, p. 277.

[95] Bronsen, p. 277.

[96] "Equipment for Pennies," *The Magazine for Ducks and Geese,* Fall 1954, p. 15.

[97] Roth's comments are quoted from a letter to Lillian Kinisberg dated February 14, 1965. This letter is found in the Henry Roth Collection.

[98] Howard, p. 76.

[99] Ribalow, p. xxviii.

[100] Appendix, p. 277.

[101] Appendix, pp. 306-307.

[102] These quotations are from three letters from G. B. Thomas, Jr. to Henry Roth dated April 20, 1961, November 14, 1961, and September 18, 1962. The letters are part of the Henry Roth Collection.

[103] Alfred Kazin, "Neglected Books," *The American Scholar,* 25 (Autumn 1956), 486.

[104] Leslie A. Fiedler, "Neglected Books," *The American Scholar,* 25 (Autumn 1956), 478.

[105] Walter B. Rideout, *The Radical Novel in the United States 1900-1954* (Cambridge: Harvard Univ. Press, 1956), p. 186.

[106] Charles Angoff and Meyer Levin, eds., *The Rise of American Jewish Litera-*

ture: An Anthology of Selections from the Major Novels (New York: Simon and Schuster, 1970), p. 116.

[107] Bronsen, p. 278.

[108] Irving Howe, "Life Never Let Up," *The New York Times Book Review,* 25 Oct. 1964, p. 1.

[109] Howe, p. 61.

[110] Martha MacGregor, "The Week in Books," *New York Post,* 8 Nov. 1964, p. 47.

[111] Howard, p. 75.

[112] Howard, p. 75.

[113] The quotation is from a postcard dated January 17, 1965 from Henry Roth to his father, Herman Roth. The postcard is part of the Henry Roth Collection.

[114] WFAU interview.

[115] Howard, p. 75.

[116] A handwritten copy of the letter is part of the Henry Roth Collection.

[117] WFAU interview.

[118] Appendix, p. 308.

[119] "The Meaning of *Galut* in America Today: A Symposium," *Midstream,* 19 (March 1963), 32-33.

[120] Appendix, p. 308.

[121] Bronsen, p. 278.

[122] Appendix, p. 301.

[123] Appendix, p. 308.

[124] All the quotations in this paragraph are from the Appendix, p. 309.

[125] Appendix, p. 309.

PART II

CALL IT SLEEP: A CLOSE READING

Chapter

CHAPTER I

CELLAR, PICTURE, COAL, AND RAIL: THE SYMBOLIC STRUCTURE

In a letter to the critic Harold Ribalow, Henry Roth once wrote, "There is one theme I like above all others, and that is redemption." [1] Redemption, the underlying theme of Roth's only major work, *Call It Sleep,* is developed in the novel by means of an intricate pattern of symbols. Although the novel is superficially constructed in an episodic manner, certain symbols, specifically cellar, picture, coal, and rail, provide a firm unifying structure, as well as the names of the four books of the novel. Since the symbolism comprises the core of the construction of the novel, an exploration of the meaning and interrelationship of the four major symbols will provide insight into the major themes. I shall discuss the meaning and development of the major symbols in the order of the four books of the novel itself, first "Cellar," followed by "Picture," "Coal," and "Rail."

"Cellar"

A nine-page prologue by an omniscient narrator establishes the emotional patterns which dominate the early life of David Schearl, the protagonist. However, with the opening lines of the first book, "The Cellar," the reader plunges directly into David's mind:

> Standing before the kitchen sink and regarding the bright brass faucets that gleamed so far away, each with a bead of water at its nose, slowly swelling, falling, David again became aware that this world had been created without thought of him. He was thirsty, but the iron hip of the sink rested on legs tall almost as his own body, and by no stretch of arm, no leap, could he ever reach the distant tap. (p. 15)

Having once entered David's mind, the reader rapidly learns that the most profound and general emotion of this child's sensitive mind is terror. Indeed, "Everything he knew frightened him" (p. 137). This all-pervading fear is one of the profound emotional connotations of the cellar, a symbol the multiple meanings and emotional equivalents of which Roth develops throughout the first book of the novel. Walter Allen praised *Call It Sleep* as the "most powerful evocation of the terrors of childhood ever written."[2] The symbol of the cellar provides a major source of the power and depth of this evocation.

At first, David simply connects the cellar with its physical attribute, darkness; for him, "It bulged with darkness" (p. 20). He contrasts the cellar's gloom with the street, where "a dazzling breaker of sunlight burst over his head" (p. 20). David's fear of the cellar is unfocused until he forms other emotional connections with it. His crude neighbor friend tells him " 'Rats on'y come out innuh da'k, w'en yuh can't see 'em, and yuh know we'a dey comin' f'om, dey comin' f'om de cellah. Dot's we'a dey live innuh cellah—all rats' " (p. 49). For David, this hideous revelation confirms his hitherto generalized fears: "The cellar! That explained it. That moment of fear when he turned the bottom landing before he went out into the street. He would be doubly terrified now" (p. 49). Gradually the cellar becomes more than a place of darkness and rats, as David learns to link it with bodily corruption and shameful sexuality. His sexual initiation repels him, and because his "initiator" is crippled, her physical deformity becomes part of his associations with the symbol of the cellar. Moreover, since the sexual activity occurs in a cellar-like place, a dark closet, David makes a direct mental connection between the two places. When the girl drags David into the closet, he senses "darkness, immense and stale, the reek of moth-balls threading it" (p. 53). Even their more innocent sex play displeases him: "His lips touched hers, a muddy spot in vast darkness" (p. 53). When she attempts to persuade him to proceed further, he reacts with extreme revulsion.

This sexual counterpart of the cellar symbol has a particularly profound effect upon the child; he feels his world disintegrating, especially his relationship to his mother, his only source of comfort and security. In his shame after his sexual initiation, he feels alienated even from her: "But she didn't know as he knew how the whole world could break into a thousand pieces, all buzzing, all whining, and no one hearing them and no one seeing them except himself" (p. 55). His terror is both conscious and unconscious; he dreams of " 'a woman with a child who turned loathsome, a crowd of people following a blackbird' " (p. 57).

When David first sees a funeral procession, he does not understand what the black carriages and black box are. However, when he does realize their meaning, he recoils in absolute fear: "That was—! Yes! That was! He suddenly understood. Mama said—Inside! Yes! Man! Inside! His flesh went cold with terror" (p. 61).

In his mind David connects all the abhorrent symbolic equivalents of the cellar, including his own loathsome sexual experience, death, and his fear of Luter, who is Albert's friend and Genya's would-be seducer. The thought of one leads irrevocably to the others:

> His thoughts returned to Luter. He would come again this evening. Why? Why didn't he go away. Would they have to run away every Thursday? Go to Yussie's house? Would he have to play with Annie again? He didn't want to. He never wanted to see her again. And he would have to. The way he did this afternoon beside the carriages. The black carriage with the window. Scared. The long box. Scared. The cellar. No! No! (p. 64)

His thoughts are connected by free association based upon the emotional connotation of the cellar, which symbolically unites all his fears.

Just as David fails to overcome his sexual anxieties and feels estranged from his mother, later his fear of death causes another breach between them. When he asks his mother about death, she reveals her disbelief in an afterlife: "I know only that they are buried in the dark earth and their names last a few more lifetimes on their gravestones" (p. 69). His mother's acceptance of this sad reality is contrasted to his horror: "The dark. In the dark earth. Eternal years. It was a terrible revelation" (p. 69). David's inability or unwillingness to accept the "facts" of human existence foreshadows his subsequent search for transcendent meaning. His mother's attitude underlines David's growing sense of isolation.

David's mind, which moves by associations, especially among physical images, even connects marriage and death, because he sees carriages at both events. For him, "Everything belonged to the same dark. Confetti and coffins" (p. 70). Similarly, David's mind makes intuitive leaps concerning the nature of the universe about him from his own limited experience. His dim awareness of Luter as a negative, potentially dangerous figure focuses when David sees him coming to visit his mother one afternoon: "He knew it! He knew it! That's why he had come. That game! He was going to make her play now. Like Annie. In the closet!" (p. 89). His grief about the sexual corruption of the universe, which is represented by this relationship between Luter and his mother, distracts him from a game he is playing with the neighborhood children. When they subsequently taunt him, he pushes one youngster down and flees. This experience with the neighbor children gives rise to the last and deepest emotional connotation of the cellar for David, that of intense guilt. Believing he has killed his playmate, he flees from his friends and is forced to take refuge in the cellar, the horror of which is now absolute:

> Darkness all about him now, entire and fathomless night. No single ray threaded it, no flake of light drifted through. From the impenetrable depths below, the dull marshy stench of surreptitious decay uncurled against his nostrils. There was no silence here, but if he dared to listen, he could hear tappings and creakings, patterings and whispers, all furtive, all malign. It was horrible, the dark. The rats lived there, the hordes of nightmare, the wobbly faces, the crawling and misshapen things. (p. 92)

Two incidents contrast dramatically with this careful build-up of dark, negative connotations of the cellar. Following his sexual initiation with Annie and his physical recoil from it, David experiences a self-purification in the snow. Just as the central physical attribute of the cellar is darkness, and its emotional connotation to David is filth, the snow represents whiteness, light, and purity. He plunges into the snow, thinking "how miraculously clean it was, all about him, whiter than anything he knew, whiter than anything, whiter" (p. 59). His yearning for something beyond normal experience is manifest in this incident as it was when he recoiled from his mother's explanation of death; he already realizes "Sidewalk snow never stayed white" (p. 59).

Similarly, David's desire for a mystical experience is connected with light and darkness in a second incident in the first book. When his mother tells him about a miracle near her home in Austria where "two peasants saw a light among the trees—yet nothing burning" (p. 120), David is intensely interested and believes in the possibility of such miracles of light, despite his mother's gentle cynicism. These two incidents are connected by their imagery of light, purity, and brightness, and contrast effectively with the physical and emotional darkness of the cellar.

In addition to the cellar, a second set of symbols develops in the first book; the symbolic nature of the three family members is made clear. Maxwell Geismar contended that "In terms of modern psychology, the family trio at the center of *Call It Sleep* is a classic example of the oedipal relation—described so beautifully, so completely, that one realizes that the author, too, wrote this classic fable in all innocence of spirit."[3] Genya, Albert, and David certainly exist as distinct, individual characters, but they are also symbolically the mother, the father, and the child in Freudian terms. The intense sexual charge of the mother-son relationship is apparent from the opening pages: Genya lifts David into her arms "with a throaty chuckle" (p. 18). As his sexual knowledge develops, "a new sense of shyness invaded him" (p. 86) and he is ashamed for her to see him undressed. Likewise, when he begins to realize that she is attractive to him as a sexual object, his reaction is guilt: "The shadow between her breasts, how deep! How far it—No! No! Luter! When he looked! That night! Mustn't! Mustn't! Look away! Quick!" (p. 64). When the neighbor boys furtively spy on his mother while she is taking a bath, David's reaction is direct and sexual, like that of a lover: *"She! Mine! Aaa, mine!"* (p. 294).

Similarly, the father is described as immensely powerful and dangerous, fearful to the son: "David often dreamed of his father's footsteps booming on the stairs, of the glistening door knob turning, and of himself clutching at knives he couldn't lift from the table" (p. 22). David's primordial fear magnifies his father into a god of wrath: "I saw my father lift a hammer; he was standing on a high roof of darkness, and below him were faces uplifted, so many, they stretched like white cobbles to the end of the world" (p. 28). The symbolic connection of the father with darkness and the victims with whiteness echoes the imagery of the cellar and the snow.

The son's sexual jealousy of the father is made explicit later in the novel when David sees him partially undressed: "Strong, how strong his father was, stronger than he'd ever be. A twinge of envy and despair ran through him" (p. 177). David believes "No, he'd never be that strong, and yet he had to be, he had to be. He didn't know why, but he had to be!" (p. 177).

"Picture"

In Book II, the action and thematic development are governed by the controlling symbol of a picture of a field with corn flowers growing, which is symbolic of David's mother's past in Austria. On a narrative level, the arrival of David's maternal aunt from Europe parallels this concern with the past. Unlike the cellar, the symbolic meanings of which are significant only to David's mind and fears, the picture has immense importance for the other characters as well, particularly his mother. Indeed, it is the other characters' concern about the picture and about the past that shapes David's reaction to these things. Moreover, unlike the cellar, the emotional meanings of which were various but all negative, the meaning of the picture is much more ambiguous, containing both negative and positive aspects.

In Book I, David's reaction to the past in Europe is one of "warm, nostalgic mournfulness" (p. 23). His mother too seems to long for the green and quiet of old Europe as opposed to the noisy, hectic city life of New York. Their gentle longing is in direct opposition to Aunt Bertha's hilariously vulgar conclusion about their village: "Veljish was still as a fart in company. Who could endure it? Trees! Fields! Again trees! Who can talk to trees?" (p. 153).

In Book II, the suddenness of Aunt Bertha's appearance in the Schearl home is paralleled by Genya's surprising purchase of a picture from a pushcart. David's initial reaction to the picture is neutral and unemotional. For him it is only "a picture of a small patch of ground full of tall green stalks, at the foot of which, tiny blue flowers grow" (p. 172). Genya reacts intensely to the picture: "David had hardly ever seen his mother so animated, so gay before" (p. 172). Furthermore, although David's first reaction is noncommittal, later "he began to wonder vaguely why it had followed him all afternoon, why it had tugged at the mind from the ambush of the mind" (p. 188). Just as Genya's and Bertha's reactions to their village differ radically, so do their opinions about the value of the picture. Aunt Bertha sarcastically asks Genya, " 'Are you starting a museum?' " (p. 187). Similarly, Albert's reaction to the picture directly reflects his attitude toward the past. He comments, " 'Why did you get a picture of corn anyway?' " and suggests that instead of a picture of corn, he would have bought a picture of " 'a herd of cattle . . . or a prize bull with a shine to his flanks and the black fire in his eyes' "(p. 190). Although he too recognizes the call of the past, his past is not that of Genya.

The deeper significance of the picture to Genya is revealed when she tells Bertha about her past in Europe. Genya recounts her intense love affair with a church organist, an illicit affair which was discovered by her parents. Her father's reaction was bitter rage and intense shame. Her lover refused to marry her, claiming that he was too poor to support her, and revealed his engagement to an older, wealthy woman. Genya's last sight of her lover and his bride is symbolically embodied in the picture. Genya tells her sister that when her lover and his new wife passed, " 'I felt empty as a bell till I looked at the blue cornflowers at my feet. They cheered me. That was the last I saw of him I think' " (p. 203). The love affair, the great event of Genya's past, has multiple emotional meanings for her. On the one hand, when she talks about the love affair, "her voice took on a throbbing richness" (p. 262), on the other hand, she admits that the end of the affair was "the fullest cup of death" (p. 200).

David only understands a portion of this overheard conversation because it is conducted partly in Polish, "that alien, aggravating tongue that David could never fathom" (p. 195). Although he does not understand the meaning of the past or the emotional connotations of the picture, he realizes their importance to his mother: "Blue corn flowers? Likes them! Corn! That was—! Inside on the wall! Gee! Look at it later!" (pp. 203-204). The past is another cause of alienation from his mother, but in this instance he feels superior to both his mother and aunt. He has overheard them, despite their concern that he not hear Genya's confession: "Easy fool them. But they didn't fool him. Didn't scare him either. Didn't change . . . Gee! The picture! Not now, though. Look at it later, when nobody's here . . . Green and blue it's s—Sh!" (p. 207). Having no personal past himself, David feels superior to the past of others.

Genya's purchase of the picture, which reflects her intense involvement with the past, is similar to Albert's subsequent purchase of the bull's horns, which have multiple meanings for him just as the picture of the cornfield does for her. On the most superficial level, Albert's purchase reflects nostalgia. In the first book, Luter laughs at Albert's preoccupation with cattle: " 'I like especially the way he [Albert] never speaks of Tysmenicz without leading in the cattle he once tended' " (p. 43). On this level, the cattle, like the corn, symbolize the peaceful, secure rural world of the past. When David first sees the horns he senses their strange potency: "There pulsed from them still a suggestion of terrific power, a power that even while they lay motionless made the breast ache as though they were ever imminent, ever charging" (p. 298). David recognizes that it was not "for memory's sake only that his father had bought this trophy" (p. 298). Pondering the meaning of the horns, David discovers the dual aspects of his father's power: its violence and its intense sexuality. In David's mind, the horns bridge two images: "that man outstretched on the sidewalk," a victim of his father's rage, and "that mysterious look of repose on his mother's face when he [David] had come in," her sexual contentment (p. 298).

But the horns have two other, darker meanings for Albert. The first is reflected in his terrible, anguished revelation to Genya in Book IV. He believes that his mother told Genya that he allowed his father to be trampled to death by a bull:

> Didn't she tell you that my father and I had quarreled that morning, that he struck me, and I vowed I would repay him? There was a peasant watching us from afar. Didn't she tell you that? He said I could have prevented it. I could have seized the stick when the bull wrenched it from my father's hand. When he lay on the ground in the pen. But I never lifted a finger! I let him be gored! Didn't she tell you that? (p. 390)

Coupled with this passionate revelation is Albert's unspoken fear of cuckoldry, also symbolized by the horns.

"Coal"

The symbol of the cellar involves uniformly negative emotional connotations, while the picture's meanings are ambiguous. The symbol of the coal, on the other hand, combines opposing or conflicting meanings. Because it is black and dirty, coal has inevitable connections with uncleanliness for David. When he is told the story of Isaiah's purification by God's coal, he is unable to reconcile the blackness of the coal he knows with purity: "But coal makes smoke and ashes. So how clean?" (p. 230). He cannot accept the purifying aspects of coal, for he connects coal with the cellar; he knows that "in a cellar is coal" (p. 231).

This blackness and filth are of course directly opposed to the purifying power of the coal in the Biblical chapter of Isaiah which the rabbi tells: " 'one of the angels flew down to the altar and with tongs drew out a fiery coal. . . . And with that coal, down he flew to Isaiah and with that coal touched his lips. . . . . And the instant that coal touched Isaiah's lips, then he heard God's own voice' " (p. 227).

In this episode, focused on Isaiah and the coal, it becomes apparent that David is symbolically the mystic, as well as the child. Leslie Fiedler remarked that David "is portrayed not only as a small boy and a Jew but also as a 'mystic,' a naive adept visited by visions he scarcely understands until a phrase from the sixth chapter of Isaiah illuminates for him his own improbable prophetic initiation."[4] David's symbolic self-purification in the snow is a previous indication of his intense desire for mystical illumination. Indeed, his profound revulsion and terror of the cellar also reflect his extraordinarily delicate sensibility. Prior to hearing about Isaiah's purification by God's coal, David realizes that he is "waiting for some sign, some seal that would forever relieve him of watchfulness and forever insure his well-being" (p. 221). Even before his acquaintance with the Isaiah story, David occasionally believes that he has come to grips with the past of the picture and the terrors of the cellar: "Those curious secrets he had gleaned long ago from his mother's story seemed submerged within him and were met only at reminiscent street-corners among houses or in the brain. Everything unpleasant and past was like that, David decided, lost within one. All one had to do was to imagine that it wasn't there, just as the cellar in one's house could be conjured away if there were a bright yard between the hallway and the cellar stairs" (p. 221). However, David has obviously not yet been able to deal with "everything unpleasant and past"; thus far, these elements have been "submerged" and "conjured away."

Although he is profoundly affected by the story of Isaiah and the coal, David is still unable to deal with the past and his terrors. This inability to come to grips with the cellar, the picture, and the paradoxical nature of the coal causes him to conclude simply that "Only God had angel-coal. Where in God's cellar I wonder? How light it must be there" (p. 231). The remainder of the novel can be seen as David's search for God's coal, the purifying mystical experience, which he finally finds in the rail.

As the coal is a symbol combining blackness and filth with purity and lightness, the rabbi himself embodies these contrasting qualities. He is physically repulsive:

> He appeared old and was certainly untidy. He wore soft leather shoes like house slippers, that had no place for either laces or buttons. His trousers were baggy and stained, a great area of striped and crumpled shirt intervened between his belt and his bulging vest. The knot in his tie, which was nearer one ear than the other, hung away from his soiled collar. What features were visible were large and had an oily gleam. (p. 212)

Moreover, he is abusive to his pupils, almost to the point of sadism. Nonetheless, it is the rabbi who recognizes David's extraordinary nature, who compliments him for his "iron head" (p. 217) and calls him a "true Yiddish child" (p. 365).

Following the revelation about God's coal, David's need to reconcile good and evil grows increasingly intense, and the conflict between his mystical desires and gross reality becomes even more pronounced. When he believes that he has sinned by lighting a candle for an old woman on the Sabbath, he ponders the seeming impossibility of God's omnipresence: "How can He look in every dark, if He's light—the rabbi said—and it's real dark. How can He see in the real dark and we can't see Him. What's real dark? Real dark. Gee! That time—Annie—closet. Cellar—Luter, Sh! Don't! Gee! Sin it was. Hurry up! Sin it was! Every place, sin it is. Didn't know. Hurry up! Coal He touched him. Hurry up!" (p. 240). The mad, hallucinatory rush of David's thoughts in this passage reflects his extreme inner conflict and lack of reconciliation.

The lack of reconciliation, the central symbolic meaning of the coal, is reflected in another incident in the book, when David is confused because his holy burning of unkosher food for Passover has a noxious odor: "Gee, how feathers stink! No, they don't! It's holy and He's looking. Feathers don't stink! No!" (p. 246). For David the burning sacrifice, like the coal and the rabbi, contains unresolved good and evil.

Despite the lack of resolution represented in the symbol of the coal, David has two subsequent mystical experiences which indicate further steps on his journey toward the final revelation which will reconcile his conflicts. The first of these experiences parallels his purification in the snow, both in emotional effect and in light imagery. Watching the sun dance on the water, he believes that he is climbing the sunrays and is hypnotized by the light which grows "Brighter than day . . . Brighter . . . Sin melted into light" [ellipses Roth's] (p. 248). However, when he is abruptly awakened from his vision, "It was as though he had seen it in another world, a world that once left could not be recalled. All that he knew about it was that it had been complete and dazzling" (p. 248).

The second mystical experience occurs when neighborhood rowdies force David to push a "sword" into the trolley track and thus shock himself. This experience differs from the others David has had in two important ways. First, he is *forced* into the event rather than seeking it willingly, and therefore his reaction does not unite his painfully divided universe; he must *seek* the revelation, in order for it to fulfill his needs. Second, the images used to describe the experience involve power and sexuality as well as light. David must come to accept power as a correlative of mystical light just as he must accept the power of his father's horns as generative sexuality as well as violence. Addition of images of sex and power to light imagery gives the vision a new depth and completeness: "Like a paw ripping through all the sable fibres of the earth, power, gigantic, fetterless, thudded into day! And light, unleashed, terrific light bellowed out of iron lips. The street quaked and roared, and like a tortured thing, the sheet zinc sword, leapt writhing, fell back, consumed with radiance" (p 253).

The rabbi's reaction when David tells him about finding God's coal in the tracks is scorn: " 'Fool!' he gasped at length. 'Go beat your head on a wall! God's light is not between car-tracks' " (p. 257). Nonetheless, David feels less afraid of the cellar and the dark following this first electric shock. Later when he is in the cellar, he says, "Gee! Used to be darker. Funny. Gee! Look! Look! Is a light! In the corner where baby-carriages—No. Looks like though. On the stairs too. Ain't really there. Inside my head. Better be inside. Can carry it" (p. 261). Moreover, he is beginning to reconcile good and evil and to see God's light everywhere: "Funny. Still can see it. There. And over there. And over in the corner where it's really dark. It sticks inside all the time, gee, you can't never be scared" (p. 261). As A. Sidney Knowles asserted, "learning the lessons of experience, growing up, becomes for David—as it does for Stephen Dedalus—a matter of surviving and reconciling the very diversity of existence."[5] In "The Coal" David confronts the diversity and begins to move toward the final reconciliation embodied in his vision of the rail.

"Rail"

Following his revelation about Isaiah, his experiences with the light on the water, and the first car-track incident, David finds a brief period of partial reconciliation: "For him the mere passing of time was a joy. The body was aware of a lyric indolence, a golden lolling within itself. He felt secure at home and in the street—that was all the activity he asked" (p. 262). However, the period of contentment is only transitory; when his father insists that David join him on his milk-delivery rounds one day, his happiness "was gone now. He was haunted again" (p. 274). As David anticipated, the deliveries prove catastrophic. When two men steal milk from him, his father beats one of them almost to death with his whip. For David, his father is temporarily transformed into a hideous god of wrath: "For a moment longer, David's father towered above him, rage billowed from him, shimmering in sunlight almost, like an aura; then with a last, fierce glance about the empty streets, scooped up the broken whip, stalked to the wagon, leaped in, and leaning out flogged the horse with the end of the rein" (p. 281). Not only is his father transformed into a symbol of rage, but the rage is directed at David: " 'False son! You! The cause!' "

(p. 282). David's intense anguish about his father's rage begins anew the disturbing cycle of cellar-associations. When he returns home, "He could not bring himself to enter the darkness. All the old fears lurked there again. Why had they returned?" (p. 286).

Following this incident, David experiences another temporary revelation on the roof of his tenement, which parallels the previous experiences in the snow and by the water. In David's mind, "The light swarmed down through the glass of the roof-housing, silent, untenanted light; evoking in his mind and superimposing an image of the snow he had once vaulted into and an image of light he had once climbed" (p. 295). Walter Rideout stated that "what David sees when he first comes out on the roof illustrates very well the combination in Roth's style of realistic and apocalyptic, and the extent to which symbolism penetrates the book."[6] The roof becomes a symbol of release and purity, contrasting vividly with the cellar and its symbolic connections with rats, fear, bodily corruption, and impure sexuality. Rideout also noted that David "identifies various parts of the two tenements in which the Schearls successively live with feelings of terror, revulsion, security, release; and these places, as they are refracted through David's mind become for the reader a complex and powerful system of symbols concerned with human consciousness."[7]

On the roof David meets Leo, the neighbor boy, and forms a relationship with him which acts as a powerful catalyst in David's later actions. His envy of Leo makes it clear that David is seeking personal power and a vision that will enable him to overcome his fears: "*—Not Afraid! Leo wasn't afraid!*" (p. 305). David connects Leo's Christianity with his mother's past and the over-heard conversation about the organist. However, after asking Leo what an organist is, David abruptly changes the subject; the past is to remain buried in his subconscious, at least temporarily. David's jealousy of Leo's religious symbols, his crucifix and rosary, is portrayed in light imagery, reinforcing the light-dark pattern used throughout the novel. When he sees the picture of Jesus and the Sacred Heart, David is awestruck: " 'He's all light inside' " (p. 323). Unable to accommodate Leo's story of Jews as Christ-killers, David falls back into admiration of Jesus's purity: " 'He's light inside and out, ain't he?' " (p. 323).

Leslie Fiedler observed that "No book insists more on the distance between the foulness man lives and the purity he dreams; but none makes more clear how deeply rooted that dream is in the existence which seems to contradict it."[8] The incident which most clearly demonstrates the disparity and inter-connection between dream and reality is when David reluctantly agrees to take Leo to see his cousins and "play dirty," so that Leo will give him the rosary. David recognizes the impossibility of juxtaposing the rosary and illicit sex; after making the agreement with Leo,

> Hope and fear and confusion had drained him of thought. His mind was numb and suspended now, as though he were drowsy with cold. Without word, without image, he sensed again the past and future converging on the morrow. And either he found a solvent for his fears or he was lost. He walked into the dreary rain as into an omen. (p. 328)

Following the incident with his cousins and Leo, David flees from the horror of the cellar and Leo's sexuality to his Hebrew school, where the rabbi instructs him to read a passage which proves to be the same chapter of Isaiah by which he was so moved previously. For a moment, the passage again transforms him: "Past radiance threw a last parting beam into the depths of his mind"; then "A cadence like a flock of pigeons, vast, heaven-filling, swept and wheeled, glittered, darkened, kindled again, like wind over prairies" (pp. 366-367). However, when the rabbi tells him " 'Blessed is your mother, my son!' " the mention of the word "mother" moves David irrevocably back to his guilt, the cellar, and her unreconciled past, the picture. He tells the rabbi a distorted version of his mother's past, for he has not understood her conversation. This compulsive "confession" is similar to the confessional aspects of the picture and the horns; the mother, father, and child all feel a need, if only subconsciously, to understand the meaning of the past.

Realizing the immensity of his act in telling the rabbi, David dashes madly through the streets. He stops at the trolley tracks and "With all the horror of one tottering over an abyss, he stared at the cobbles, the gleaming tracks" (p. 378). This scene dramatically foreshadows his final apocalyptic vision, but here the ultimate desperation which will drive him to the tracks is not yet upon him, and he returns home.

A terrible confrontation between David, his parents and the rabbi, develops around the involved meanings of two of the major symbols, the cellar and the picture. When the rabbi goes to the Schearl home to tell David's parents about the boy's strange tale, they react most strongly when the tale correlates with the picture on the wall. The rabbi's last words, " 'She met him among the corn,' " cause them both to gasp. David's wild tale drives Albert to reveal his past, the meaning of the bull's horns. He makes it clear that his anxiety about their marriage has been based upon a fear that David is not his child and that he is a cuckold. He tells Genya: " 'My sin balances another,' " and adds " 'All these years my blood told me! Whispered to me whenever I looked at him, nudged me, told me he wasn't mine!' " (p. 391).

Before any of the three family members can begin to deal with these revelations about the past, about the picture and the horns, David's aunt and uncle arrive to complain about the seduction of their daughter in the cellar. But before his uncle can complain about David's involvement in Leo's misdeeds, the child reaches his limit of guilt and compusively confesses. Nevertheless, the climactic horror is yet to come. When Albert beats him with the whip David compulsively hands him, the rosary falls out of David's pocket. The rosary provides a connection between Genya's picture and the filth of the cellar; for Albert, the rosary is " 'a proof of my word! The truth! Another's! A goy's! A cross! A sign of filth!' " (p. 402). Fleeing insanely from his home, David reaches the bottom of despair; the cellar, the picture, and the coal have driven him to absolute desperation, absolute need of purification and resolution.

As David races through the streets, his mad thoughts are interspersed in the conversation of the street people. Allen noted that David's "climactic flight through the streets is brilliantly done, counterpointed against a chorus of voices representative of the varied life of the city."[9] Expelled from his family, he is forced to depend upon the people in the street, and it is the people who will carry him home after his shock on the rail. Unlike all his previous mystical experiences, into which he drifted or was forced by others, this experience is conscious and willed. David knows, *"Now I gotta make it come out"* (p. 409). The "it" is God's coal which he believes is buried in the car-tracks. David must have a revelation which will unify the cellar, the picture, and the coal. Standing over the tracks with the milk ladle which he will plunge into the slot, he thinks, *"there's light in the crack"* (p. 410) and later, *"In the crack be born"* (p. 411). As Knowles asserted, in this realization "two themes are united: the generative touch of the fiery coal upon the lips of Isaiah is equated with the generative act of sex."[10] The act of plunging the ladle into the car-tracks is obviously symbolic sexual intercourse. The vision which ensues is overpowering to David. *"Incredible, barbaric power"* and *"a siren of light"* flood his senses and brain; *"His brain swelled and dilated till it dwarfed the galaxies in a bubble of refulgence"* (p. 419). David sees *"the white, frosty light within the red iris*" (p. 425). The color imagery of red and white represents the power and light which must be united in God. His vision is hallucinatory, with images shifting, coming together, and pulling apart again as David floats back to consciousness. From the joy of the first flash, he descends to a terrifying vision of his father with a murderous hammer, to a coffin and confetti, then "*David touched his lips. The soot came off on his hand. Unclean*" (p. 426). His mind goes back in time and he recalls images of the earlier books, especially "The Cellar." He descends "*down into darkness, darkness, that tunneled the heart of darkness, darkness fathomless*" (p. 429). He descends to the bottom of the symbolic cellar in despair, but miraculously he is now able to find the meaning of the vision: "*Coal! In a cellar is . . . Coal! And it was brighter than the pith of lightening and milder than pearl . . . And made the darkness dark because the dark culled its radiance for that jewel*" (p. 430). David has found God's coal, and by this discovery he is able to transcend the horrors of the cellar, the oppression of the picture, the conflict of the coal: "*Horror and night fell away. Exulted, he lifted his head* (p. 431) and he reawakens to consciousness.

Three analogues of redemption—sexual, political, and Christian—support and universalize David's personal mystical redemption in chapter xxi. As noted previously, David's insertion of the milk ladle into the rail has direct sexual connotations. When he runs from home toward the tracks, the voice of a "goggle-eyed yid" (p. 417) preaches political revolution. The revolutionary's cry—" 'Only the laboring poor, only the masses embittered, bewildered, betrayed, in the day when the red cock crows, can free us' " (p. 417)—parallels David's simultaneous vision of "*A sense almost palpable, as of a leashed and imminent and awful force*" (p. 417). The sexual and political themes combine in the speech of "the kindly faced American woman" who declares, " 'And do you know, you can go all the way up inside her for twenty-five cents. . . . The Statue of Liberty' " (p. 415). David's near-electrocution evokes the suffering of Christ on the Cross as the street voices talk of Mary and the "T'ree Kings" and David's vision includes images of "*the last smudge of rose, staining the stem of the trembling, jagged chalice*" (p. 418). The revolutionary's red cock recalls the cock's crow when Peter three times denied Christ, and a street voice asks sarcastically, "How many times'll your red cock crow, Pete, befaw y' gives up? T'ree?' " (p. 418). In the climactic moment of David's vision, the three analogues, the sexual, the political revolutionary, and the Christian, completely combine as the red cock stands for the penis, revolution, and the Biblical cock: " 'a red cock crowing. Over a statue of. A jerkin'. Cod. Clang! Clang! Oy! Machine! Liberty! Revolt! Redeem!' " (p. 419).

The "proof" of David's new-found wisdom is soon apparent in his relationship with his father; after he is carried home to his parents "a vague, remote pity [for his father] stirred within his heart like a wreathing, raveling smoke tenuously dispersed within his being" (p. 440). At last, his vision completed, his reconciliation final, he falls asleep, feeling "strangest triumph, strangest acquiescence" (p. 441). The vision of the rail has united and transcended the first three symbols.

NOTES

[1] Harold U. Ribalow, "The History of Henry Roth and *Call It Sleep*," *Call It Sleep* (Paterson, N. J.: Pageant Books, 1960), p. xix.

[2] Walter Allen, "Two Neglected American Novelists," *The London Magazine*, 2 (May 1962), 79.

[3] Maxwell Geismar, "A Critical Introduction," *Call It Sleep* (Paterson, N. J.: Pageant Books, 1960), p. xliii.

[4] Leslie A. Fiedler, "Henry Roth's Neglected Masterpiece," *Commentary*, 30 (Aug. 1960), 106.

[5] A. Sidney Knowles, Jr., "The Fiction of Henry Roth," *MFS*, 11 (Winter 1965 66), 395.

[6] Walter B. Rideout, *The Radical Novel in the United States 1900-1954* (Cambridge, Mass.: Harvard Univ. Press, 1956), p. 313.

[7] Rideout, p. 186.

[8] Fiedler, p. 105.

[9] Allen, p. 80.

[10] Knowles, p. 399.

CHAPTER II

USE OF MOTIFS

One of the principal virtues of *Call It Sleep* is Roth's brilliant manipulation of motifs to unify and enrich the novel and to reinforce the reader's psychological identification with the protagonist, David Schearl. Roth's own comments about his use of motifs in the novel are illuminating:

> I think the motifs were conscious—I think I felt the *need* of them. When you speak about the evolution of the form and the recognition of the individual—how to achieve form in the course of a long work like that—this is one of the things that I recognized that I needed. Really it gives added interior structure.[1]

By tracing three motifs—the Thor, the *Chad Godya*, and the *zwank*—through *Call It Sleep*, I hope to indicate the intricacy of Roth's motif patterns and their relationship to the artistry and extraordinary psychological power of the novel.

The Thor motif exemplifies how Roth uses recurrent themes and verbal patterns to achieve what he calls "added interior structure." The other two motifs, the *Chad Godya* and the *zwank*, are examples of a special and more complex sub-class, the motif of transformation: in the climactic chapter of the novel motifs from the earlier books are transformed in David's mind and he in turn is transformed by them. The mystical vision in the climactic chapter is convincing and moving primarily because, by following David's ever deepening and changing awareness of these motifs, the reader, in a sense, is able to experience the child's vision with him.

I use the expression "Thor motif" for purposes of simplification rather than as an assertion that in *Call It Sleep* Roth aimed at a direct parallel to Germanic mythology. Since Albert possesses certain qualities in common with the Teutonic figure, I use the term "Thor motif" to refer to the related cluster of images which define and characterize David's tyrannical father. Like Thor, Albert is, to David, a god-like figure of wrath, with his arm upraised in anger. And, like Thor, Albert is directly associated with a hammer (or hammer-substitute) which he wields wrathfully. Albert also has two other qualities traditionally attributed to Thor; in Germanic mythology Thor's "powerful voice rose above the tumult of battle and filled the enemy with terror," while his eyes "flashed fire" and "flashed like lightning" when he was infuriated.[2] All three Thor-like qualities are prominent in Roth's presentation of Albert: the fearful hammer, the terrible voice, and the fiery visage and nature. In *Call It Sleep* these qualities are significant both in the action and the language of the novel; not only does Albert wield an actual hammer, but his voice is described as hammer-like.

Early in the novel, in chapter ii of "The Cellar," Albert forces David to accompany him to a printing shop where he has just quit working. There one of Albert's former co-workers tells David, " 'Your ol' man near brained me wid a hammer' " (p. 25). David hears how his father " 'looked like he wuz boinin' up' " and twisted a rail in his hands (p. 26). David's smallness and fragility in contrast to his father are underscored when Albert's former employer refers to the Schearl son and father as David and Goliath (p. 26). Not surprisingly, the incident impresses David intensely, and the memory enters the deepest recesses of his psyche. Early in *Call It Sleep* the image of Albert with arm upraised in "burning" fury is established, an image that is repeated, with variations, throughout the novel to provide a graphic and potent emblem both for David and the reader.

Shortly after the fearful revelation about his father, David has a tussle with a neighborhood child, Yussie, in which David kicks Yussie's nose, making it bleed. Albert's reaction is swift and brutal: again with arm upraised, this time against his own child, Albert beats David first with his hand and then with a clothes hanger. The incident is especially horrible to David because of its unconscious symbolic significance. At the moment when Albert stands with his arm raised above him, David thinks: *"The hammer in that hand when he stood! The hammer!"* (p. 83). As in the first incident at the printing shop, Albert is again described as "boinin' up." Here the "blazing eyes" and "white heat" of Albert's features transfix the child. Similarly, Albert's voice is "the voice of the clothes hanger biting like flame into his flesh" (p. 84). To David, Albert's face "seemed slowly to recede, but recede without diminishing, growing more livid with distance, a white flame bodiless" (p. 83).

Later in "The Cellar," Albert, who senses a change in Luter's attitude toward him, vows to respond appropriately if things continue to disintegrate at his new printing job. Genya urges Albert not to do anything rash, and David involuntarily envisions "a dark roof, a hammer brandished over pale and staring cobbles" (p. 125). In David's experience, Albert had never radiated "so fell, so electric a fury. It was as though his whole body were smouldering, a stark, throbbing, curdling emanation flowed from him, a dark, corrosive haze that was all the more fearful because David sensed how thin an aura it was of the terrific volcano clamped within" (p. 127).

When Albert returns home from the printing shop with his thumb mangled, he blames Luter for the injury. Albert's curses against his false friend evoke the same burning imagery; Albert says: " 'God's flame make a candle of him' " (p. 135) and " 'May he burn with them' " ("them" refers to Luter's presents given on previous occasions) (p. 136).

In contrast with the burning, destructive imagery in this scene are images of traditionally gentle animals, animals associated with sacrifice rather than prey. Before Albert is hurt on the job, he vows to injure Luter and says: " 'I'm no lamb' " (p. 126). After his injury, Albert is disgusted with himself for having been hurt without inflicting pain on his enemy and complains: " 'they led me out like a sheep' " (p. 135). The imagery of fire and the contrasting animal imagery seem to reflect Albert's vision of the universe: one is either a destructive, burning figure of wrath or a victim.

The "Thor motif" (Albert with raised arm wielding a hammer in fury) appears with slight variation in Book IV, "The Rail." Having left the printing trade and become a milkman, Albert no longer possesses a murderous hammer. But the image and psychological meaning are the same for David and the reader when Albert takes a whip to a man who steals milk from him. As in the earlier scenes, Albert is magnified to immensity, and his wrath is fiery and god-like.

In the highly dramatic confrontation scene preceding David's flight toward the rail, the powerful Thor-image of his father forces itself into David's mind and then into actuality. Having confessed his part in arranging the sexual play between his cousin Esther and Leo, David cannot keep himself from handing Albert his whip with which to beat him. The language Roth uses to describe Albert in this scene supports the involuntary nature of David's action: Albert "hammered the air in David's direction" (p. 390);

his voice "broke like a rod of stiff metallic words across his [David's] back" (p. 393) and "struck with the brunt of thunder" (p. 399). The hammer movement and thunder sound directly recall the previous uses of the Thor motif. Again, Albert's raised arm "hung in the air, hung motionless," (p. 399) as before the first beating in "The Cellar." It seems to David that

> one compulsion rallied the body and brain like a standard. A dream? No, not a dream. Not a dream, nor the memory of a dream. An act, ordained, foreseen, inevitable as this very moment, a channel of expertness, imbued for ages, reiterated for ages, familiar as breath. (pp. 399-400)

For Albert, too, the scene seems pre-ordained, destined, and he asks David, ' 'Is it your fate you're begging for?' " (p. 400).

The Thor motif occupies a central position in David's flow of images when he is knocked unconscious by the short-circuiting of the rail. As befitting a representation of unconscious mental activity, the imagery here is shifting and phantasmagoric. Albert possesses supernatural powers and comes leaping *"from roof-top to roof-top, over streets, over alley ways, over areas and lots"* . . . *"with a feathery ease"* (p. 426). Significantly, Albert searches until he finds a hammer which *"snapped like a whip"* (p. 426); this simile makes explicit the parallel between the hammer and the whip. As Albert brandishes the whip-like hammer, *"the cobbles stretched away in the swirling dark like the faces of a multitude aghast and frozen"* (p. 426). This imagery recalls the "faces uplifted, so many they stretched like white cobbles to the end of the world" in David's first dream in "The Cellar." In David's unconscious mind, Albert not only possesses a whip-like hammer, but his voice is the voice of a god of wrath which *"thundered"* and *"beat like a hand upon his back"* (p. 428). The Thor images horrify David and evoke other images of death and corruption in his unconscious flow of impressions. He seeks to flee, but his father's *"inexorable voice"* forces him to descend into darkness.

At the climax of his phantasmagoric mystical experience, when David finally achieves his vision of *"nothingness beatified,"* the glory of his vision is expressed in connection with the destruction of this hideous image of Thor: silence *"struck that terrible voice upon the height, stilled the whirling hammer"* (pp. 430-431). And with the destruction of this image of his father, *"Horror and the night fell away"* (p. 431).

David's concern with *Chad Godya,* an Aramaic song recited by Jews at the conclusion of the Passover feast, is particularly fitting. Although this song is, on one level, a simple nursery rhyme, it has been regarded as an allegorical version of the principle of *jus talionis:* "eye for eye, tooth for tooth" (Exodus XXI, 24).[3] *Chad Godya* is about a progressive series of destructions ending with "And then the Almighty, blessed be He, killed the angel of death, who killed the butcher, who killed the ox, who drank the water, that quenched the fire, that burned the stick, that beat the dog, that killed the cat, that ate the kid my father bought for two zuzim. One kid, one only kid." Since David is searching throughout the novel for the meaning of the universe, a sense of God's order and justice, it is fitting that he should catch upon this nursery rhyme as a possible clue.

Chad Godya is quoted in its entirety in *Call It Sleep* in chapter iv of "The Coal" as it is recited by David in the cheder. The immense significance of the song to David is revealed both thematically and stylistically. David learns *Chad Godya* at the very time that he first hears about Isaiah's purification by God's coal. *Chad Godya* is therefore linked in David's mind with the Isaiah story, which seems to suggest the possibility of redemption. When David recites *Chad Godya* aloud for the rabbi, the psychological impact on him is emphasized by Roth's first extended use of italics in *Call It Sleep: "(Gee! Last. Nobody after. Didn't know before. But sometime, Mama, Gee!)"* (p. 233).

Moreover, the fact that *Chad Godya* is a Passover song is strikingly apt. The Jewish holiday of Passover celebrates God's bringing the Jews "from slavery to freedom, from sorrow to joy, from mourning to feasting, from darkness to full light, from bondage to redemption."[4] These Passover conceptions coalesce in the novel in the central motif of "deliverance." The word "deliverance" itself sounds, then echoes at least nine times through the novel, foreshadowing and reflecting David's great "deliverance" in the climactic chapter. At the end of "The Coal," for example, Roth observes that "Deliverance was in the air—The Passover—deliverance from Egypt and from winter, from bondage and death!" (p. 260). *Chad Godya* and Passover are external, public symbols of David's internal, psychological search.

Shortly after David learns *Chad Godya,* the reader sees him attempting to derive profound significance from the song. Typically, David's mind moves by associations, and his thinking is largely rearranging, fitting together disparate pieces. When his mother tries to answer his question, " 'Who is God?' " with a metaphor that " 'He was brighter than the day is brighter than the night,' " David immediately thinks of *Chad Godya.* The "scale" implied in his mother's metaphor "reminded him of the steps of the chad godyuh [sic]" (p. 241). He envisions the *Chad Godya* as a movement from a world of darkness toward God's light; significantly, this light-dark imagery is basic to the texture of the entire novel.

The imagery of David's stream of consciousness during the electrocution scene derives from his tortured memories and associations, which are shifted and transformed by his imagination into a redemptive vision. During this electrocution experience, David combines the *Chad Godya* with another motif, that of "the man in the wires." Moreover, "the man in the wires" is itself the product of the merging in David's unconscious of two motifs: "the man in the tugboat" and "the wires." In Book I, "The Cellar," David flees from home when guilt, fear, and sexual nausea overpower him. Racing down the streets, he becomes conscious of the telephone poles with their "wires on their crosses swinging into the sky" (p. 93). He believes that the wires connect heaven and earth, that "the tall spars were climbing into the sky" (p. 94).

The motif of "the man in the tugboat" first appears in Book III, "The Coal." In this book, David has a mystical experience (one of several in the novel) while gazing at the river. Watching the sun rays on the water, he believes that he is climbing the rays and is hypnotized by the light which becomes "Brighter . . . brighter . . . Sin melted into light" (p. 248). But he is abruptly awakened from this vision by "the man in a tugboat": "In a doorway amidships, his back to the bright brass engine, stood a man in his undershirt, bare outstretched arms gripping the doorpost on either side" (p. 248). This man, standing in an obviously Christ-like pose, whistles to David and yells, " 'Wake up, Kid!' " (p. 248).

In the climactic chapter, the motif of "the man in the tugboat" combines with that of "the wires" to become "the man in the wires," which later coalesces with *Chad Godya.* While David is unconscious from the electrical shock, the telephone poles with their "crosses swinging into the sky" (p. 93) merge into "the man in the tugboat" with his "bare outstretched arms gripping the doorpost on either side" (p. 248) to produce "the man in the wires": *"And a man in a tugboat, hair under armpits, hung from a pole among the wires, his white undershirt glittering"* (p. 425). Two pages later in the electrocution scene, this combined motif of "the man in the wires" blends with the *Chad Godya* motif when David thinks: *" 'Chadgodya!'* [sic] *moaned the man in the wires. 'One kid one only kid' "* (p. 427).

In the scene from "The Coal," David, the kid (or child), is awakened from a transcendent vision to mundane reality by "the man in the tugboat," but in the climactic scene David equates himself with the *Chad Godya* kid (goat) and so is likewise saved by "the Almighty, blessed be He." This transformation of the child to the goat reflects the convulsive movement of David's child-like mind and also parallels a major "misinterpretation" or transformation of David's: throughout the last two books of *Call It Sleep,* David confuses the Biblical coal or "burning ember" with the black combustible mineral used for fuel. Through these connections, transformations, and "errors," the reader *experiences* David's mind at work. It is, in fact, through such "mistakes" that the psychological power of *Call It Sleep* is most deeply felt. These very "errors" underlie Walter Allen's assertion that in *Call It Sleep* Roth "plunges us into a child's mind more directly and more intransigently than any other novelist has gone." [5]

Like The *Chad Godya* motif, the *zwank* motif brings together several thematic strands in the climactic chapter of *Call It Sleep,* and the transformation indicates David's redeeming imaginative vision. When the word *zwank* first appears in David's stream of consciousness during the electrocution, it may seem to represent merely a sound—like "khi-r-r-r-f" and "S-s-s-s" and "Klang" which also appear. The noise-like aspect of the word is certainly intended, but the word *zwank,* which is Yiddish for "tongs," also brings together several important themes.

In "The Cellar," when David questions his mother about death, she replies that the dead "are cold; they are still. They shut their eyes in sleep eternal years" (p. 69). Unable or unwilling to understand the meaning of "eternal years," David asks what she means. Her answer is metaphorical; she picks up a sugar cube with tongs and explains, " 'This is how wide my brain can stretch. . . . No wider. Would you ask me to pick up a frozen sea with these narrow things?' " (p. 69). She never finishes the comparison, but says only, " 'The sea to this—' " (p. 69). While the tongs here symbolize the mind's inability to grasp the infinity of the universe and the mystery of life and death, they reappear with an opposite significance in "The Coal."

When David is in the *cheder,* the rabbi translates from Hebrew into Yiddish the Biblical story of Isaiah's purification with God's coal. David hears how " 'one of the angels flew to the altar and with the tongs drew out a fiery coal' " and touched Isaiah's lips with it (p. 227). Moments later, David ponders the Isaiah story and says to himself, "—with a zwank, he said it was. Zwank" (p. 230). In the Biblical story, the *zwank* is the very means of reaching understanding or redemption. Not until the electrocution scene can David connect this *zwank* with his mother's use of the word.

In David's phantasmagoric stream of consciousness both these thematic threads are united and transcended. When the word *zwank* first appears in "The Rail" scene, the sound itself seems most important, as previously suggested: "Khi-r-r-r-rf! S-s-s-s- (*—Zwank! Zwank! Zwank!* . . .)" (p. 426). However, as David's mind goes back in time, the word *zwank* assumes its semantic and imagistic significance; he spells out the word God, *"And shrank and was a cube of sugar gripped be—) . . . (tween the softly glowing tongs . . ."* (p. 428). His mother's awful words about the mind's limitations echo with a slight variation: *" 'So wide we stretch no further—' "* (p. 428). David descends into seemingly endless darkness until at last he finds God's coal: *"And made the darkness dark because the dark had called its radiance for that jewel"* (p. 430). Significantly, the very next words are *"Zwank! . . . Zwank! Zwank! Zwank! Nothingness beatified reached out its hands"* (p. 430). The tongs of David's mind have stretched wider; David has been purified by God's coal; the two *zwank* motifs coalesce.

These three motifs—the Thor, the *Chad Godya,* and the *zwank*—suggest the formalistic subtlety and psychological depth of this modern American classic. Speaking about *Call It Sleep,* Roth said,

> During the time I was writing, especially towards the end, the whole novel was in my consciousness at once. I thought of it [*Call It Sleep*] musically—that's how I really felt about it. My attitude toward it was what a musician must feel about his composition.[6]

Roth's evocative comments touch upon one of the most remarkable achievements of *Call It Sleep:* the brilliant manipulation of motifs which enrich and unify the novel and which enable the reader to enter David's consciousness and share his transfiguring vision in the climactic chapter.

NOTES

[1] Appendix, p. 296.

[2] E. Tonnelat, "Teutonic Mythology—Germany and Scandanavia," *New Larousse Encyclopedia of Mythology,* 1968.

[3] George Alexander Kohut, "Had Gadya," *The Jewish Encyclopedia,* 1904.

[4] Gotthard Deutsch, "Haggadah Shel Pesah," *The Jewish Encyclopedia,* 1904.

[5] Walter Allen, "Two Neglected American Novelists," *The London Magazine,* 2 (May 1962), 79.

[6] Appendix, p. 296.

CHAPTER III

LANGUAGE AND LANGUAGES

The patterns of symbols and motifs do not alone account for the unusual power of *Call It Sleep;* equally important is Roth's subtle exploitation of language—and more precisely languages—to anchor those patterns in a highly textured and convincing reality. Polish, Yiddish, Hebrew, Italian, German, and many dialects of English all go into the mixing bowl, and the result is a novel that breathes the complex social and ethnic reality of New York City. Roth's three major motives in his use of language and languages are 1) to characterize and individualize his figures; 2) to evoke the complex verbal atmosphere in which the action takes place; and 3) to explore the psychological connotations of the various languages, especially in the mind of the young protagonist.

In the prologue Roth sets the pattern for the handling of language which continues throughout the novel, just as he establishes thematic and symbolic motifs. The first character whose voice we "hear" is Genya, who timidly says to her husband, Albert: " 'And this is the Golden Land' " (p. 11). By stating that "she spoke in Yiddish," Roth immediately informs the reader of the pattern he is using in *Call It Sleep*. This simple and direct way of announcing his procedure is indicative of Roth's methods in general. Despite its apparent complexity, the novel poses no serious problems for the careful reader; Roth always makes sure that the reader knows which language his characters are speaking.

Having asserted that his characters are speaking Yiddish, Roth translates that language into English, then closes the prologue with two sentences in Yiddish itself. Although the two sentences remain untranslated, their meaning is clear; Genya asks Albert if they are going to live in New York (Nev York), and Albert answers that they will live in Brownsville (Bronzeville). The fact that Roth chooses to end the prologue with this short, untranslated exchange in Yiddish is suggestive of his use of language throughout *Call It Sleep.* Roth wants the reader not only to realize what language his characters are speaking, but also to experience the *feel* of that language, its sound and texture. In *Call It Sleep* Roth evokes the languages of his characters just as he evokes the qualities of light and air through which they move; like light and air, language is part of the atmosphere, the ambience of experience. Roth wants the reader to know his characters and their world emotionally as well as intellectually.

In the first chapter of "The Cellar," Roth introduces his second "language"—the broken English spoken by his immigrant characters, a language which Horace Gregory described as "at first a difficult and awkward tongue, ugly and harsh, yet slowly gaining speed and flexibility."[1] We first hear this language when David leaves his apartment and goes downstairs. Yussie, a neighbor friend, shows David a dismantled clock and remarks " 'It still c'n go' "; David answers: " 'So wot makes id?' " (pp. 20–21). After this exchange, Roth immediately notes, "In the streets David spoke English" (p. 21). This simple explanation also suggests the emotional connotations of English that develop in the novel: English is the language of David's peers, and of the streets, which to David signify blaring noise and threatening movement.

The reader's initial reaction to this garbled street language is no doubt surprise, and possibly distaste. Roth's use of this "difficult and awkward tongue" is a central critical question in the novel. Unlike the "correct" English which stands for Yiddish, this street language poses problems for the reader, for it is, at least at the beginning of the novel, difficult to understand. Although the difficulty of this street language is undeniable, what is gained through its use makes the reader's effort worthwhile.

One reason for this broken English, of course, is Roth's desire for verisimilitude. His characters speak English falteringly and with great difficulty. To render their speech without attempting to capture its sound and tone would be to falsify its essence. The language the characters speak in *Call It Sleep,* whether Yiddish (rendered in "correct" English) or broken English, is essential to their meaning. In a sense, to hear them is to know them.

This method of character-revelation by means of speech can best be seen in a comparison of Genya and her sister, the comical Aunt Bertha. Shortly after Bertha's arrival from the Old World, "David soon observed that his mother and Aunt were worlds apart in temperament. His mother was grave, attentive, mild in her speech; his aunt was merry, tart and ready-tongued" (p. 146). Genya is more than simply mild in speech, however. She is perceptive and acutely sensitive to the tragic side of life. Her most memorable words embody this tragic sense, and she often expresses herself in suggestive metaphors accompanied by telling gestures. Even before she reveals her past to Bertha in "The Picture," Genya's emotionally rich character is revealed by her speech. In "The Cellar," when she tells David about her grandmother, this story imparts a sense of the past, of an old and rich culture which Genya experienced in Europe but of which David is deprived. Genya describes her grandmother as a strange, gentle woman, deeply attuned to the seasons, who in old age said, " 'it is wrong being the way I am. Even a leaf grows dull and old together. Together!' " (p. 68). Genya tells David of her grandmother's self-willed death and how she looked "like early winter snow." She adds, " 'And I thought to myself even then, let me look deeply into her face for surely she will melt before my eyes' " (p. 68).

The language of Genya's explanation to David of death and human limitations is similarly metaphorical and evocative. Her gesture of lifting a cube of sugar with tongs and saying, " 'This is how wide my brain can stretch' " is graphic, immediate, and tragic. Not only is death a mystery to Genya, but life is inescapably sad. Later, when Luter spurns Albert, as Genya knew he would after she refused his sexual advances, she tells David: " 'This is the way of the years, my son. Each new one shows you both hands this way—' She held out her two closed hands before her. 'Here, choose!' And opening them. 'And they're both empty' " (p. 140). Such words and gestures make Genya an unforgettable figure; in Irving Howe's words, "Genya brings radiance and dignity to every page on which she appears." [2]

As Genya's depth and perception are revealed through her speech, so are the limitations of her life in America. After passages like those quoted above, which, of course, represent her Yiddish speech, it is a shock to the reader when Genya first speaks English. When David gets lost and is taken to a police station, Genya goes there to take him home. Her terrible isolation from the society around her is forcefully expressed by the poverty of her language. After Genya's melodic, metaphorical Yiddish speech, it is painful for the reader when she is reduced to repeating, " 'T-tanks so—so viel" and "Herr—Mister. Ve—er—ve—go?' " (p. 106). Walter Allen remarked that "Roth makes us sharply aware, as no other novelist except Willa Cather has done, in a book like *My Antonia,* of the degradation, the diminution in human dignity, that was one aspect of the immigrant's lot as he moved from a society with a traditional culture to another with no culture at all."[3] The few blocks surrounding their apartment are Genya's "pale" in America: her pathetic broken English marks the borders of her world.

Genya's sister Bertha is also subtly characterized by her speech, which is as highly metaphorical and suggestive as Genya's, but in a sexual way. The tartness, irony, and deflating quality of Bertha's speech capture the essence of Yiddish. Describing the special quality and flavor of Yiddish, Leo Rosten said that it "is a tongue that never takes its tongue out of its cheek."[4] He added that while it is "steeped in sentiment, it is sluiced with sarcasm," and "In its innermost heart, Yiddish swings between *schmaltz* and derision."[5] He concluded, "Were I asked to characterize Yiddish—its style, its life story, its ambience—in one word, I would not hesitate: irrepressible."[6] Bertha's speech reflects all these special qualities, particularly in her pungent curses and sharp metaphors. According to Bertha, "Veljish was as still as a fart in company" (p. 153).

Bertha's speech and the character her speech reveals make her the most "Jewish" character in *Call It Sleep*. Indeed, among the many purposes she serves in the novel is that of showing by contrast how more universal and less narrowly "Jewish" the other characters are. Bertha herself comments upon certain non-Jewish aspects of Genya's personality, saying "You were good enough, the gentlest of us all. But you weren't truly Jewish. You were strange. You didn't have a Jew's nature" (p. 165). Although Bertha is unable to explain what makes Genya seem non-Jewish, she insists upon the reality of her perception. Bertha tells Genya that she was "a mopish calf-eyed creature," who read German romances which made her non-Jewish in a subtle, yet undeniable way.

In addition to the metaphors and earthiness of Bertha's speech, Roth carefully reinforces the fact that all the major characters are speaking Yiddish by inserting certain colorful phrases that are obvious literal translations. For example, David's parents refer to him as "sweet fragment," "the prayer," and "what will pray for me after my death." Periodically placed, such expressions confirm, if only unconsciously, the reader's realization that the characters' "correct" English stands for their Yiddish.

Besides using language to characterize his figures and to suggest the verbal landscape, Roth emphasizes the impact of language and its problems on David. David moves uneasily among various languages, sometimes using English, sometimes Yiddish, to fulfill the various roles into which he is forced. When his father quits a printing job in a murderous fury, dragging David to the shop to collect his wages and belongings, David practices aloud the speech he will make to his father's employer, repeating his father's instructions in Yiddish. His father screams, " 'Say it in English, you fool' " (p. 25), demonstrating that in some circumstances, Yiddish is inadequate.

Not only can a particular language be inadequate in certain circumstances, but language and words in general can be untrustworthy. When Annie, David's neighbor friend, tries to tempt him into "playing dirty," David is misled by her words and by his misunderstanding of their intent. Simply repeating her phrases and pretending to understand her meaning, he thinks at first: "it was the easiest game he had ever played" (p. 52); then somehow he finds himself in a closet with her. Later in "The Cellar," when David is lost, his terror and confusion are again due to language. Here his pronunciation of English betrays him: his pronunciation of his address as "on a hunnder 'n' twenny six Boddeh Stritt" (p. 97) is interpreted as "Bodder," "Porter," and "Barhdee" by the police and bystanders who try to direct him home. Believing himself captive forever in the police station, David thinks: "Never believe. Not anything. Everything shifted. Everything changed. Even words. Words, you said. Wanna, you said. I wanna. Yea. I wanna. What? You know what. They were something else, something horrible!" (p. 102). These words, recalling his fateful conversation with Annie, reflect his fear of words and language. To David, words, like people, "sidewalks, even streets, houses" (p. 102) are faithless, shifting treacherously.

Part of David's problem with language is that each of the four languages he hears—English, Polish, Yiddish, and Hebrew—has different emotional connotations to him. English is the language of the street, Yiddish the language of the home, Polish an unfathomable foreign language, and Hebrew "a strange and secret tongue" (p. 213). The very number and diversity of languages represent barriers between people and are causes of alienation, to David. Hearing a parrot and canary sing together, "He wondered if they understood each other. Maybe it was like Yiddish and English, or Yiddish and Polish" (p. 174).

English is the language of David's peers as well as of the street, and he is inevitably drawn more and more into it and away from Yiddish—thus Roth underscores David's subtle but definite growing alienation from his mother. Some of the young people use English as a weapon against the older generation, as a way of asserting themselves. For example, when Yussie argues with Genya about whether she will visit his mother, he ends the disagreement by changing from Yiddish to English; "Yussie switched into English as if to avoid any further discussion" (p. 81). Since David's primary identification is with his mother, he does not wish to separate himself from her by speaking English. Thus when Yussie is telling David a long, involved story in English during the crisis created by the injury to Albert's hand, David tries to get rid of Yussie by reverting "desperately to Yiddish" (p. 140).

Nonetheless, through the course of the novel, as David grows older, he is drawn into English without even realizing it. His mother tells him, " 'Your Yiddish is more than one-half English now. I'm being left behind' " (p. 120). Not only is she being left behind by David, but also by the latecomer to America, Bertha. Unlike Genya, whose pathetic limitation in English is poignantly revealed in the police station scene, Bertha plunges headlong into English, relishing the multi-lingual puns, especially the sexual ones, just as she rushes gustily into the Metropolitan Museum. Besides revealing Bertha's earthy character, these puns, such as "kockin" (excreting) and cocaine, reinforce the fact that the characters are speaking Yiddish most of the time.

In "The Picture," when Genya finally decides to give in to her sister's curiosity and tell Bertha about her past in Austria, she begins her narrative in Polish so that David cannot understand. To David, Polish means secrets and exclusion from a past he cannot comprehend. Fittingly, the only actual Polish word Roth uses is "lupka," love, for Genya's past is, in essence, her tragic love affair. Furious at being excluded, David vows revenge: "And if the time came when he knew something they didn't know, he'd pay them back in the same coin. He'd learn to talk the way the girls talked in the street—alligay walligay" (p. 198).

As mentioned previously, to David, Hebrew is "a strange and secret tongue" (p. 231). As a child, he literally believes, "If you knew it [Hebrew] then you could talk to God" (p. 213). David's search for understanding becomes connected with his lessons in the *cheder*; he thinks that "Perhaps the sign would be revealed when he finally learned to translate Hebrew" (p. 221). In the course of the novel, David never does learn to translate Hebrew, but the very sound of the words enchants him. Roth writes the Hebrew in transliteration to suggest the flow and sound of the language. Because Roth wants the reader to experience *with* David, he does not provide word-for-word translation. David does not understand Hebrew, and it is enough if the reader, like David, experiences the Hebrew, as "a chant, a hymn, as though a soaring presence behind the words pulsed and stressed a meaning" (p. 367).

David's child-like belief that Hebrew is literally God's language parallels a belief traditionally held by Jewish mystics. In *Major Sources of Jewish Mysticism,* Gershom Scholem observed that the Kabbalists held a "metaphysically positive attitude toward language as God's own instrument."[7] Scholem explained that

> To them, Hebrew, the holy tongue, is not simply a means of expressing certain thoughts, born out of a certain convention and having purely conventional character, in accordance with the theory of language dominant in the Middle Ages. Language in its purest form, that is, Hebrew, according to the Kabbalists, reflects the fundamental spiritual nature of the world; in other words, it has a mystical value.[8]

The word-magic implied in this theory of language has its negative as well as its positive side in David's mind. When he hears about Isaiah's complaint that his lips are unclean, David tries to discover the cause of Isaiah's uncleanness. He concludes that "he said dirty words, I bet. Shit, pee, fuckenbestit" (p. 231). To David these are not simply "dirty words" —improper language. The fact that he has thought them horrifies him, and he concludes: "It's a sin again" (p. 231).

In the same way that coal symbolizes conflict and unresolved tensions and the rabbi himself sums up these conflicting meanings, so the languages in "The Coal" underscore the tension. David believes in the sacredness of Hebrew and "ever since he had begun attending cheder, life had leveled out miraculously, and this he attributed to his increasing nearness to God" (p. 221). Hebrew represents one end of the spectrum of languages, or, in the terms of the novel, the top "rung on the long ladder" of the *Chad Godya* (p. 233), while, according to the rabbi, English lies at the other end. The rabbi denounces the young generation, the generation of English speakers: "What was going to become of Yiddish youth? What would become of this new breed? These Americans? This sidewalk-and-gutter generation?" (p. 374). In the *cheder,* his rejection of the new world parallels his denunciation of English: he shrilly tells his pupils: " 'and don't speak to me in goyish' " (p. 228). For Rabbi Pankower, English itself is defiled.

In "The Rail" the incompatibility of the implications of the several languages reaches a climax. Significantly, when Leo, David's gentile friend, wants to persuade David's cousin, Esther, to join him in the cellar, he attempts, as a ploy, to speak Yiddish. He persuades David to teach him a few phrases which he flaunts to prove his Jewishness. When Esther doubts that he is a Jew, he triumphantly exclaims: " 'Shine maidel, dere! Dat's wutchoo are. See? Tookis! Mm. Oh boy! Ain' dat good!' " (p. 344). The combination of broken English and the broken Yiddish for "pretty girl" and "ass" is excruciating. Later in "The Rail," after David has fled the scene of his cousin's corruption and his own guilt, he runs to the *cheder,* the world of sacred Hebrew. Reciting the words about Isaiah's purification, he falters as his own sense of corruption and guilt conflict with the sacred tongue. His thought, "Mother," destroys his absorption; "A howl of terror beat down all mystery" (p. 367).

In the climactic chapter of *Call It Sleep,* chapter xxi of "The Rail," Roth uses various dialects of English—as well as phrases of other languages—to render the milieu through which David runs madly from fear and guilt toward his own "purification" at the trolley tracks. We hear, and thus *feel,* the very texture of the lives of the masses: Bill Whitney's musing and cursing, Callahan's snickering, O'Toole's obscene sexual bragging, Jim Haig's nostalgic longing for fish and chips. The multi-faceted, multi-lingual, life of the city is captured in the languages of these voices, as well as those of the Armenian peddler, the Jewish pretzel seller, "the kindly faced American woman," and the "gilt-spectacled fanatic." At the moment of David's near-electrocution, when he plunges a milk ladle into the trolley tracks in search of a mystical vision, their voices, previously disparate and jarring, join momentarily into a kind of cosmic voice which Roth renders as poetry:

"W'at?

"W'ut?

"Va'at?

"Gaw Blimey!

"W'atsa da ma'?" (p. 419)

Similarly, when David's recovery from his near-electrocution becomes apparent, the voices of the masses join in thanksgiving:

"Mimi! He's awright! He's awright"

"Yeh?"

"Yeh!"

"No kiddin'! No kiddin'!"

"Yeh!"

"Yuh!"

"Yeh!"

"Oi, Gott sei dank!" (p. 431)

As David subsides from his triumphant, but transient vision of glory, so the languages drift back into separate tongues, accents, voices. As David is carried home by a doctor and policeman, we again hear the war of languages. Genya moans in Yiddish, the doctor tries to give her instructions in German, and Albert answers the policeman's questions in broken English. David has returned to the fallen world, the world of languages after the tower of Babel.

In his exploitation of languages for characterization and atmosphere and in his exploration of the psychological connotations of these languages, Henry Roth adumbrates a central theme of *Call It Sleep:* David Schearl's search for his own voice.

NOTES

[1] Horace Gregory, "East Side World," *The Nation,* 140 (27 Feb. 1935), 255.

[2] Irving Howe, "Life Never Let Up," *The New York Times Book Review,* 25 Oct. 1964, p. 60.

[3] Walter Allen, "Afterword," *Call It Sleep* (New York: Avon Books, 1964), p. 445.

[4] Leo Rosten, *The Joys of Yiddish* (New York: Pocket Books, 1970), p. xvii.

[5] Rosten, p. xvii.

[6] Rosten, p. xvii.

[7] Gershom G. Scholem, *Major Trends in Jewish Mysticism,* (London: Thames and Hudson, 1955), p. 15.

[8] Scholem, p. 17.

CHAPTER IV

CALL IT SLEEP AS A PSYCHOLOGICAL NOVEL: STREAM OF CONSCIOUSNESS AND OTHER TECHNIQUES

Call It Sleep is a profound psychological study of David Schearl, who is at once a sensitive child and a mystic longing for divine illumination. By describing *Call It Sleep* as a psychological novel, I do not mean to suggest that there are two neat categories of novels, psychological novels and nonpsychological or social novels, and that *Call It Sleep* falls simply into the former category. The term "psychological novel" is itself redundant, for traditionally novelists have explored motive, character, feeling, and thought. In fact, it seems unlikely that any significant novelist is not profoundly interested in just these matters. Similarly, all novels may be said to be social novels. Lionel Trilling made this point forcefully in his essay "Manners, Morals, and the Novel," when he asserted that the novel "is a perpetual quest for reality, the field of its research being always the social world, the material of its analysis being always manners as the indication of the direction of man's soul." [1]

As absolute terms, "psychological" novel and "social" novel are untenable. Yet the terms do seem to tell us something about the basic differences between novels. Some novelists seem more interested in exploring the internal life of a character or characters, while others explore reality in its external social manifestations. The difference is one of emphasis or focus.

Call It Sleep is primarily a psychological study of David Schearl. It is also something more. Roth provides a rich, almost palpable sense of an external world, the complex social reality in which David and the other characters move. But while never forfeiting the sense of the exterior, social scene, Roth focuses on the fluid, intense psychic life of his protagonist. *Call It Sleep* is above all a psychological novel.

One of Roth's principal fictional techniques is his use of stream of consciousness. Since there is considerable critical disagreement about whether stream of consciousness is a genre or a technique, and if a genre, what techniques it encompasses,[2] I will define my use of the term at the outset. For the purpose of this chapter, I will use the term stream of consciousness to refer to those passages in which Roth provides the reader with what seems to be a direct quotation from David Schearl's mind.

In *Call It Sleep* Roth combines stream of consciousness passages with a variety of other fictional techniques in order to achieve psychological intensity. These stream of consciousness passages are so interwoven with the other techniques that to treat these passages alone would be to rend the carefully contrived fabric of the novel.

Roth varies his techniques, such as typographical experimentation, in the four books of the novel in order to achieve a different effect in each book and thus provide contrast and variety in this long novel. Therefore I will analyze Roth's use of all these various techniques, including stream of consciousness, as they appear in each of the four books.

Because "The Cellar" anticipates most of the technical devices employed in *Call It Sleep* and introduces many of the thematic and symbolic motifs, this first book demands special attention. As noted previously, the first paragraph establishes David as the center of consciousness in the novel. Besides showing the reader that the sink is being observed from a point of view other than that of the narrator, the opening paragraph makes clear that the point of view is that of a small child. The childish questioning about where the water comes from and goes brings the reader directly into a child's sense of the mystery in the common-place—although the language is that of the narrator. Moreover, by a subtle use of diction Roth reinforces special qualities of David's childlike mind and observation. In the first few paragraphs of this opening book, Roth employs verbs to describe objects that suggest animation and human activity; water "lurked" and "gurgled," a chair "squealed," and a window "chuckled." Likewise, the tip of the faucet with water beads on it is seen as a dripping nose; and when Genya stops sweeping in order to listen to David's request for water, her pause is described obliquely: "the unseen broom stopped to listen" (p. 17). Although none of these first few paragraphs place the reader entirely in David's head or behind his eyes, they enable the reader to sense how the universe appears to David.

Another early paragraph in Book I shows how Roth achieves psychological intensity and the reader's identification with David by other indirect and subtle means:

> He went out into the hallway. Behind him like an eyelid shutting, the soft closing of the door winked out the light. He assayed the stairs, lapsing below him into darkness, and grasping one by one each slender upright to the banister, went down. David never found himself alone on these stairs, but he wished there were no carpet covering them. How could you hear the sound of your own feet in the dark if a carpet muffled every step you took? And if you couldn't hear the sound of your own feet and couldn't actually see anything either, how could you be sure you were actually there and not dreaming? A few steps from the bottom landing, he paused and stared rigidy at the cellar door. It bulged with darkness. Would it hold? . . . [ellipsis Roth's] It held! He jumped the last steps and raced through the narrow hallway to the light of the street. Flying through the doorway was like butting a wave. A dazzling breaker of sunlight burst over his head, swamped him in reeling blur of brilliance, and then receded . . . [ellipsis Roth's] A row of frame houses half in thin shade, a pitted gutter, a yawning ashcan, flotsam on the shore, his street. (p. 20)

Written in third person, the paragraph nonetheless stays very close to David's mind, his sense of the world around him. As in the first paragraph of "The Cellar," especially well-chosen verbs support Roth's pschological effects. Here Roth gives the reader an intense sense of David's fear of the dark and the cellar: the comparison of the close of the door to the "winking" of an eyelid imparts a particularly sinister feel to the event, as does the "bulging" of the darkness. The credibility of David's fear is profound because the reader is convinced of Roth's psychological insight into the child's mind; David's fear that he is dreaming when he cannot hear his own footsteps is particularly convincing because it suggests the deeper psychological roots of his fears. Roth here comes close to placing the reader directly behind David's eyes. The words, "Would it hold? . . . It held," bring us swiftly into the actual event as it unfolds. The reader is forced to live through David's experience with him: the ellipsis in this passage marks David's mad dash past the cellar. Moreover, by using indirect narration in this paragraph rather than stream of consciousness, Roth enables the reader to see what David is doing as well as to experience his reactions. The concluding passage of the paragraph, beginning with the words "A row" reveals another of Roth's devices for achieving psychological intensity: the use of a sentence fragment to record David's immediate sensory impression. This use of a sentence fragment to indicate David's immediate sensory impression appears again later in "The Cellar" when Annie drags David into the closet. David senses, "Darkness, immense and stale, the reek of moth balls threading it" (p. 53).

Later in Book I, Roth uses another device to increase the reader's psychological identification with David, without destroying the reader's sense of the external physical world in which David moves. In the scene in which Luter stays with David while his parents attend a theatrical performance, the reader experiences David's inexplicable, yet nonetheless potent, suspicions of Luter. First the reader enters David's childish reverie about Puss in Boots: "If one had these on one's feet instead of shoes, one might bound instead of walk. High as the roof; far away at once. Like Puss in Boots. But if the mouse changed back into an ogre inside the puss—just before he died—I'm a mouse—an ogre—Then poor Puss would have swelled and swelled and—" (p. 36). Luter's intense preoccupation distracts David, and he becomes completely absorbed in Luter's disturbing change from bland affability to self-absorbed cunning. In the following paragraph, Roth presents his material in such a way that the reader both follows Luter's physical movements and at the same time experiences David's reactions to them:

> Deliberate, brown-clad legs approached (what?) passed by him (he relaxed) stopped before the wall (peered over his shoulder) the calendar. Luter thumbed the leaves (black, black, black, red, black, black) held up a thin sheaf, and with puckered lips, stared at the date as though something far more intricate and absorbing than the mere figures were depicted there. Then he lowered the upturned leaves slowly, cautiously (Why? Why so carefully? They had only one place they could fall to) and rubbed his hands. (p. 36)

While in general Roth presents David's impressions in the parenthetical insertions, it is noteworthy that Roth uses both third person and first person in these insertions. Since it is more effective to say "he relaxed" than to dramatize David's mind relaxing, Roth chooses this technique.

Besides using parenthetical expressions to represent David's reactions, Roth occasionally modifies his sentence structure and rhythms to reproduce the very motion of David's mind; thus, although the material is presented indirectly, the texture of David's emotions is sharply defined. For example, when David tries to avoid meeting Annie and Yussie, he is faced with the necessity of running past the dread cellar in order to escape seeing them: "he must—before they saw—the darkness, the door, the darkness. The man in the box in the carriage. Alone. He must" (p. 62). The jerkiness of phrase and repetition of key words suggest David's frenzy and confusion as he tries to steel himself to pass the cellar.

Similarly, in another scene in "The Cellar" Roth deliberately slows the flow of his prose to reproduce the horrible stillness and nightmare timelessness of the moment before Albert beats David:

> Nothing existed any longer except his father's right hand—the hand that hung down into the electric circle of his vision. Terrific clarity was given him. Terrific leisure. Transfixed, timeless, he studied the curling fingers that twitched spasmodically, studied the printer's ink ingrained upon the finger tips, pondered, as if all there were in the world, the nail of the smallest finger, nipped by a press, that climbed in a jagged little stair to the hangnail. Terrific absorption. (p. 83)

The repetition of the word "terrific," the beating quality of the repeated "T" sounds, the extraordinarily minute observation of Albert's hand, give the scene an appalling slowness and horror—qualities the event has for David himself.

Another technique which adds to the psychological intensity of the novel is Roth's use of italics for heightened emotion, especially shocked horror: *"The hammer in that hand when he stood! The hammer!"* (p. 83). Previous to this sentence about the hammer, Roth used italics twice in "The Cellar" to register the protagonist's psychological discoveries. First, when Annie explains about sex to him, David repeats with shock her word *"knish"*—a vulgarism in Yiddish for the vagina (p. 53). Later when his mother tells him that there is no afterlife, that the dead lie in their graves forever, he repeats with terror, *"Eternal years"* (p. 69). The italicized passage quoted above concerning the hammer indicates that David suddenly recalls two related events: first, his trip to Albert's former place of employment where David learned about his father's attack with a hammer on another man, and second, his subsequent dream vision of his father in which Albert stood with a hammer on a high roof of darkness.

In "The Cellar," Roth dramatizes David's reactions most fully in two scenes: when he learns about death from Genya, and when he flees through the streets believing that he has killed a playmate. The first scene is thematically important because it reveals David's association of many dark, negative experiences and images, and because it establishes the negative focus of "The Cellar" as symbol and book. The second scene has similar thematic importance, and it also foreshadows David's mad, hallucinatory dash toward the rail in Book IV.

The scene in which David learns about the finality of death from his mother has already been mentioned in connection with the use of italics to emphasize David's emotionally charged reaction to his mother's explanation. Indeed, in this scene Roth uses a number of devices to show David's heightened sensitivity—including setting off David's silent repetition of Genya's words by a dash and separate paragraph: "—Dark. In the grave. Eternal years . . ." [ellipsis Roth's] (p. 70). However, Roth's primary method in this scene is to reproduce David's developing associations and thoughts—that is, to record his stream of consciousness. As evening approaches, the uneven shifting quality of the twilight with its "flecks, intricate as foam" reminds David of a past event. The flecks of light seem to him "like popcorn blowing in the big window in that big candystore. Blowing and settling. That day. Long ago" (p. 70). This memory recalls one of the first scenes of the book in which David accompanies Albert to the printing shop where Albert had quit in a murderous rage. On that day, David and his father had passed an ice cream parlor where "gaudy, colored popcorn danced and drifted, blown by a fan" (p. 24). This subtle visual association is extremely important because the memory it recalls is an event which has cemented David's vision of his father as a looming, crazy figure of god-like wrath. Moreover, the shifting, unsteady quality of the light which David compares to the popcorn is of special significance to David, because he consistently associates light with good and dark with evil. The link between the past and the present, between "flecks" of twilight and popcorn is visually imagistic, and, although the popcorn is not "logically" connected with Albert's rage in the way the hammer is, the very randomness of the association seems psychologically convincing.

After associating the flecks of light with blowing pieces of popcorn, David's mind moves from these tiny drifting things to the actual snow falling outside the apartment window, and then to another memory, this time of confetti which was thrown at a newly-married couple. Recalling how the bridal couple entered a black carriage, David shifts his focus to this object and then recalls that on another occasion, he saw a black carriage carry off a coffin. The second stream of associations is noteworthy in that the recollection about the wedding evokes a scene which Roth never previously dramatized—unlike the scene of Albert's return to the printing shop. Because Roth is careful to make the meaning of this memory clear, the reader never loses David's trend of thought. Further, this second group of associations shows David linking the distant past (the wedding), to the more recent past (the funeral he saw earlier in the day), to the actual present (the sabbath eve).

After dramatizing the rapid movement of David's mind as it flits from image to image, from past to present, Roth ends the section with David's conclusion about the significance of his flowing associations: "Everything belonged to the same dark. Confetti and coffins" (p. 70). This conclusion makes the thematic significance of Book I clear for the reader.

The second major use of stream of consciousness in "The Cellar" occurs during David's flight from his neighborhood when he believes he has killed a friend. This early scene establishes David's highly emotional nature and his tendency to flee when trapped by guilt and fear. Before his fight with the neighbor boy, David recognizes Luter approaching, associates Luter's visit to Genya with his own unpleasant sexual initiation with Annie, and concludes "He was going to make her play now. Like Annie. In the closet!" (p. 89). This fearful conclusion distracts David, making him unable to "follow the leader," much to his friends' annoyance. Subsequently the boys tease David about Albert's beating him; then David pushes a youngster down and flees. In this scene Roth uses a variety of means to make the scene psychologically vivid. When David first runs to the cellar to hide, Roth shows the boy's terror by presenting his thoughts as jerky and frantic: "The door. . . . No! No! Not there! No . . . Must . . . No! No! . . . Policeman . . . Run out . . . No, they'd catch" [ellipses Roth's] (p. 91). Roth follows this with a brilliant description of the darkness of the cellar, a description which provides words and images equivalent to the child's wordless apprehension of its repulsiveness. As Faulkner in the first section of *The Sound and the Fury* convinces the reader that he has captured an idiot's vision of the universe, so in descriptions like these Roth seems absolutely right in conveying how a sensitive child would perceive the cellar, or, more precisely, how this particular sensitive child would perceive it.

David's subsequent flight through the streets and brief stay in the police station are presented in detail. In these scenes Roth dramatizes other aspects of David's mind than horror and fear. For example, we see him playing games with the telegraph poles as he runs beside them; pretending to race them up the hill, he addresses them as "Mr. High Wood" (he talks to and argues with objects throughout *Call It Sleep).* Likewise, we see David arguing with himself about when it is time to return home:

> —Time to look back.
> —No.
> —Time to look back.
> —Only to the end of that hill. There where the clouds fell.
> —Time to look back. (p. 94).

One of Roth's reasons for reproducing David's thoughts at this time so fully is that the telegraph poles become highly significant to David in the future. Here he sees the telegraph poles with "the wires on their crosses swinging into the sky" and thinks they are "climbing into the sky" (p. 94). Later he comes to associate this entire race through the streets with Isaiah's purification by God. Therefore it is important to Roth that the reader experience David's perceptions of the telegraph poles as they register in his mind; through David's stream of consciousness the reader grasps both David's misapprehensions and the importance of the telegraph poles.

Besides registering David's reactions to the poles, Roth captures David's more random thoughts and memories, thus making the child a believable, rounded figure. When he passes a cat "licking a paw," David thinks hungrily of things his mother may prepare for dinner. The stream of consciousness passage reproduces the sing-song quality of David's thoughts as they parallel his footsteps: "sour cream. Sour. Cream. Sour Cream. Like it, like it. I—like—it. I like cake but I don't like herring" (p. 95).

When David is taken to the police station, Roth uses stream of consciousness techniques in two different sections to evoke the quality of David's feelings during this traumatic experience and to foreshadow parallel plot developments in the later books of the novel. David believes himself tricked by an old woman who promises to take him home but instead takes him to the police station; accordingly, his thoughts revolve around the words, "never believe." He connects childhood games, coffins, sex, and words in general with the cellar—all of life seems untrustworthy (p.

102). This fearful conclusion remains even after his mother comes for him. After he is home, he thinks (significantly the thought is rendered in italics) "*—Don't believe. Don't believe. Don't believe. Never!*" (p. 114). This deep lack of faith, this intuition of the evil of all existence, which forms the emotional basis of "The Cellar," anticipates David's search for meaning and redemption in the final book.

After immersing the reader in David's long "never believe" reverie, Roth captures the sense of simultaneity, of the instantaneous break in David's thoughts, by a typographical device:

> Slow, cunning. Trust noth—
> On the stairs outside, heavy feet tramped down . . .
> [ellipsis mine] (p. 103)

This substitution of a dash for the omitted letters of a word to achieve a sense of simultaneity anticipates Roth's extended use of this technique in the climatic chapter of "The Rail."

David's other long reverie in the police station is set off by the sound of a whistle, a sound that recalls the first chapter of "The Cellar," when David can tell time only by whistles: when David hears the factory whistle, he knows he can return to the safety of his home from the dangers of the street. The stream of consciousness section here reveals certain aspects of David's mind which Roth develops more fully in later scenes, especially David's attempt to "move" within his own mind, to transfer himself to another scene by intense mental effort. Hearing the wail of the whistle, David realizes that he cannot escape physically from the police station and thinks: "Be two Davids, be two! One here, one outside on the curb. Now watch! Wait till she looks out! Now watch! See? There she is behind the curtain. Yes, that thick lace curtain—only in the winter it was there. Now she parts them—two hands like that—stoops" (p. 104). The power of David's imagination and his extraordinary sense of mental reality are both captured in this passage.

The second book of the novel, "The Picture," is quite different in focus and effect from "The Cellar." Having laid a solid basis of negative psychological connotations of the cellar in the first book, in "The Picture" Roth provides relief from David's tortured associations. Book I takes the reader to the depths of David's mind and achieves an almost unbearable intensity. The succeeding book offers a contrast to the pounding, accumulating negative movement of the first book.

During much of Book II, the fictional mode is comic rather than tragic. Indeed, the change of fictional modes parallels the Schearls' physical move from Brownsville (and their apartment house with the cellar) to the Lower East Side and its "avalanche of sound" (p. 143). In addition, the introduction of Aunt Bertha, whom Walter Allen called "a very considerable comic creation,"[3] with her physical immensity, sloppiness, and sharp Yiddish wit moves the focus temporarily away from David.

Maynard Mack, in his introduction to *Joseph Andrews,* suggested certain criteria for differentiating between the comic and tragic modes of fiction; his comments may well be applied to Roth's technique in the opening chapters of "The Picture." Mack asserted that "comedy presents us with life apprehended in the form of spectacle rather than in the form of experience," and added that for the comic vision "we must be not inside the character but outside him."[4]

Chapter iii of "The Picture" exemplifies Mack's analysis of comedy. In that chapter Aunt Bertha and David visit the Metropolitan Museum. In an early review of *Call It Sleep,* Horace Gregory remarked that Bertha's "trip with David to the Metropolitan Museum is, I think, one of the best single episodes in contemporary fiction."[5] Roth achieves his considerable comic success in this chapter by observing David and his aunt from the outside, as figures of fun who doggedly trail a couple through the museum hoping to find the way out. Unlike in "The Cellar," here the reader is scarcely aware of David's psychological state, lest we experience his inner fear rather than laugh at his outward comic condition. Much of the comic effect is achieved by Roth's concentration on physical description and on Bertha's hilarious comments. For example, we read that "sweat runneled his aunt's cheeks, hung down from her chin, fell sometimes, spotting the bosom of her green dress" (p. 147); we hear Bertha's instructions to David about following the couple: "We must cleave to them like mire on a pig" (p. 149).

Besides subtly shifting the focus in the opening scenes of "The Picture" for comic relief and variety, Roth, throughout the book, keeps the reader at a far greater psychological distance from David than in "The Cellar." This change in technique may be seen in Roth's use of italics and stream of consciousness. In the first book, he uses italics four times, while in "The Picture" only once; on that occasion, David inwardly exclaims *"That was it!"* (indicating the picture of corn which he and Bertha just noticed) (p. 187). The italicized exclamation follows shortly one of the few stream of consciousness passages in "The Picture." When Genya brings home the picture she has bought from a street vendor, David is unconcerned with it until he notices his mother's extreme animation while she hangs it up. Later, when he is wandering through the streets, David muses on the events of the day, his thoughts shifting from the nuts his mother has forgotten to ask for in the Chinese laundry to the impending visit of Bertha's suitor. Meanwhile he tries to remember a half-buried thought about the picture: "He had been wondering about something he'd told himself. Yes. Something. But now he couldn't remember. Not chinee-nuts. No. Company was coming. Maybe, no" (p. 173). Roth's depiction of David's thoughts here gives the reader a sense of his uncomprehending, yet emotionally alert, awareness of the picture and dramatically anticipates Genya's revelation of its meaning for her.

The other major passage of stream of consciousness in Book II focuses on David's growing concern about the picture. When he overhears his mother's revelations about her love affair, David immediately recognizes the connection between the story and the picture. His mother's words, " 'I felt as empty as a bell till I looked at the blue corn flowers at my feet' " (p. 203), awaken an immediate intuition in David's mind: "—Blue corn flowers? Likes them! That was—!" (p. 203). Later Bertha curses Genya's unfaithful lover, who deserted her for an older rich woman, saying " 'may it be that the maker of the road [the rich woman's brother] and his sister and his brother-in-law meet with years as black and as long as that road!' " (p. 204). Again David's intense reaction is immediately registered in a stream of consciousness passage: "—Road. Black! Black! Where did I hear it before? Black? Not now" (p. 204). Bertha's curse, of course, reinforces the light/dark imagery of the novel, emphasizing the evil of blackness. But her curse also recalls one of Genya's earlier speeches in "The Cellar." In that book, when Genya is painfully uneasy and distracted about Luter's hostility toward Albert, she tries to find relief from her thoughts by listening to David's recollections of his day. Trying to amuse her, David tells his mother about seeing a new green sidewalk being laid down and a boy poking a hole in it with his foot. Ironically, this seemingly neutral recollection has a potent effect on Genya: "Her face had sagged strangely, lips parting before a slow emission of breath. The taut, pale planes of her cheeks seemed to have slipped the chin-bone, overlapped it" (pp. 129-130). When David asks her why she reacts so strongly to his little reminiscence, she only replies, " 'Nothing! Nothing at all! I did that too when I was a girl, stepping on a road, new-made. But mine was black! Nothing! Nothing at all' " (p. 130). Unable to fathom the meaning of his mother's unusually strong reaction, David simply stores the memory—as does the careful reader. This memory emerges from David's unconscious when he hears Bertha's curse on Genya's unfaithful lover and the engineer of the new black road to Genya's village in Austria.

Roth's decision to use few stream of consciousness passages and psychological distancing in "The Picture" is aesthetically sound for two reasons. First, his method provides the reader with a palpable sense of the external physical world surrounding David, rather than limiting the reader's vision to David's distorted perceptions of it. Second, although we glimpse David's emotional reactions to the picture and his mother's revelation, we do not experience his extreme psychological confusion, which for dramatic purposes Roth saves until "The Rail." Here we only touch upon David's intense reaction to Genya's revelations, his confusion, and the fact that he puts off trying to figure out the precise emotional significance. Although David wonders what an "orghaneest" is and why his mother liked goyim, he does not yet come to any real conclusions. Just as he ends thinking about the black road by saying "Not now," his last words in "The Picture" have the same anticipatory inconclusiveness: "Gee! The picture! Not now, though. Look at it later, when nobody's here . . . Green and blue it's—Sh!" [ellipsis Roth's] (p. 207). Roth's relative distance from David in "The Picture" gives the reader a clear sense of the world surrounding the child—especially of Genya's emotional depth. This distancing also fills the reader with curiosity about what David will make of his mother's revelations, and dramatically prepares for the child's tortured and confused explanation to the rabbi in the final book of the novel.

Similar to "The Picture" in its brevity, "The Coal" is decidedly different in tone and technique. While Book II alleviates the reader's tension and broadens the focus to capture a more tangible sense of external realities, Book III again thrusts the reader directly into David's mind, focusing especially on his search for transcendence. Having little plot in the sense of physical events, this book concentrates on David's internal development, particularly his deepening religious feelings. Not surprisingly, in "The Coal" Roth uses stream of consciousness passages more extensively than in either of the two earlier books to render this internal development and to make David's growing intuitions *felt* by the reader rather than simply reported by the author. The extensive use of stream of consciousness serves another general aesthetic purpose: as David recalls images and memories from the earlier books, digesting and reassembling them, the reader too is able to "knit together" the manifold threads of the novel into an increasingly complex whole. Related to this increasing employment of stream of consciousness is Roth's unusual use of typography, including capitalization, dashes, and dots for various psychological effects.

One of the early uses of stream of consciousness in book III is noteworthy for two reasons. First, it makes clear how Roth uses David's memory and imagination as unifying devices aesthetically; David's recollections serve to mold *Call It Sleep* into an organic whole. Seeing neighborhood children teasing a girl whose underpants have been exposed when her dress was raised by the wind, David thinks: "Knish and closet. Puh! And that time when two dogs were stuck together. Puh! Threw water that man. Shame! Shame!" (p. 223). The attentive reader recalls David's sexual initiation with Annie in the closet in "The Cellar," as well as her vulgar expression for the vagina, "knish." The fact that "knish" was the first word Roth italicized in *Call It Sleep* makes the verbal echo especially prominent.

Second, the way Roth moves almost imperceptibly in and out of David's mind in this passage is also significant. Just prior to the words quoted above, Roth writes: "With what prompt spasms the mummified images in the brain started from their niches, aped former antics and lapsed. It recalled that time, way long ago" (p. 223). With the change in complexity of diction and imagery beginning with "way long ago," the reader glides gracefully into David's words and mind from the narrator's polished prose.

In the central scene of Book III, in which David hears about Isaiah's purification with God's coal, Roth combines a wide variety of techniques, including stream of consciousness and typographical experimentation, to counterpoint multiple layers of action and reflections and of external and internal reality. We hear the rabbi teaching Mendel about Isaiah, and their conversation is written in transliteration of the Hebrew, "Beshnos mos hamelech Uziyahu vaereh es adonoi" as well as in translation into pure English (for Yiddish) "In the year that King Uzziah died, Isaiah saw God" (pp. 225-227). At the other verbal extreme, we hear the babble of schoolboys' voices, cursing and arguing in broken English: " 'Dere! Chinky shows! Id's mine! How many fences didja go? I tore it f'om a tree in duh pock, mine bean shooduh! T'ree fences. So a lighten den, wise guy!' " (p. 230). As Leslie Fiedler observed, "Such grossness [as the boys' talk] is necessary to make clear the challenge of the angelic chorus singing 'Holy, Holy, Holy' even as that chorus is necessary to define the full horror of mouths that can scarcely blaspheme intelligibly." [6] David, whose thoughts are revealed by his stream of consciousness musings, tries to mediate between the holiness of the Bible and the corruption of his contempories. Besides counterpointing the various voices against David's stream of consciousness, Roth also inserts parentheses into David's flow of thought to insure that the reader has an external as well as an internal view of David's activity. For example, pondering about why Isaiah said he had an unclean mouth, David thinks: "But your mouth don't get dirty. I don't feel no dirt," and Roth inserts the information "(He rolled his tongue about)" (p. 231).

Later in the scene, when David recites *Chad Godya,* Roth indicates the child's intense reaction to the implications of the Passover song by registering his astonishment in italics. The memory link to the past, the connection between Book I and this scene, is a verbal echo ("but sometime") rather than a visual image (p. 233). Early in "The Cellar," when Genya had told David that the dead do not awaken, he had not been able to accept this bleak vision and twice insisted, " 'But sometime' " (p. 69).

Roth reproduces David's stream of consciousness in "The Coal" for another special effect: to reinforce the fact that, although David is a seeker after mystical transcendence, a spiritual quester of sorts, he is nonetheless a child. Roth shows us David making childish errors and misperceptions, and thus assures that we do not forget his youth and inexperience. In this way, Roth reinforces David's credibility as a character. David's primary "error" in this book is, of course, that of not differentiating between the coal or burning ember which purified Isaiah and black combustible fuel (in the cellar). While with the coal David tries to give magical properties to a natural element, to add mystery to the coal bin, he also wrongly "de-mystifies" events on another occasion. Hearing thunder while in the *cheder,* he thinks the noise is a "bed on wheels" scraping along a floor (p. 226). Thus when he tells the rabbi he saw a light like Isaiah's in the car tracks, Reb Pankower laughs hysterically at David's childish errors: " 'Yesterday he heard a bed in the thunder! Today he sees a vision in a crack. Oy! Chah! Chah! Chah!' " (p. 257).

Roth's increased use of stream of consciousness in "The Coal" is part of his greater stylistic experimentation in this book. One example is the description of the brass banisters of the Schearls' apartment house: "It had a corrupt odor, brass, as of something rotting away, and yet where the sun struck the burnished metal, it splintered into a brilliant yellow light. Decay. Radiance. Funny" (p. 242). The three last words indicate David's subjective reaction and also show a condensation from sentence fragments to single words to register sensual perception and reaction.

Significantly, Roth's typographical experimentation in "The Coal" is most extensive in the scene dramatizing David's mystical vision at the river—just as the most experimental chapter in the entire novel is the mystical vision at the trolley tracks in the final book. Roth's short paragraphs, in "The Coal," alternating poetic description with David's thoughts and memories, give the effect of a "dialogue" between the child and the natural world, between David's private reality and the phenomenal universe:

> His gaze shifted to the left. As the cloud began to pass, a long, slim lathe of sunlight burned silver on the water—
>
> —Gee, didn't see before!
>
> Widened to a swath, a lane, widened.
>
> —Like a ship just went.
>
> A plain, flawless, sheer as foil to the serried margins. His eyes dazzled.
>
> —Fire on the water. White.
>
> His lids grew heavy.
>
> —In the water she said. White. Brighter than day. Whiter. And He was. (p. 247)

This passage with its astonishing literal epiphany of God, "And He was," succeeds because of Roth's manipulation of techniques usually associated with poetry. In his stream of consciousness, David combines memory and vision, recollection and awe. His words, "In the water she said," recall Genya's explanation several pages earlier that God lives "in the earth and in the water and in the world" (p. 241). The breaking up of a syntactically complete sentence of description by the insertion of a brief paragraph of David's thoughts (for example, between the words "water" and "Widened" in the passage quoted above brings internal and external reality into close conjunction, and suggests the sense of oneness with the universe that a mystical experience usually involves.

As David's mystical vision subsides, Roth uses a wide variety of punctuation and typographical devices to capture the various levels of reality—dashes, dots, and literal transcription of sound effects, such as "Ug chug" and "cucka cucka." David's reawakening from his dream-like state is marked typographically by the capitalization of these conflicting sounds: "Ug chug, ug chug, ug—TEW WEET!" (p. 248). The tugboat's engine and whistle bring him back to earth. Technically and thematically, this scene foreshadows the treatment of the climatic chapter in "The Rail."

When the three gentile boys cruelly provoke David into thrusting a sword into the trolley tracks, the release of power both terrifies and awes him. He flees to the *cheder* for security, for a reassertion of his everyday life. The intensity of the two events, the river vision and the first rail incident, their seeming similarity and yet antagonism (David is forced by anti-Semites into the second act) overwhelms him emotionally. His subsiding into a relaxed state and his subsequent discovery that God is to be found everywhere, including in the coal in the cellar, is precisely captured in a stream of consciousness reverie. In the *cheder* yard, he finds the "realities warm and palpable" which he seeks in the comforting sounds and smells of Jewish cooking, especially the steady chopping of food and herbs. His reverie reflects and parallels this constant "chop, chop" and achieves a slow, chanting rhythm: "In the river, showed him, showed. In the dark, in the river was there. Came out if He wanted, was there. Stayed in if He wanted, was there" (p. 254-255). The hypnotic beat and repetition work slowly toward a climax of realization in which Roth uses special typography to show the leap David's mind makes:

> —In the dark, in the hallways, was there. In the dark, in the cellars was there. Where cellars is locked, where cellars is coal, where cellars is coal, is
> —Coal!
> —Coal! (p. 255)

In addition to being by far the longest of the four books of the novel, "The Rail" is the most densely wrought and complex section. In this book Roth intertwines and transposes multiple thematic and imagistic strands, bringing them to an intensely dramatic climax in chapter xxi. Moreover, in "The Rail" as a whole Roth paradoxically achieves both his deepest psychological insight and his widest view of the surrounding social scene.

One example of the increased psychological intensity in "The Rail" is the extensive use of italics throughout the book, particularly in chapter xxi, in which Roth counterpoints long sections of italicized passages pertaining to David's mystical experience with unitalicized sections describing the movements of the city inhabitants around him. In addition to this climactic chapter, Roth uses italics on fourteen occasions in "The Rail"— from David's simple cries of "awakened terror" while in the cellar with Leo and Esther ("—*Ow*!"), to longer sentence fragments (*"From somewhere an obscure drum of hooves"*) which describes Albert's angry approach when he comes to take David on his milk rounds (p. 272).

Later in "The Rail" after two strangers steal Albert's milk despite David's efforts to protect the bottles, the child becomes frenzied, anticipating his father's rage. Knowing that he cannot physically escape his father, he attempts a mental escape; he tries "to flee from himself as he had once done in the darkness behind his palms" (p. 278) in the police station scene in "The Cellar." He tries to escape to his mother in his imagination by mentally going home through his neighborhood streets to his apartment. Imagining his route homeward, he is thwarted first as mental pictures of his old apartment building in Brownsville with its cellar crowd his mind, then by the image of baby carriages whose smell of milk he involuntarily associates with his present predicament. His past memories (the cellar) and his present reality (the milk) combine to prevent his mental journey homeward.

Subsequently David tries to escape reality by literally denying his own identity, by becoming someone else. This attempt occurs after David, in order to obtain rosary beads, helps Leo "play dirty" with Esther and then tells the rabbi a confused story about his mother's past. David's motivation behind this complusive revelation is complex, but it is primarily based on his intense desire for self-justification. First, David hopes to excuse his activities with Leo by shifting the blame to his mother. In his words, "If she like a goy, so I liked. There! She made me. How did I know? It's all her fault and I'm going to tell too. Blame it on her. Yours, Mama! Yours!" (p. 385). Even more psychologically significant is the fact that the basis of David's tale is that Genya and Albert are not his parents—and thus, in his own mind, David is someone other than himself.

Roth makes David's complex motivation clear in several stream of consciousness passages. In a wild torrent of words, David insists, " 'I'm somebody else—, *else*—ELSE! Dot's who I am. . . . Can't tell on me. I ain'. So tell! Tell her! Tell Tanta Berta! Tell my modder! I ain'!' " (p. 371-372). Indeed, this attempt to be someone other than himself is made manifest by the very language of David's thought processes. Ordinarily ashamed to curse even to himself, he now revels hysterically in words like "fugimbestit" and "sonn'va-bitch" and calls the rabbi "ol smoke-mout'-stink" and "ol' geezer" (pp. 371-372). Even more tellingly, he takes his tormentors, the anti-Semitic gentile boys who have forced him to push the sword into the trolley tracks, as models of behavior and speech. David's words, " 'Lager beeuh comms f'om—,' " before urinating in the street exactly reproduce Pedey's words and actions in "The Coal." Besides reinforcing David's complex and confused motivation in telling the rabbi the story about his mother, this mimicking of the gentile boys' behavior anticipates David's return to the rail. Thus the stream of consciousness passage looks forward and backward, linking the novel psychologically and aesthetically.

Formally the arrangement and technique of chapters xvi, xvii, and xviii are highly significant for the variety and psychological effect achieved. In chapter xvi, for the first time since the prologue, Roth removes the reader entirely from David's presence; here the reader follows the rabbi on his journey from the *cheder* to the Schearl apartment. The following chapter, in contrast, consists almost entirely of David's stream of consciousness as he mentally tortures himself with memories and anticipation before returning home. In the third of these chapters, the reader again leaves David, but this time to witness a dramatized scene between Nathan and Bertha at their candy store before Nathan slips off to demand David's punishment for allowing Leo to play sexually with Esther. The effect of this arrangement is both dramatically and psychologically effective, in that the scenes with the rabbi and the Sternowitz couple contrast with the intensely private, internal movement of the middle chapter, balance each other, and provide a building sense of fatality; the external forces (the rabbi and the Sternowitz couple) which David has set in motion by his tale about his mother and his activity with Leo seem inexorable—both to David and the reader.

Chapter xvii, which consists largely of David's tortured thoughts before returning home, combines another technique with the stream of consciousness passages. This technique may perhaps best be explained by T. S. Eliot's theory of the "objective correlative." In this chapter, an external event, a plot fragment, seems to evoke exactly the required emotion in both character and reader. At the close of chapter xvii, Roth writes:

> A boy stood leaning against the brass banister on the top step of the stoop. He held in his hands the torn tissue of a burst red balloon which he sucked and twisted into tiny crimson bubbles. As David, fainting with terror, dragged himself up the stone stairs, the other nipped at a moist, new-made sphere. It popped. He grinned blithely.
>
> "Yuh see how I ead 'em? One bit!" [sic]
>
> David stopped, stared at him unseeingly. In the trance that locked his mind only one sensation guttered with a bare significance. The chill of the tarnished railing under his palm, the chill and the memory of its lustre and the flat taint of corruption.
>
> "Now, I'll make a real big one!" said the boy. "Watch me!" The stretched red rubber hollowed into a small antre in his mouth, was engulfed, twisted, revealed. "See dot! In one bite!"
>
> Pop!
>
> Despair . . . [ellipsis Roth's] (p. 379)

In a way that cannot be precisely explained, this scene of the boy popping the balloon captures the essence of David's despair—his overpowering sense of his own corruption and that of the world. The other boy's youthful blitheness seems particularly malevolent, and his wanton destructiveness as he "tortures" the balloon—sucking, twisting, and finally popping it—parallels and evokes David's psychological distress. Thus in this chapter the stream of consciousness and narration support each other in the most intimate way possible.

For the dramatic confrontations involving the Schearls, Rabbi Pankower, and the Sternowitz couple in chapter xix, Roth uses conventional narration and dialogue, with little stream of consciousness. However, in the last sentences of the chapter Roth again uses a technique mentioned previously: the modulation of the narrator's prose to evoke David's emotional condition and to achieve psychological closeness to the protagonist. Thrown out of his parents' apartment, the child runs downstairs to the street and tries to decide what to do next. The chapter closes:

> The street.
>
> The street. He dared to breathe. And stumbled to the sidewalk and stood there, stood there. (p. 403)

Because of the modification of his prose, Roth has no need to tell us that David is breathing heavily, overwrought from the scene in the apartment and his flight. The prose itself captures David's breathless panting, his pounding heart.

In the succeeding chapter Roth combines a variety of stylistic techniques and anticipates the climactic scene both thematically and technically. In long passages of stream of consciousness, David reveals both his extreme youth and his anguish, a combination that is, of course, particularly poignant. He plays childish games with the window and with himself; he asks the window: " 'Yuh gonna lighd winder? Winder! Winder! Yuh gonna lighd winder?' " (p. 407) and gives the window several chances to do so, as he would a playmate. Likewise, he prepares himself emotionally for his possible electrocution by daring and double-daring himself. The childishness of these games is especially moving because their motivation is so unchildish—in a sense, so unnatural. David's games effectively contrast with the innocent, unself-conscious hide-and-seek game played by the other children during this chapter. David's concern about and conversation with the window about lighting is psychologically significant; he obviously equates the window's lighting with emotional stability. Part of him believes that all his conflicts will be alleviated if only the light in his apartment goes on. Moreover, the "illumination" is of symbolic value both to him and to the reader, and the failure of the light to go on in the Schearl apartment reinforces the necessity of David's journey to the trolley tracks in search of God's light.

Chapter xx technically anticipates the subsequent climactic chapter in the duality of its movement—deeper internally and broader externally. In the stream of consciousness sections we move deeper into David's emotions and complex motivations. As he anticipates how he will explain his possession of the rosary beads to his father, we relive his deeply intertwined stream of associations. On the other hand, David's psychic movement into himself and his God-preoccupation are shown against the large, social scene. Besides the children's games mentioned previously, we hear the voices of old Jewish men discussing card games and see brief images of passersby. While David moves toward his decision to try to find God's coal in the trolley tracks, we see: "Humanity. On feet, on crutches, in carts and cars. The ice vendor. The waffle wagon. Human voices, motion seething, throbbing, bawling, honking horns and whistling" (p. 407).

The setting at the trolley tracks is both realistic and symbolic, both literally accurate and emblematic: "To the left, the chipped brick wall of the warehouse shut off the west and humanity, to the right and behind him, the ledge of the dump heap rose; before him land's end and the glitter on the rail" (p. 409). Cut off from humanity by the desperation of his religious need, sensing the corruption, the "dump heap" of man's condition, David turns to the "glitter" of God's coal. The phantasmagoria of the scene parallel David's convulsive words, about which Roth says:

> The small sputter of words in his brain seemed no longer his own, no longer cramped by skull, but detached from him, the core of his surroundings. And he heard them again as though all space had impelled them and were shattered in the framing, and they boomed in his ears, vast, delayed and alien. (p. 409)

Besides conveying David's condition, this passage also provides an explanation of and justification for the extraordinary techniques of the next chapter.

Because of the extreme complexity of chapter xxi and the central importance of the two concluding chapters of *Call It Sleep,* I will discuss chapters xxi and xxii of "The Rail" separately and in detail in my following chapter. Although *Call It Sleep* achieves its greatest psychological intensity and Roth exhibits his greatest technical virtuosity in chapter xxi, it is well to examine what the novel achieves up to that point; the climactic chapter is no mere technical *tour de force,* and its effectiveness rests securely on Roth's careful manipulation of his materials throughout the novel. Using stream of consciousness on various occasions in *Call It Sleep,* Roth combines these passages with a variety of fictional techniques. Using typographical experimentation, modifying his prose to reflect his protagonist's emotional condition, making his settings both symbolically and psychologically significant, ordering the arrangement of chapters for dramatic effect, Roth continually shapes his novel to make it psychologically intense. Moreover, the modification of these devices and techniques in the four books of *Call It Sleep* provides for variety and balance and assures the reader's growing sensitivity to and identification with David's psychic nature and mystical quest.

NOTES

[1] Lionel Trilling, "Manners, Morals, and the Novel," in *Approaches to the Novel: Materials for a Poetics,* ed. Robert Scholes (San Francisco: Chandler Publishing Co., 1971), p. 237.

[2] On the one hand, Lawrence Edward Bowling, in "What Is the Stream of Consciousness Technique?" (*PMLA*, 65 [1950], 345), stated that "the stream of consciousness technique may be defined as that narrative method by which the author attempts to give *a direct quotation of the mind*—not merely of the language area but of the whole consciousness." On the other hand, in *Stream of Consciousness in the Modern Novel* (Berkeley and Los Angeles: Univ. of Calif. Press, 1954), p. 4, Robert Humphrey asserted that "there is no stream of consciousness technique," and explained that stream of consciousness is a genre using four basic techniques: direct interior monologue, indirect interior monologue, omniscient description, and soliloquy. Melvin Friedman, in *Stream of Consciousness: A Study in Literary Method* (New Haven: Yale Univ. Press, 1955), p. 5, agreed with Humphrey that stream of consciousness is a genre but listed interior monologue, internal analysis, and sensory impression as the techniques encompassed.

[3] Walter Allen, "Afterword," *Call It Sleep* (New York: Avon Books, 1964), p. 446.

[4] Maynard Mack, "Introduction," *Joseph Andrews* (New York: Holt, Rinehart, and Winston, 1961), p. xv.

[5] Horace Gregory, "East Side World," *The Nation,* 140 (17 Feb. 1935), 255.

[6] Leslie A. Fiedler, "Because I am a Man of Unclean Lips." *The Griffin,* Oct. 1960, p. 12.

CHAPTER V

CHAPTERS XXI AND XXII OF "THE RAIL": CLIMAX AND DENOUEMENT

In his 1971 book on Jewish American writers, Allen Guttmann remarked that "the twenty-two pages of Chapter xxi [of "The Rail"] are among the most remarkable in American literature, comparable perhaps to Captain Ahab's defiant worship of the fiery God who torments him."[1] The bases for the themes and techniques (including stream of consciousness) employed in this climactic chapter are firmly established in the earlier sections of the novel; indeed, throughout *Call It Sleep* Roth carefully shapes his material toward this climax and thus creates a sense of artistic inevitability. The success of the chapter partly derives from Roth's employment of certain archetypal motifs and themes, which, because they develop organically out of the material, reinforce the narrative. In the concluding chapter, Roth "grounds" the deep psychological exploration and panoramic vision of the climax in the everyday family life of the Schearls. This concluding chapter functions as a denouement, bringing to a satisfying close the intricately developed themes and motifs.

While chapter xx closes with David's desperate internal self-admonition, *"Now I gotta make it come out"* (p. 409), in the opening paragraphs of the climactic chapter Roth does not mention the child. Abruptly we find ourselves in the Royal Warehouse, following old Bill Whitney, the night watchman, on his rounds. As in earlier sections of the novel, Roth's linguistic versatility, his ability to suggest an extraordinary range of dialects, is strikingly evident in this brief vignette. Bill Whitney and the other minor "characters" who appear in this chapter define themselves largely by their speech; their words and voices reveal and differentiate their characters so effectively that by the middle of the chapter, Roth does not have to identify the various speakers by name: " 'You're de woist fuckin' liar I ever seen he sez an' ducks over de goider' " is clearly a retort of the foul-mouthed Husky O'Toole; " 'Yuh god mor'n a pair o' sem'ns?' " is an utterance of one of the Jewish card players; and " 'It's the snug ones who'll preach it wuz to be' " is a complaint of the night watchman, Bill Whitney.

While Whitney represents one voice of the city—one of the nameless millions whose banal lives simply continue as David experiences his near-electrocution—Whitney also serves a symbolic function. Like the setting of the rail scene which is both realistic and symbolic, Whitney is both a man of the people and "the watchman": "The key he turned the clocks with on every floor of the building—the proof of his watch and wakefulness" (pp. 409-410). By beginning the climactic chapter with a picture of the eternal watchman, Roth provides a kind of frame around his basic apocalyptic material.

As representative of the masses, Whitney and the other minor figures serve to broaden the novel's focus. As Sanford Pinsker observed, chapter xxi "widens the social scope until it includes a kind of thirties' panorama" and achieves "the same effect that John Dos Passos matches [sic] in his lengthy trilogies."[2]

After the brief vignette about the slow-witted night watchman, Roth inserts the first passage of italicized prose about David's personal crisis. Counterpointing the narrative sections dealing with the life of the city, these italicized sections trace David's movements, external and internal, from his approach to the rail, through the electrical shock and unconscious vision, to his reawakening on the street. At the same time that the vignettes provide the social panorama, the italicized passages of the chapter direct the reader's attention more and more deeply into David's psyche. As in the previous books of the novel, the italics indicate heightened emotion, intense dramatic pitch. In these italicized sections Roth freely combines third person narration, internal analysis, and stream of consciousness passages; stream of consciousness, here as elsewhere in *Call It Sleep,* is simply one of several techniques Roth employs to achieve psychological intensity.

The first italicized section opens with the words *"Resounded, surged and resounded, like ever swelling breakers: —Double! Double! Double dared me!"* (p. 410). Because of the inversion of subject and verb and because of the etymology of the word "resounded" (to sound again), the passage points backward and forward. The passage looks back to the last italicized line of chapter xx as well as forward to David's repeated resolve.

The words *"Where there's light in the crack,"* make the sexual implications of David's action clear. The sexual meaning of his thrusting the milk ladle into the tracks is dramatically prepared for in the previous book. In Book III, when David tells the rabbi about seeing a coal like Isaiah, the rabbi is especially amused by David's tale when the child says that "It [the trolley tracks] gave a big light in the middle, between the crack!" (p. 257). David's use of the word "crack" with its obvious sexual connotation is particularly hilarious to the rabbi, who repeats the word four times, laughing harder each time (p. 257). Because of this foreshadowing incident in "The Coal," the appearance of the expression, *"where there's light in the crack"* in chapter xxi is aesthetically fitting.

Besides describing the child's crisis, the italicized sections serve a structural function: the placement of these passages between the non-italicized portions serves to separate the individual vignettes at the beginning of the chapter and makes the various "scenes" distinct. The appearance of one of the italicized passages indicates a change of locale; in this way, the italicized sections guide the reader through the complex material of chapter xxi.

The second of the city scenes, the vignette about Husky O'Toole and his cohorts in Callahan's bar, introduces a different tone from that of the Bill Whitney material. Whitney's musings are pathetically simple-minded, but O'Toole's words are rude and coarse. His sexual innuendos and curses are especially striking considering the novel's date of publication. The sexual license suggested by O'Toole's speeches and in the corresponding female voices heard behind the "Family Entrance to Callahan's" are reminiscent of the second half of "A Game of Chess" in *The Waste Land.* Like Eliot, who uses fragments of conversation about abortion and infidelity to suggest the raw sexuality of the lower classes, so Roth records extremely frank conversations about sex and lets the speakers' words define them. Moreover, like Eliot, Roth uses the theme of sexual depravity for other reasons: first, to suggest that even this most basic human activity is debased in the modern world, and second, to symbolize contemporary sterility and debasement in general, especially on the religious level. The fact that the main female character's name is Mary and that she speaks to Mag (a possible abbreviation for Magdalene) provides an ironic parallel to the Christian motif—especially since in *Call It Sleep* Mary has an abortion rather than an infant. O'Toole's particularly coarse nature is also striking, in that later in the chapter, it is he who retrieves David from the rail and tries to give him artificial respiration.

The vignette about Mary (the woman whose words correspond to those of O'Toole in sexual frankness) underlines one of Roth's techniques in the climactic chapter. Mary's speech and the conversation of many of the other minor characters include many puns—and almost invariably the word-play is obscene. For example, Mary and her friend snigger together about the word "cut," using the word to mean the female genitals as well as an incision. Against this background of off-color puns, Roth employs another type of word-play in the climactic chapter and for a number of artistic reasons. These elaborate puns serve to connect the various vignettes so that they contrast and comment upon each other. Even more important, the puns come to suggest a "link" between various levels of human activity and connect a "lower" material world to a "higher" spiritual one.

One of the most prominent examples of this type of word-play is the pun on the words "card-cod." The word "card" first appears in chapter xxi in the Callahan beer-saloon vignette; when O'Toole impresses his companions, the hunchback and the weazened coal-heaver, with his wit, the latter tells O'Toole " 'Yer a card!' " (p. 411). In the next vignette, which deals with Jim Haig, an oiler on a British tramp steamer, the lonely Britisher muses about missing fish and chips and says to himself that someone should open " ' a 'omely place in New York—Coney Island fer instance. Loads o' prawfit. Taik a big cod now—' " (p. 411). The card-cod identification becomes apparent in the vignette about the Jewish card players; in their Yiddish accent, they pronounce the word card as cod. One of them laughs: " 'Cha! Cha! Cha! Dot's how I play mit cods!' " (p. 413).

Later, when we hear Jim Haig continue in his same nostalgic vein about fish and chips, the word "cod" assumes a deeper significance. The traditional association of Jesus with the fish makes Haig's remark, " 'Christ knows how many chaps can be fed off one bloody cod,' " (p. 417) particularly striking. The statement evokes Christ as feeder of the poor with loaves and fishes as well as Christ's body as sacramental "food." The various meanings and associations of "cod" coalesce and receive a sexual gloss in the lines before David short-circuits the rail: "Dere's a star fer yeh! Watch it! T'ree Kings I god. Dey came on huzzback! Yee! Hee Hee! Mary! Nawthin' to do but wait fer day light and go home. To a red cock crowin'. Over a statue of. A jerkin'. Cod. Clang! Clang! Oy! Machine! Liberty! Revolt! Redeem!" (pp. 418-419).

Roth employs the association of Jesus and the fish in other sections of *Call It Sleep* as well. Earlier in "The Rail," when Leo tries to persuade David to introduce him to Esther and Polly, the gentile boy uses a rosary as an enticement; much to David's surprise, Leo removes this magical object from a box with the word God "printed right above a large, black fish" (p. 327). Later in chapter xxi, the fish reemerges in David's unconscious vision in a somewhat different form: the child envisions *"a wooden box with a sliding cover like the chalk boxes in school, whereon a fiery figure sat astride a fish"* (p. 428). Thus while the puns of the minor characters in the climactic chapter are scatological, Roth's word play has eschatalogical implications.

Roth employs another, more erudite pun in this chapter in the expression, "hura mezda," which appears in the vignette about the Jewish card players. One of the Jewish men teases another about having been with a Negro prostitute the previous night and asks him, " 'Vus dere a hura mezda, Morr's?' " (was there a whore-master, Morris?) (p. 414). Roth himself observes that in constructing *Call It Sleep* he felt and tried to express "a kind of floating mysticism" or pantheism. Part of this general mystical attitude is embodied in the word-play. In Roth's words, "I picked here, there, and everywhere." About the pun in question, Roth remarks, "What I was thinking of was ahura mazdah, who is the god of light in Persian religion or Zoroasterism. I punned away." Although obscure, this Joycean pun does support the basic light/dark antithesis and imagery of the novel and underlines David's search for God's light in the climactic chapter.

In addition to the vignettes, Roth employs a number of other techniques in chapter xxi of "The Rail" to suggest the texture of the city life around David. Among these is the onomatopoeic reproduction of nonhuman sounds or noises, such as "ppprr," "whawmmmmm," "w-w-whack," "crritlkt," "khir-r-r-r-f," and "S-s-s-s." As with his orthographic rendition of various dialects, these "noise" reproductions are evidence of Roth's desire to suggest actual sounds.

Roth also effectively uses Whitmanesque catalogues in this chapter to suggest the endless variety of human life: "Eyes, a myriad of eyes, gay or sunken, rheumy, yellow or clear, slant, blood-shot, hard, boozy, or bright swerved from their tasks, their play, from faces, newspapers, dishes, cards, seidels, valves, sewing machines, swerved and converged" (p. 419). Even more reminiscent of Whitman's techniques is Roth's skillful use of repetition and parallelism. Following the example of F. O. Matthiessen, who arranged a prose account by Thoreau into free verse to show its similarity to Whitman's poetry,[4] I will write part of one paragraph of chapter xxi as verse to indicate Roth's careful manipulation of devices usually associated with poetry:

> The voice of the pale, gilt-spectacled, fanatic face rang out above all other sounds:
> above the oozy and yearning "Open the door to Jesus" of the Salvation Army singing in the park;
> above the words of the fat woman swaying in the car as she said, "So the doctor said cut out all meat if you don't want gallstones. So I cut out all meat, but once in a while I fried a little boloney with eggs—how I love it!"
> Above the muttering of the old gray-bearded Jewish peddlar [sic] (he rocked his baby carriage on which pretzels lay stacked like quoits on the upright sticks) "Founder of the universe, why have you tethered me to this machine? Founder of the universe, will I ever earn more than water for my buckwheat? Founder of the universe!"
> Above the even enthusiasm of the kindly faced American woman: "And do you know, you can go all the way up inside her for only twenty-five cents. For only twenty-five cents, mind you! Every American man, woman and child ought to go up inside her, it's a thrilling experience. The Statue of Liberty is—." (p. 415)

Roth also effectively uses catalogues and parallels in sentence structure in earlier sections of *Call It Sleep*. On the first page of the prologue, Roth begins three sentences with the words "all day" or "all that day." The first sentence catalogues the various peoples coming to America; the second, their clothes; and the third, the sounds of their voices upon reaching the New World. In both the prologue and the climactic chapter, the catalogues set the intimate portrait of David Schearl (and his family) against the larger social scene, and emphasize both the family's uniqueness and its position as one among many.

In describing David's electrical shock, Roth avoids vagueness and abstraction by using a great many concrete metaphors and similes. For example, in one italicized passage we read that David is *"blind as a sleep walker,"* the glitter of the tracks fixes him *"like a brand, drawing him with cables as tough as steel,"* and the dipper in the *"long, dark grinning lips"* of the rail is *"like a sword in a scabbard"* (p. 413). Roth also uses a special type of animal imagery to achieve vividness. When David first feels the surge of electrical power released by the short circuit, Roth describes the power as being *"like a paw,"* and then speaks of *"the hawk of radiance"* and the *"rams of darkness"* (p. 419). Similarly, he says that the ensuing flash of light is "as if leviathan leaped for the hook and fell back threshing" (p. 422).

In presenting David's vision when he is knocked unconscious by the electrical shock, Roth recalls and reorders images and verbal echoes from the previous books of the novel. The unconscious vision shows David transforming his memories and associations and thus transcending them. The first line describing David's unconscious state is striking in that it suggests the apocalyptic by combining seeming opposites: *"Like the red pupil of the eye of darkness . . ."* (p. 424). This paradoxical *"eye of darkness"* is like *"the enormous bell of the very heart of silence"* earlier in chapter xxi (p. 411). The emotional tone of the unconscious phantasmagoria is shifting; in fact, a temporary happy emotional state is apparent in the earliest section when we see *"the man in a tugboat"* who is grinning and whistling pleasantly while *"yellow birds flew to the roof"* and *"wires twanged brightly"* (p. 425). Not only does Roth employ images from the earlier books, but also he uses verbal echoes which have strong emotional significance for both David and the careful reader. For example, in David's vision a coffin *"bulged"* (p. 426), while in the early pages of Book I, the cellar "bulged with darkness" (p. 20). The verbal echo evokes a wealth of cellar-associations, and the verb itself suggests a violent overflowing of evil.

The extraordinarily complex intertwining of motifs and themes in David's vision can best be seen if one takes a single passage as an example. After the series of cellar-associations evoked by the appearance of Albert, Roth writes: *"The man in the wires writhed and groaned, his slimy, purple chicken-guts slipped through his fingers"* (p. 426). In "The Coal," when David first hears the rabbi describe Isaiah's purification, the child wonders when he will learn the meaning of the Hebrew words he simply reads or mechanically repeats. Pondering what he will learn, David thinks: "First you read, Adonoi elahenoo abababa, and then you say, And Moses said you mustn't, and then you read some more abababa and then you say, mustn't eat in the traife butcher store" (p. 226). Thoughts about *traife* (unkosher food) give rise to memories of seeing unkosher food, which seems repulsive to him, including "chickens without feathers in boxes" (p. 226). David even remembers seeing a chicken killed by a kosher butcher: "And then the man with the knife went zing! Eee! Blood and wings. And threw him down. Even kosher meat when you see, you don't want to eat" (p. 226). The association of "chicken-guts" with uncleanliness and the horror of death combines with another association in "The Rail." Visiting Leo in his apartment, David sees a picture "that for all of David's staring would not take on a reasonable shape because the light was too dim" (p. 319). To David, the picture of Jesus and the Sacred Heart seems to be a picture of a man "only his guts are stickin' out" (p. 321). Later David thinks: "Guts like a chicken, open. And he's holding them" (p. 321). Thus, the one sentence in chapter xxi about the man with chicken-guts unites multiple associations from the earlier books.

Immediately following the appearance of the Christ-like "man in the wires," *"David touched his lips. The soot came off on his hand. Unclean"* (p. 426). David touches his lips, of course, because like Isaiah, he believes his lips are unclean. In David's mind, the uncleanliness of his mouth relates both to his speech (especially cursing) and to the eating of non-kosher food (as suggested in the previous paragraph about chicken-guts). The choice of the word "soot" rather than some other kind of filthy matter is significant; soot, "the fine dispersion of black particles chiefly carbon, produced by the incomplete combustion of coal . . . or other fuels," recalls the negative half of the coal symbol, its association with the cellar.

The next sentences, *"Screaming, he turned to flee, seized a wagon wheel to climb upon it. There were no spokes—only cogs like a clock-wheel. He screamed again, beat the yellow disk with his fist"* (pp. 426-427) also evoke images and memories from the first pages of the novel. Early in "The Cellar" Yussie shows David a clock he has dismantled and gives him "a bright yellow gear" (p. 21). "Brooding, engrossed in his thoughts, engrossed in the rhythmic, accurate teeth of the yellow cog in his hand" (p. 22), David falls into a sleep-like state and is "filled with a warm, nostalgic mournfulness" for the Old World (p. 23). When David accidentally drops the yellow cog he is fingering, "The sudden sound moored him again, fixed him to the quiet, suburban street, the curbstone" (p. 23). Through the image of the cog, David's early failure to escape into a dream-like state in Book I foreshadows his thwarted desire to flee from his father in his unconscious vision.

Besides evoking, combining, and transforming motifs in chapter xxi of "The Rail," Roth employs experimental typography to shape this climactic chapter of *Call It Sleep.* The basic two-part division of the chapter into italicized and unitalicized sections embodies in the *form* David's personal trauma: the disparity between external and internal realities. By the technical juxtaposition of these two kinds of sections, Roth forces the reader to experience the building tension and conflict between David's psychological and religious needs and the social world in which he lives. Roth also manipulates the typography for other aesthetic and psychological reasons. By dividing the material into brief sections and even dividing individual words, Roth forces the reader to proceed slowly, and constantly to double back to pick up various threads, various voices. In this way, the multiple levels of meaning and the complex juxtapositions are thrown into relief. Roth also divides single words into syllables to underline his themes typographically. For example, in the following passage he underscores the Christian parallel developed in the chapter by splitting the word "crossing" (meaning intersection) to emphasize the "cross" syllable:

> *and there was the last crossing of*
> *Tenth Street, the last cross—*
> "Heazuh a flowuh fer ye, yeller-belly, shove it up yer ass!"
> *ing, and beyond . . .* (p. 418; ellipsis mine)

Moreover, by interspersing the italicized portions concerning David's mystical experience with the unitalicized sections, Roth can use single words or phrases to create a feeling of tension for the reader. Roth employs this type of "strategic word-placement" when David reaches the abyss of his mystical experience. Roth follows the words, *"And He was not"* (p. 429) with more than a half-page of unitalicized passages indicating the reaction of the crowd and the efforts of the interne to revive David. As the reader's anxiety builds about whether or not David will survive, Roth inserts the single word "(*But—*)" within the unitalicized narative and conversation.

David's return to consciousness is also indicated typographically in three successive sections. In the first section, David is still completely unconscious, and all the material is presented in italics: "(*Mister! Whistle, Whistle! Whistle! Whistle, Mister! Yellow birds!*)" (p. 431). As the child begins to revive, the italics disappear and are replaced by capitalization: "(Whistle, mister! WHISTLE!')" (p. 431). Finally Roth observes: "(A spiked star of pain of consciousness burst within him)" (p. 431), and the transition to normal typography (and consciousness) is complete.

Chapter xxi is aesthetically satisfying and psychologically compelling because it fulfills the artistic expectations developed throughout the novel. The achievement is extended by drawing into the climax certain archetypal mythical and mystical motifs.

Asked about his knowledge and use of mythology when writing *Call It Sleep,* Roth observed:

> I did very little of it [developing mythological motifs] consciously. What would happen is that while writing I would think of some particular point I could make that would heighten the novel's effect. In the process, I would sometimes get an insight into the fact that this had a mythological overtone. And that was very satisfying. But if the addition did not contribute to the general flow of the narrative, whether it had mythological overtones or not, I wouldn't have included it. I will say that this is a cardinal rule or guide: the primary thing had to be its potential for heightening the narrative flow.[5]

These comments by the author are especially revealing about the importance of narrative integrity and the organic development of mythological motifs in *Call It Sleep.*

In *Rites and Symbols of Initiation,* Mircea Eliade suggested *why* the embodiment in literature of certain mythological themes, especially initiatory motifs, satisfies the psyche of the reader. He asserted that

> initiation lies at the core of any genuine human life. And this is for two reasons. The first is that any genuine human life implies profound crises, ordeals, suffering, loss, and reconquest of self, "death and resurrection." The second is that, whatever degree of fulfillment it may have brought him, at a certain moment every man sees his life as a failure.[6]

But modern man's need and desire for religious renewal or initiation go unfulfilled because he lives "in a basically desacralized cosmos."[7] For the modern man, part of this unsatisfied need is met through non-religious, especially aesthetic gratification. In Eliade's words,

> Reading itself, as a distraction and escape from the historical present, constitutes one of the characteristic traits of modern man. Hence it is only natural that modern man should seek to satisfy his suppressed

> or inadequately satisfied religious need by reading certain books that, though apparently "secular," in fact contain mythological figures camouflaged in the guise of everyday happenings.[8]

David's experience when knocked unconscious by the power of the short-circuited rail parallels typical initiation rites in general form and in some particular details. The three major stages of initiation: torture, ritual death, and resurrection,[9] parallel the structure of David's unconscious vision. In *Call It Sleep,* the "torture" is embodied in the reappearance of the terrible images of evil, death, and uncleanliness from the earlier books, especially "The Cellar." This torture section of the unconscious vision climaxes in the commandment of the Thor-like Albert to *"Go down!"* (p. 428). David's descent into darkness clearly parallels a mythical descent and ritual death. Similarly, the joyful imagery of the closing section of the vision with its flowering ember *"swimming without motion in the motion of its light"* (p. 430) signifies a resurrecton from this death-like state.

In addition, Roth's handling of the material of the climactic chapter resembles the typical initiation rites described by Eliade in more detailed and minor aspects. The very "setting" of David's initiation is "mythically" right; typically, initiation rites occur on "sacred ground" and involve the "separation of the novices from their mothers."[10] By the time David flees to the trolley tracks in chapter xxi, the rail itself is special and holy to him because it was there that he first "saw a coal like—like Isaiah" (p. 257). The child himself seems to recognize that his mystical experience must occur in a special, uncommon place. In "The Coal," when he first hears Rabbi Pankower's description of Isaiah's confrontation with God, David thinks: "—Where did he see Him? God? Wonder if the rabbi knows? Wish I could ask. . . . Way, way, way, maybe. Where?" (pp. 229-230). Already anticipating seeking God himself, David associates this distant sacred place (where Isaiah saw God) with his own brief flight from home in Book I: "Some place, me too . . . When I—When I—in the street far away . . . [ellipses Roth's] Hello, Mr. Highwood, goodbye Mr. Highwood. Heeee! Funny!" (p. 230). The separation of the novice from his mother mentioned by Eliade is, of course, apparent in *Call It Sleep* in the terrible scene in which Genya "thrust him [David] from her, slammed the door after him" (p. 402) in order to save him from Albert's insane wrath.

The very fact that in searching for God's coal David seeks to repeat Isaiah's experience is significant. Eliade observed that " 'sacred history'—

mythology—is exemplary, paradigmatic," and in initiation the novice repeats "the exemplary gesture of the mythical Hero."[11] If Isaiah is David's mythical hero in *Call It Sleep,* then the child's desire to imitate the prophet's experience parallels the usual initiation pattern. For David, the two essential aspects of the Isaiah story are the prophet's woeful assertion of his unworthiness, "Behold, my lips are unclean" (p. 227), and Isaiah's subsequent purification by God's coal or ember. Both motifs are prominent in the phantasmagoric scene. As noted previously, in his unconscious vision, David tries to flee after touching his lips and finding them unclean (p. 426). The purifying coal or ember essential to the Isaiah story appears both at the beginning and at the climax of David's vision. As David is knocked unconscious, *"One ember fanned"* and then *"dilated, spun like a pinwheel, expanding, expanding"* (p. 424). Signaling his resurrection from his death-like descent, the purifying ember later reappears: *"Not cold the ember was. Not scorching. But as if all eternity's caress were fused and granted in one instant"* (p. 430).

The second stage of initiation, the ritual death, involves not only descent into an Underworld but also frequently a "theme of regression to the embryonic"[12] or bodily dismemberment—that is, some type of reduction or destruction of the novice's body. In the climactic chapter, Albert's order to *"Go down,"* is followed by David's descent into *"darkness fathomless"* (representing the underworld), and a "dwindling" of David himself: *"Each step he took, he shrank, grew smaller"* until finally: *"And now the seed of nothing, and nebulous nothing, and nothing, And he was not"* (p. 429).

In the resurrection or rebirth stage of David's vision, the *"yellow birds"* which earlier *"filled the sky"* (p. 426) triumphantly reappear; *"exalted,"* David cries: *"Whistle, Mister! Yellow birds!"* (p. 431). These birds are memory images from the scene in "The Coal" in which David experiences a fleeting epiphany while watching the sun move across the river. But the birds are also archetypal symbols; in Eliade's words, "bird symbolism is always connected with an ascension" and "the ascent to heaven symbolized by the flight of birds is characteristic of archaic culture."[13]

Besides embodying archetypal patterns of initiation, the climactic chapter of *Call It Sleep* has direct parallels with Jewish mystical experience. That this should be so is not surprising, for primitive "initiatory ordeals . . . are still traceable even in the experiences of the great mystics."[14] Moreover, the parallels with Jewish mysticism, both in form and in the language in which these experiences are expressed, are found in earlier sections of *Call It Sleep* as well. The great scholar of Jewish mysticism Gershom Scholem observed:

> The lower ranges of God's manifestation form the object of steady human contemplation, but the highest plane which meditation can reach at all, namely the knowledge of God as the mystical *Mi* (Who), as the subject of the mundane process, this knowledge can be no more than an occasional and intuitive flash which illuminates the human heart, as sunbeams play on the surface of water—to use Moses de Leon's metaphor.[15]

Both Scholem's meaning—and the metaphor in which it is expressed—are present in the novel (in *Call It Sleep* the metaphor is an actual event). In "The Coal," David experiences a brief epiphany as "a long slim lathe of sunlight burned silver on the water" (p. 247). Furthermore, the crucial aspect of this mystical experience is its "occasional and intuitive" nature: "What was it he had seen? He couldn't tell now. It was as though he had seen it in another world, a world that once left could not be recalled. All that he knew about it was that it had been complete and dazzling" (p. 248).

The structure of chapter xxi also embodies parallels to the experience of mystics, even its paradoxes. Scholem remarked that "not the least baffling of these paradoxes—to take an instance which is common to Jewish and Christian mystics—is that God is described as the mystical Nothing."[16] Likewise, Scholem explained that "Only when the Soul has stripped itself of all limitations and, in mystical language, has descended into the depths of Nothing, does it encounter the Divine."[17] This mystical descent into nothingness and experience of God as the mystical Nothing are central structural motifs in David's unconscious vision. In his descent, David sheds *"The husks of being, and himself tapering always downward in the funnel of the night . . . and now the seed of nothing, and nebulous nothing, and nothing, And he was not"* (p. 429). In his gradual ascent David screams: " *'Now find! Now find!' And nothingness whimpered being dislodged from night, and would have hidden again"* (p. 430).

Roth's phrase, *"nothingness whimpered being dislodged from night and would have hidden again,"* parallels a paradoxical Jewish mystical interpretation of Psalm CXXX; Scholem observed that, according to Jewish mystics, the phrase from this psalm " 'Out of the depths I have called unto Thee' means not 'I have called unto Thee from the depths (where I am)' but 'from the depths (in which Thou art) I call Thee up.' "[18] In chapter xxi of *Call It Sleep,* David descends to the "heart of darkness" to find God who must be *"dislodged from night and would have hidden again."*

Finally, even the erotic imagery of the climactic chapter, including the sexual symbolism involved in David's pushing the phallic milk ladle into the "long, dark grinning lips" of the rail, is typical of mystical narratives. As Scholem noted, "With few exceptions mystical literature abounds in erotic images." [19]

The final chapter of *Call It Sleep,* chapter xxii of "The Rail," serves functionally as a denouement in which the tension of the climax subsides. The two chapters are best examined in conjunction, for while chapter xxi provides the most profound internal exploration as well as the widest panorama of the social scene, the last chapter presents the necessary third "type of reality": David's domestic, everyday, essentially familial atmosphere. Chapter xxii returns to the immediate context and the daily atmosphere of the novel, and, in a sense, provides the link between the two extremes explored in the previous chapter. In mood and tone as well as in theme, the final chapter comments upon chapter xxi. Not only does the final chapter "ground" the climax in the daily life and the most basic familial setting, but it is an ironic commentary on the climax. This is not to say that the final chapter negates the transcendent climax, but only that it provides another view, a qualifying comment.

An early and subtle form of ironic comment on David's mystical quest occurs in the first paragraphs of the last chapter. When David reawakens from his unconscious state, he sees "the ever-encroaching bodies, voices, faces at all heights, gestures at all heights, all converging upon him, craning, peering, haranguing, pointing him out, discussing him" (p. 432). He thinks this reality is "a nightmare" and "deliverance was in the thought" (p. 432). In this context, the use of the word "deliverance" is extremely ironic in several ways. On the one hand, although the interne and the policeman have successfully revived him, David's first thought when reawakening to consciousness is a desire to escape the nightmare of reality surrounding him. On the other hand, since the transcendent vision of "eternity's caress" is his deliverance, why does he reawaken to a nightmare which "wasn't a dream" (p. 432)? In other words, why is he still hoping for deliverance?

The interne's comment: " 'I don't see why he was out so long anyway. Weak, I guess' " (p. 433) is an example of a more obvious form of irony. While in the reader's mind David has assumed heroic proportions because of the intensity of his mythical quest and experience, from the interne's point of view, the child's long period of unconsciousness is a result of his weakness.

An important type of ironic "circle" is completed in the last pages of the novel. While the chatty, self-praising policeman fills out the police report describing David's "accident," he questions Albert about the boy; these questions and Albert's answers: " ' My sawn. Mine. Yes. Awld eight. Eight en'—en' vun mawnt' " (p. 437) are the original "questions" of the novel and the basis of Albert's deep-seated anxiety about David. Beginning in the prologue, Albert's basic concern is about David's exact age and whether the child is his son.

The beautifully evocative, and ambiguous final paragraph provides a "circling back" or completion of a pattern both technically and thematically. Here Roth depends largely on the techniques of cataloguing, repetition, and parallelism—all techniques first used in the opening pages of the prologue.

It is noteworthy that Roth remains true to the "gritty" reality of his vision to the very end. The catalogue of things into which "every wink of the eyelids could strike a spark" is profoundly urban and absolutely part of David's life: the beards, roller skates, stoops, and rails touch the "thinginess" of David's world. Roth does not cancel them out by evoking a more traditional, pastoral beauty; instead, in *Call It Sleep* he reveals the beauty of the city, even of the ghetto.

The three long sentences of the last paragraph—each beginning with the words, "It was only toward sleep"—catalogue what David sees, hears, and, most important, feels: "It was only toward sleep" that "every wink of the eyelids could strike a spark"; that "ears had power to cull again and reassemble"; and that David could feel "not pain, not terror, but strangest triumph, strangest acquiescence." Using repetition with a slight but significant variation, Roth follows these three catalogues by saying, "One might as well call it sleep." The earlier "he" referring to David changes to the impersonal "one"; in this way Roth universalizes David's experience.

Roth uses the sleep/awake theme with great subtlety throughout the novel, beginning, of course, with the title and ending in the last paragraph. But what exactly the "it" of *Call It Sleep* signifies remains unexplained, perhaps inexplicable. In *Call It Sleep* David is often dreaming, and others accuse him of sleeping. In the first chapter of "The Cellar," David fingers a yellow cog wheel while listening to the girls on the street sing a plaintive song, and he soon enters a dream-like reverie: "His body relaxed, yielding to the rhythm of the song and to the golden June sunlight. He seemed to rise and fall on waves somewhere without him. Within him a voice spoke with no words but with the shift of slow flame" (p. 23). Similarly, in "The Rail," when Leo and Esther are "playing dirty," David experiences an intense reverie about the rosary beads; Leo rudely awakens him, saying: " 'I tolju he wuz sleepin'. He's a'ways sleepin', aincha Davy?' " (p. 349). The most prominent use of the sleep or dream motif to signify a mystical or imaginative reverie occurs in "The Coal" when David sees rays of sunlight dance on the river and "sin melted into light" (p. 248). In all of these scenes David is awakened to reality: in "The Cellar," by the sound of the cog wheel hitting the ground when he drops it; in "The Rail," by Leo's insulting words about him to Esther; and in "The Coal," by the voice of the man in the tugboat who yells, " 'Wake up, Kid!' " (p. 248).

A second major use of the sleep/awake contrast has a different significance, for in this metaphorical usage, sleep and death are equated. In "The Cellar," Genya tells David what happens after death and denies the existence of an afterlife: " 'They [the dead] shut their eyes in sleep eternal years' " (p. 69). Horrified, David asks when the dead wake up, and Genya answers: " 'There is nothing left to awaken' " (p. 69).

These two "meanings" or associations of the sleep/awake contrast coalesce in David's unconscious vision, his climactic sleep or dream. Because of the Christ-like pose and associations of "the man in the wires," his earlier commandment to David to "Wake up, Kid," comes to signify an awakening from sleep-like death. That is, in David's mystical vision or sleep, he discovers the way to escape his mother's prediction about the finality of death; he finds the way *not* to "shut his eyes in sleep eternal years."

Like the light/dark imagery which is central to the novel, the sleep/awake contrast is psychologically satisfying because it is archetypal. In Northrop Frye's words,

> We have identified the central myth of literature, in its narrative aspect, with the quest-myth. Now if we wish to see this central myth as a pattern of meaning also, we have to start with the workings of the subconscious where the epiphany originates, in other words in

> the dream. The human cycle of waking and sleeping corresponds closely to the natural cycle of light and darkness, and it is perhaps in this correspondence that all imaginative life begins. The correspondence is largely an antithesis: it is in daylight that man is really in the power of darkness, a prey to frustration and weakness; it is in the darkness of nature that the "libido" or conquering heroic self awakes. Hence art, which Plato called a dream for awakened minds, seems to have as its final cause the resolution of the antithesis, the mingling of the sun and the hero, the realizing of a world in which the inner desire and outward circumstance coincide.[20]

The final two chapters of "The Rail" provide a fitting conclusion to Roth's exceptionally artful and moving novel. In chapter xxi, Roth brings the major themes and motifs to a brilliant climax; and because the material organically embodies certain mythological and mystical motifs, the climactic chapter is particularly satisfying to the reader. Besides providing an ironic commentary on the climax, the final chapter binds the psychological and panoramic climax to the daily, familial setting and brings to a complex denouement this extraordinary novel.

NOTES

[1] Allen Guttmann, *The Jewish Writer in America: Assimilation and the Crisis of Identity* (New York: Oxford Univ. Press, 1971), p. 54.

[2] Sanford Pinsker, "The Re-Awakening of Henry Roth's *Call It Sleep*," *Jewish Social Studies,* 28 (1966), 157.

[3] Appendix, p. 300.

[4] F. O. Matthiessen, *American Renaissance: Art and Expression in the Age of Emerson and Whitman* (London, Oxford, New York: Oxford Univ. Press, 1941), p. 583.

[5] Appendix, pp. 295-296.

[6] Mircea Eliade, *Rites and Symbols of Initiation: The Mysteries of Birth and Rebirth,* trans. Willard R. Trask (New York: Harper & Row, 1965), p. 135.

[7] Eliade, p. ix.

[8] Eliade, pp. 134-135.

[9] Eliade, p. 91.

[10] Eliade, p. 4.

[11] Eliade, p. x.

[12] Eliade, p. 98.

[13] Eliade, p. 70.

[14] Eliade, p. 1.

[15] Gershom G. Scholem, *Major Trends in Jewish Mysticism* (London: Thames and Hudson, 1955), p. 221.

[16] Scholem, p. 5.

[17] Scholem, p. 25.

[18] Scholem, pp. 33-34.

[19] Scholem, pp. 225-226.

[20] Northrop Frye, "The Archetypes of Literature," in *Myths and Literature: Contemporary Theory and Practice,* ed. John B. Vickery (Lincoln: Univ. of Nebraska Press, 1966), p. 95.

PART III

INFLUENCES AND MOVEMENTS

CHAPTER I

HENRY ROTH AND JAMES JOYCE

In 1923, the year after *Ulysses* appeared in book form, T. S. Eliot remarked with obvious admiration (and possibly less obvious warning): "I hold this book to be the most important expression which the present age has found; it is a book to which we are all indebted, and from which none of us can escape."[1] The following year, when he was a college freshman, Henry Roth read a copy of Joyce's great work given to him by Eda Lou Walton; by the time he began to write *Call It Sleep* in 1929, Roth had also read the available critical commentary on *Ulysses*. Ironically, the publication of *Call It Sleep* in December, 1934, followed the first American edition of *Ulysses* by only eleven months. Since the first reviews of *Call It Sleep,* Roth's novel has been compared to *Ulysses;* indeed, one recent critic said that "comparison of the two is inevitable."[2] Moreover, Roth himself stresses the fact that he was strongly impressed and influenced by Joyce. A comparison of the two novels is instructive in terms of literary history because it "places" Roth in a literary tradition. The comparison is also useful in "placing" *Call It Sleep* in a more profound sense; it tells us what *Call It Sleep* is by clarifying what it is not.

Speaking about what he thinks he gained from Joyce, Roth observes, "What I gained was this awed realization that you didn't have to go anywhere at all except around the corner to flesh out a literary work of art—given some kind of vision, of course."[3] Roth's comment about only having to go "around the corner" for material reflects his similarity to Joyce in two ways. First, both novelists are profoundly autobiographical writers. Harry Levin even remarked about Joyce that "His youth in Dublin . . . furnished his only subject matter," and that "Joyce's life is so inextricably woven into his work, we shall be confronted with the details of his biography as soon as we turn to the pages of his books."[4] Roth's autobiographical impulse is obvious not only in *Call It Sleep* but in his subsequent career as well; his short stories clearly relate to his own experience, and at least one of the reasons for Roth's failure to complete his second novel was the fact that its focus was *not* autobiographical.

The work of both Joyce and Roth reveals a profound preoccupation with their fathers. In his 1970 book on Joyce, John Gross commented, "Of all Joyce's emotions, as they figure in his work, the strongest were undoubtedly those centering on his father."[5] Similarly, the figure of Albert looms darkly over *Call It Sleep,* and Roth's most recently published story, "Final Dwarf," explores the subtle ramifications of a deeply hostile father-son relationship. Roth himself says that his actual relationship to his father "was a relationship that could not be resolved."[6]

Roth's comment about learning from Joyce that one did not have to go anywhere except around the corner connects *Call It Sleep* to *Ulysses* in another, larger way. Describing Joyce's attributes as a writer, Levin noted that "No naturalist has ventured a more exhaustive and unsparing depiction of the immediacies of daily life."[7] Joyce's depiction of the "immediacies of daily life" is nowhere more obvious than in *Ulysses,* where the daily life of the Blooms and Stephen Dedalus is recorded in meticulous detail. Roth's brilliant recording of daily life is one of the most noteworthy aspects of *Call It Sleep.* Moreover, both *Ulysses* and *Call It Sleep* record a special twentieth-century kind of daily life: the chaotic life of the modern city. Levin called the city one of Joyce's two obsessive themes (the other is the artist).[8] In *Ulysses* and *Call It Sleep* Dublin and New York achieve a sense of "felt reality" rarely equalled in other novels; the sights, sounds, and smells of the city are evoked with a seeming tangibility.

Commenting on *Ulysses,* Roth says that "in stream of consciousness I recognized that my own continual dialogue with myself could be made into literature," an observation which underscores another major and undeniable similarity between *Ulysses* and *Call It Sleep.* Joyce's masterful technical experimentation with stream of consciousness has been a major subject of critical discussion about *Ulysses* since its first appearance. In addition to the usual novelistic procedure of revealing character in action and speech, in *Ulysses* Joyce makes massive use of character revelation by the seemingly direct recording of the associative flow of psychic experience. For Roth, Joyce's use of this technique—a technique which implied a new way of looking at human beings and the universe—"was a tremendous impetus toward writing."[9]

In *Call It Sleep* Roth used another major technical device of *Ulysses:*

motifs which enrich and unify his voluminous material. In their long and complex novels, both Joyce and Roth overcome the problem of loose narrative structure by the careful manipulation of recurring motifs. In Roth's words, "When you speak about the evolution of the form and the recognition of the individual—how to achieve form in the course of a long work like that [*Call It Sleep*]—this is one of the things I recognize that I needed. Really it gives added interior structure." And in this area as well Roth credits Joyce as the great innovator and influence on him: "Again that's a Joycean thing." [10]

The new and rapidly growing interest in mythology and anthropology in the first decade of the century had an obvious and direct influence on the literature of the period; the publication of *The Waste Land* and *Ulysses* in 1922 revealed that in both poetry and fiction these new interests were to play a central role. When Roth came to write *Call It Sleep,* he was familiar with Frazer's *The Golden Bough,* with *The Waste Land,* and, of course, with *Ulysses.* Moreover, Eda Lou Walton's anthropological background provided Roth with a direct, non-literary exposure to these fields. Joyce's use of mythological and archetypal material reaches a climax in *Finnegans Wake,* but even in *Ulysses* his use of it is prominent (one might begin with the title). As I have suggested previously, Roth carefully employs archetypal initiation patterns, especialy in the climatic chapter of *Call It Sleep.*

A less obvious parallel between the two novels is their "foreshortening" tendency. As is well-known, the action proper of *Ulysses* occurs on June 16, 1904. More than simply an organizing device this foreshortening, of the usually extended period of time covered in a novel implies a basic attitude both to human life and to the novel as a form. Traditionally, the novel presents its characters' lives over a long period of time—often beginning in youth and ending in old age or even death. This time-span reflects the assumption that only by recording a successive number of events can an author reveal character and character development. Conversely, Joyce with his "one day" arrangement implicity asserts that every moment of present time contains within it the memories of the past and the fulfillment of the future: we are what we have been, and we will be what we are. Novelistically, Joyce's structure implies that a wide and deep enough study of even one day reveals, through implication, a lifetime. Although Roth's handling of time in *Call It Sleep* is not nearly so extreme as that of Joyce in *Ulysses,* the short time-span of *Call It Sleep* reflects Roth's kinship to Joyce in this matter. *Call It Sleep* is aesthetically satisfying even though it deals with only a few years in the early childhood of the protagonist. Only if one assumes that the events of these few childhood years suggest or symbolize a larger frame of reference does this short time-span seem adequate.

Although Joyce was the major artistic influence on Roth, it is useful to examine their differences closely—both to clarify the uniqueness of Roth's novel and to suggest what Joyce bequeathed to later novelists and the novel in general.

Not surprisingly, the underlying source of the essential differences between Joyce's work and Roth's is the difference of their aims. Looking at Joyce's prose works as a whole, or more precisely, as a continuum, one sees a definite progression: from naturalism to symbolism, from characters to archetypes, from plot and event to word and myth. In all, Joyce stretched the boundaries of the novel as a form to their limits—and perhaps beyond (the form of *Finnegans Wake* bears little, if any, direct relationship to traditional novel form).

Considering a few examples of critical definitions of the novel *qua* novel, one sees how the seeds of *Finnegans Wake* were buried in *Ulysses,* how even in the earlier novel, Joyce showed only limited interest in traditional novelistic goals. Marvin Mudrick asserted that "In prose fiction the unit is not, as in poetry, the word, but the event," [11] and explained that "The distinctive talent of a writer of fiction is to make events, the mark of his maturity is to offer, by way of events, a community of individual lives in the act of defining themselves." [12] Similarly, in an article sharply critical of Joyce and especially of *Finnegans Wake,* John Peter stated that "The novel is, indeed, preeminently the literary form where the quality of human life is celebrated in all its richness without abstractions, and whatever technique it uses can only be a means to this end." [13] Alan Friedman suggested that "the stream of events is the fundamental form of fiction," [14] and that we read novels "to share in creating the experience of one more world of selves, and one more, and one more." [15] The traditional novel is thus usually defined in terms of character and event, in terms of "plot" in R. S. Crane's use of the word: the "peculiar synthesis of character, action, and thought, as inferable from the sequence of words, to move our feelings powerfully and pleasurably in a certain definite way." [16]

In *Ulysses* (and more obviously in *Finnegans Wake*) Joyce had different aims from these usual novelistic goals. Whether in praise or disparagement, Joyce's critics consistently note his extra-novelistic tendencies.

Speaking specifically of *Finnegans Wake* but by implication of *Ulysses* as well, John Peter observed that Joyce made a

> retreat not only from the immediacy of human experience but ultimately from human experience itself, a retreat—from life into the "subjects" of history, mythology, and psychology; he . . . denied to the novel virtually everything in terms of which it is properly valued. It becomes a treatise, no more. However comprehensive a treatise, however subtle, it can only be, *qua* novel, an evasion.[17]

But while *Ulysses* and to a greater extent *Finnegans Wake* may be judged evasions as novels, it seems only fair to emphasize that Joyce *consciously* pursued different, broader—which is not to say more worthwhile—aims. These different aims were aptly suggested by John Gross in his book on Joyce. After enumerating Joyce's experimental techniques in *Ulysses,* Gross observed,

> These techniques pull in two directions at once. Many of them serve to heighten the surface realism of *Ulysses* and to reinforce the impression of accurate psychological notation. Many others do just the opposite: they are deliberately obtrusive, anti-illusionistic, the calculated firework displays of a virtuoso. And no one is going to get the best out of the novel unless he is to some extent ready to accept such displays for their own sake, for their wit and inventiveness, without worrying unduly about how far they can be accommodated to traditional fictional procedures.[18]

Summing up Joyce's aims, Gross suggested that, like many modernist artists, Joyce took technique as his subject.[19] While as a novel *Ulysses* may be seen as a retreat from human experience and the usual novelistic goals of significant characterization, event, and plot, these "deficiencies" can be explained and defended as arising from extra-novelistic aims and suppositions.

Joyce's non-traditional novelistic aims affect every aspect of *Ulysses,* from the treatment of character and the manipulation of motifs and symbols to the use of stream of consciousness. And Joyce's non-novelistic aims mark Roth's distance from him.

Far from aspiring to universal mythic evocation or to self-reflective "attempts to create a literary substitute for the revelations of religion"[20] in Harry Levin's phrase, Roth fixed his goals strictly within the traditional realms of the novel. The crucial aspect of *Call It Sleep* for Roth was obviously "the narrative flow"—the traditional core of a novel. All of the Joycean technical devices that Roth adopted and adapted were bent in service to this un-Joycean aim.

The way in which the two novelists manipulated symbols and motifs is an obvious dividing point between them. Much of Joyce's symbolism in *Ulysses* is mechanical and cerebral; the linking of various parts of the body with various chapters is an obvious example. As I have suggested in a previous chapter dealing with the symbolic structure of *Call It Sleep*,[21] Roth's novel is completely organized around four basic symbols: cellar, picture, coal, and rail. Part of the appeal of these symbols is no doubt their broad psychological associations; for example, the psychological suggestiveness of the cellar as a symbol of the unconscious seems undeniable. But the primary reason for the effectiveness of the symbolism is its organic relationship to the narrative structure: the symbols emerge naturally from the material; they are not imposed upon it.

Similarly, Roth's demands on the reader are quite different from Joyce's. Levin admitted that in reading *Ulysses* we "limp along after him [Joyce] down bypaths of language and learning."[22] Indeed, one of the principal joys of reading Joyce (attested to by the innumerable articles on esoteric matters) is strictly cerebal: the pleasure of deciphering. In *The Rhetoric of Fiction,* Wayne Booth distinguished between the difficulty inherent in a great work of art and the intellectual difficulty of *Ulysses:*

> I work at this play [*King Lear*] as I work at few artistic experiences, but my work is not that of figuring out, of calculating allusions, of unraveling intentions, [as it is in *Ulysses*]. It is the work of raising myself to the height required to experience the imaginative and emotional complexities of Lear's tragedy.[23]

Call It Sleep provides little of the intellectual difficulty of *Ulysses.* For example, there are few esoteric puns. The one noted previously, "ahura mazdah," is peripheral; "missing it" does not deprive the reader of the essential meaning of the novel any more than "getting it" brings the reader to the heart of the matter.

A. Sidney Knowles commented that *Call It Sleep* "is technically far less elaborate than *Ulysses* and it is therefore surprising to find that the experience of reading it is somewhat more intense."[24] Knowles credited the intensity of *Call It Sleep* to the fact that Roth focuses the novel on childhood and thus "draws us into an area of intense psychic experience that we have shared in common and that is at once simpler and more piquant"[25] [than the adult life explored in *Ulysses*]. But as my comments thus far have suggested, the greater intensity the reader feels in reading *Call It Sleep* is a natural by-product of the difference between Roth's fictional strategy and Joyce's. Joyce's more "elaborate" technique keeps the reader from experiencing the novel on a profound emotional level; the technique calculatedly draws attention to itself and away from the characters and story.

The influence of *Ulysses* on *Call It Sleep* is apparent. Roth clearly recognized Joyce as a master novelist and innovator who expanded the horizons of the novel as a genre, especially in the use of stream of consciousness, symbolism, and motifs. But the differences between the two are even more revealing. As T. S. Eliot predicted of the entire age, Roth did not "escape" Joyce's influence; nonetheless, he adapted Joyce's technical achievements while rejecting Joyce's underlying goals. Rather than slavishly imitating the technical master, Roth molded Joyce's technical innovations to his own aims. Roth produced a rich, dense, symbolic novel —but one in which the core, "the narrative flow," is solidly within the realms of the traditional novel. In *Call It Sleep* technique is everywhere subordinated to vision, to the "life" behind the words.

NOTES

[1] T. S. Eliot, "*Ulysses,* Order, and Myth," *The Dial,* 75 (1923), 480.

[2] A. Sidney Knowles, Jr., "The Fiction of Henry Roth," *MFS,* 11 (Winter 1965-66), 396.

[3] Appendix, p. 294.

[4] Harry Levin, *James Joyce: A Critical Introduction* (Norfolk, Conn.: New Directions, 1941), p. 11.

[5] John Gross, *James Joyce* (New York: The Viking Press, 1970), p. 14.

[6] Appendix, p. 307.

[7] Levin, p. 18.

[8] Levin, p. 19.

[9] Appendix, p. 294.

[10] Appendix, p. 296.

[11] Marvin Mudrick, "Character and Event in Fiction," *Yale Review,* 50 (1960), 205.

[12] Mudrick, p. 210.

[13] John Peter, "Joyce and the Novel," *Kenyon Review,* 18 (1956), 628.

[14] Alan Friedman, "The Stream of Conscience [sic] as a Form in Fiction," *Hudson Review,* 17 (Winter 1964-1965), 544.

[15] Friedman, p. 546.

[16] R. S. Crane, "The Concept of Plot and the Plot of *Tom Jones,*" in *Critics and Criticism: Ancient and Modern,* ed. R. S. Crane (Chicago: Univ. of Chicago Press, 1952), p. 622.

[17] Peter, p. 631.

[18] Gross, p. 60.

[19] Gross, p. 61.

[20] Levin, p. 29.

[21] See Chapter I of Part II above.

[22] Levin, p. 9.

[23] Wayne C. Booth, *The Rhetoric of Fiction* (Chicago and London: Univ. of Chicago Press, 1961), p. 304.

[24] Knowles, p. 396.

[25] Knowles, p. 396.

CHAPTER II

CALL IT SLEEP AS A JEWISH NOVEL

Is *Call It Sleep* a Jewish novel? Almost every critic who has analyzed the book has at least mentioned its Jewishness or referred to its position in the body of American Jewish fiction. But there is significant disagreement as to the extent or import of its Jewishness. On the one hand, Robert Alter said that, while *Call It Sleep* is written by a Jew and is about Jews, it is not essentially Jewish:

> Henry Roth's *Call It Sleep* . . . still probably the most fully achieved work of fiction by an American writer of Jewish descent, is a novel of immigrant experience, using Joycean methods for the lyrical rendering of consciousness; the principal characters happen to be Jews, but I see nothing in the conception or execution of this extraordinary book that could not be readily transferred to a novel about a family from some other immigrant group.[1]

On the other hand, Kenneth Nelson insisted that so Jewish is *Call It Sleep* that one must *be* a Jew to appreciate the novel:

> To say that one need not be a Jew to savor *Call It Sleep,* to commend it to tens of thousands of readers by declaring it to be simply the story of a little immigrant boy trying to come to terms with a very hostile world is but to debase the book, dupe the readers, and ridicule the man who spent himself writing it.[2]

Between these two extreme positions, other critics cover the middle ground. In *The Jew in the American Novel,* Leslie Fiedler remarked that *Call It Sleep* is "a specifically Jewish book, the best single book by a Jew about Jewishness written by an American, certainly through the 'thirties [sic] and perhaps ever."[3] Elsewhere Fiedler asserted that "there is surely no more Jewish book among American novels."[4] Irving Howe mentioned that *Call It Sleep* is "intensely Jewish in tone and setting,"[5] while Walter Allen noted that *Call It Sleep* is "profoundly Jewish in much the same way as *Portrait of the Artist* is sometimes described as profoundly Catholic, but it is no more a 'Jewish' novel than Joyce's is a 'Catholic' novel."[6]

The question of what makes a novel "Jewish" is fascinating and thorny, especially because of the nature of Judaism itself. One seemingly undeniable criterion of the Jewish novel is that its author be a Jew. But that in itself raises questions which are probably unanswerable: even the Israeli Supreme Court has puzzled over the question of who is a Jew. If one starts with the simple definition of Jews as the descendants of Abraham, the question of conversion immediately arises. Although by Jewish law a non-Jew converted to Judaism is "born anew," what happens if this converted Jew writes a novel? Is it then a Jewish novel? Likewise, what of the convert *from* Judaism? Is he still a Jew for literary purposes? The problem of who a Jew is, or what a Jew is, is complicated by the fact that Orthodox Judaism is traditionally seen as, in Allen Guttmann's words, "a way of life rather than a series of definitions or beliefs."[7] But since most Jews in America, including most American Jewish novelists, are non-Orthodox, how does one say finally whether or not they are indeed Jewish? Answering such a question is especially difficult because their daily life may contain little that is ostensibly Jewish. In *The Jewish Writer in America,* Guttmann concluded, "No wonder that some have attempted in desperation to define Jews on the basis of *Schicksalgemeinschaft,* a common fate, or even on the basis of *Yizkor,* the link of Memory."[8]

While the problem of who is a Jew fascinates critics of Jewish American literature, for Henry Roth the question is oddly peripheral; the question of whether or not Roth is a Jew has never been raised, despite the fact that Roth himself says he became an atheist at fourteen and at the time he wrote *Call It Sleep* "consciously . . . was already faced in opposition to things Jewish."[9] In contrast, Nathanael West, a novelist of the Thirties to whom Roth is often compared, is sometimes considered a Jewish novelist and sometimes not. Fiedler asserted that "West is, despite his own disclaimers, in a real sense, a Jew,"[10] and that it seems "inconceivable that anyone but an urban, second-generation Jew in revolt against his background could have produced the novels from *Balso Snell* to *The Day of the Locust.*"[11] Conversely, Guttmann defended his omission of

West (along with Arthur Miller and J. D. Salinger) from his survey of American Jewish writers, saying that they are "nominally Jews, but they are in no important sense Jewish writers."[12]

Although it is generally agreed that a Jewish novel must be written by a Jew (whatever that is!), other more directly literary questions arise. If a Jewish novel is not simply any novel written by a Jew but also a work about Jews or Jewishness, questions about Jewish "content" are inevitably—and rightly—raised. Just as the problem of articulating precisely who a Jew is complicates the first qualification of the "definition," so what Jewishness is muddles the second. For a large part of the American public, including Jews, Jewishness is now unrelated to anything specifically spiritual. Indeed much of what is commonly labeled as Jewish is Eastern European rather than strictly Jewish, social rather than religious: chicken soup and gefilte fish are often seen as the essence of American Judaism. The "indefinableness" of Jewishness is, of course, reflected in what a critic says about the Jewish novel; one's definition of Judaism (whether implicit or explicit) must affect one's perception about what is Jewish about a particular novel. In their efforts to distinguish the Jewishness of a novel, critics often point to things which are, if considered more closely, difficult to label specifically Jewish. In Alter's words,

> there has been a tacit conspiracy afoot in recent years to foist on the American public as peculiarly Jewish various admired characteristics which in fact belong to the common humanity of us all. The Jewish folk is imagined as possessing a kind of monopoly on vividness, compassion, humor, pathos and the like; Jewish critics and novelists are thought to be unique in their preoccupation with questions of morality.[13]

Furthermore, even more specifically "religious" definitions of Jewishness are, because of the peculiar nature of Judaism itself, questionable as literary guides. For example, central to Kenneth Nelson's analysis of *Call It Sleep,* in which he sees David Schearl as a metaphor for the Jewish people, is his definition of Judaism as "the struggle of man to become man, the history of a conscious effort to purge oneself and elevate oneself to a more human level."[14] Unfortunately, this definition applies to civilization or culture as easily as to Judaism—and suggests the difficulties involved in discussing the Jewish novel in significant terms.

One way around the impasse is to consider the American Jewish novel only in historical or sociological terms, to examine the literature for what it reveals about the experience of Jews in America and the complex interaction of these two cultures upon each other. This was Guttmann's approach in *The Jewish Writer in America* as well as that of Charles Angoff and Meyer Levin in their anthology, *The Rise of American Jewish Literature*. Angoff and Levin present "not only samples of literary development but a portrait of Jewish life in development, a social history through the novel." [15]

Considered in historical perspective, *Call It Sleep* is of exceptional interest as a Jewish novel because it reveals the unique role Judaism played in the lives of the members of the immigrant generation and their offspring at the beginning of the century. In *Call It Sleep* Judaism envelops the characters' lives and is at the center of their milieu, although the conscious and unconscious attitudes of the characters toward Judaism vary widely. Each character's relationship to Judaism suits his personality, his general outlook; thus the presentation of Judaism is believable and satisfyingly complex. Although Genya rejects the Orthodox beliefs about afterlife and miracles, she nonetheless brings to her Sabbath preparation a warmth and beauty that makes it "the hushed hour, the hour of tawny beatitude" (p. 71). Albert too is somewhat dubious about the truth of Orthodox Judaism, yet he conscientiously sends David to *cheder* saying " 'I mean I'm little enough a Jew myself. But I want to make sure he'll become at least something of a Jew also' " (p. 210). Despite her conscious rejection of Old World and embrace of New World values, Bertha is the most simply "believing" of the adult characters; when she takes David to the Metropolitan Museum where they see "an enormous figure seated on an equally enormous horse," she naively comments, " 'This is how they looked in the old days. . . . Gigantic they were, Moses and Abraham and Jacob, and the others in the earth's youth' " (p. 149). David himself recognizes the different degrees of religious observance of his mother and his aunt. Thinking about kosher laws, he comments to himself, "Mama don't care except when Bertha was looking. How she used to holler on her because she mixed up the meat-knives with the milk-knives" (p. 226).

In *Call It Sleep* not only is each character's relationship to his religion subtly drawn, but Judaism envelops the book as it is the heart of the social milieu. I have already discussed the delicate interplay of Yiddish, Hebrew, and English,[16] but it is worth noting how often Judaism is in the characters' speech and thoughts, in their allusions and comparisons.

Roth's characters reflect a generation of people whose references and allusions were derived from Judaism, not from the wider western European culture. Abraham and Moses were tangible and known, while Odysseus and Helen of Troy were outside their sphere. Thus, while religious faith is a cloak the characters can take off, their "Jewishness," like the air around them, is not removable. Casual references to Jacob and Esau, Moses and the burning bush, Solomon, and Adam and Eve are found throughout the novel, defining the characters' background and their cultural identity.

Similarly, in *Call It Sleep* the characters' daily life, as well as their frame of reference, is deeply Jewish; the Jewish holidays and observances shape their lives and mark the passing seasons. The beautiful evocation of the Sabbath has already been mentioned; the minute preparation for and emotional connotations of Passover are also evoked, from the rhythmic chopping of the bitter herbs to the ritual burning of the *chumitz* or unleavened bread.

The centrality of Judaism to immigrant life at the turn of the century is underscored in *Call It Sleep* by the fact that David's attendance at *cheder* and his attitudes toward his religious education are basic to the novel, while public school goes almost unmentioned. Surely this fact reveals something about the limited role public school played in the lives of immigrant children in the early 1900s—its foreignness and lack of significant relationship with the home life and immigrant culture. In *The Jew in American Literature,* Solomon Liptzin observed that "the novels that dealt with the generation of immigrant children who grew up between 1880 and 1914 stressed the bright, happy atmosphere of the public school and the dark gloom of the supplementary Jewish school or *cheder.*"[17] Using *Call It Sleep* as an example of this theory, Liptzin noted that David's "darkest hours were those spent in the *cheder* under the tutelage of the Hebrew teacher, Reb Yidel Pankower."[18] But Roth hardly mentions public school, and his treatment of the *cheder* and Reb Pankower is much more subtle and ambiguous than Liptzin's comments suggest. Far from simply stressing the gloom of the impoverished, dirty *cheder* and the petty tyranny of Reb Pankower, Roth makes clear that David's emotions toward his *cheder* experience are profoundly mixed. While David and the reader must at least partially agree with the other boys' evaluation of Reb Pankower—" 'He's a louser! He hits!' " (p. 213) —it is this same man who recognizes David's intellect and his strange spirituality. Moreover, Reb Pankower's biting comments about "this sidewalk-and-gutter generation" sufficiently counter his pupils' accusations about him. Similarly, the *cheder,* although undeniably dirty and impoverished, is the scene of some of David's profoundest joy; as he reads in the *cheder* about Isaiah's purification, "a cadence like a flock of pigeons, vast, heaven-filling, swept and wheeled, glittered, darkened, kindled again, like wind swept over prairies" (p. 367). Likewise, when terrified by the anti-Semitic boys, David flees to the *cheder* for security. And in his unconscious climactic vision, the *cheder* with its *"wall sunlit, white-washed"* offers momentary release from Albert's *"whirling hammer"* (p. 427).

But *Call It Sleep* is Jewish in more than language, allusion, and narrative materials; it is profoundly mystical in theme and focus. Gershom Scholem, the great scholar of Jewish mysticism, remarked that "There is no mysticism as such, there is only the mysticism of a particular religious system."[19] Obviously, David Schearl is not a Jewish mystic—he is a character in a novel. But in the *world of the novel* he is a mystic; his quest throughout *Call It Sleep* is for mystical transfiguration, for purification by God. And since his world and his experience are Jewish, it seems plausible, using Scholem's remark as a guide, to call David a Jewish mystic.

The background against which Roth develops David's transcendental search is Jewish; the basic narrative materials which Roth manipulates to describe and define David's quest develop thematically and imagistically out of two main Jewish sources: the significance and associations of the Isaiah story and the Passover celebration. Certainly the more one knows of the Jewish beliefs and traditions, the more Roth's narrative of David Schearl's quest is enriched. For example, Isaiah, the prophet whom David wishes to emulate, was himself a mystic, "distinguished from all other prophets in that he received his communications directly from God and not through an intermediary."[20] Moreover, Isaiah was the first prophet to give a detailed description of the future ideal king of Israel; significantly, in exilic times, the prophecy developed that David (the second king of Israel) would be the king in the millennium. The chief merit of Isaiah's prophecies is their consoling character—for Isaiah announced deliverance. The theme and imagery of deliverance unite the Isaiah prophecy, the Passover story, and Roth's presentation of his mystical theme. Roth's manipulation of the *Chad Godya* motif (one only kid) which has already been discussed[21] parallels the traditional Jewish belief that when the ideal future king predicted by Isaiah appears, "the lambs will not dread the wolf, nor will the leopard harm the kid."[22]

The deliverance foreseen by Isaiah is underscored by the fact that

Passover itself is the Jewish celebration of deliverance. The oldest of the Jewish festivals, Passover was originally simply a spring festival; in the month of spring when the kids and lambs were born, the Jews traditionally sacrificed a sheep or goat from the flock. Subsequently, "Spring, the time of liberation for nature, and the idea of human freedom seemed to fit very well together"[23] and the seasonal holiday (with its built-in death and rebirth structure) became the "festival of the freedom of the Jewish people, its deliverance from slavery, and its awakening to a new life."[24] After the destruction of the Temple, Passover took on still a third related meaning, for it then "attained still greater importance as the anniversary of the deliverance from the first exile and as the model for delivery from the last exile."[25] The Passover and Isaiah associations which Roth so deftly integrates into David Schearl's experience parallel and reinforce the major theme of mystical search.

The emphasis on the Jewish quality of David Schearl's mysticism is not meant to deny the Christian motifs in the novel, which are especially prominent in the climactic chapter. However, these Christian motifs, unlike the Isaiah and Passover material, exist as analogues which broaden and generalize the frame of reference, rather than providing the basic narrative materials.

In a 1963 symposium in *Midstream* on "The Meaning of *Galut* in America Today," Roth described the upbringing he was giving to his sons and said that "the fairly intensive conditioning of my own childhood with regard to Judaism, with its inculcation not only of special criteria, but also of a state of mind, has been abandoned to the extent possible."[26] Ironically, it is precisely this Judaism as *"a state of mind"* that lies at the heart of *Call It Sleep;* indeed Roth's evocation of the Jewish mystical state of mind can be seen as his special contribution to the Jewish novel as a genre.

Philip Rahv incisively observed that "the American-Jewish writers do not in the least make up a literary faction or school" and warned that

> the homogenization resulting from speaking of them as if they comprised some kind of literary faction or school is bad critical practice in that it is based on simplistic assumptions concerning the literary process as a whole as well as the nature of American Jewry, which, all appearances to the contrary, is very far from constituting a unitary group in its cultural manifestations.[27]

Each significant Jewish writer is more than simply a Jew writing about

Jews; he uses his Jewish background in a particular way and taps his own Jewish sources—whether he consciously does or does not focus on Judaism or Jewishness. What the novelist makes of his Jewishness—which aspects of his background he explores—is the important question in explaining the meaning of the label "Jewish novelist." That is, while Henry Roth, Saul Bellow, and Bernard Malamud are all Jewish novelists, the way they express Jewishness in their work is highly individual. Bellow is a novelist of the contemporary Jewish *Weltanschauung,* evoking the ironic, urban worldview of the modern Jew. Malamud is a Jewish moralist, primarily exploring the moral imperatives of Judaism. And Roth is the Jewish novelist of the spiritual quest. The range of these novelists and the distance between them reflect not only their uniqueness as authors, but also the multifaceted breadth of the Jewish experience.

Roth says that he does not consider *Call It Sleep a* Jewish novel: "I just used whatever background or material was available to me, and this was it. I did not use a Jewish background to illustrate Jewish life *per se.* I used it to fulfill certain of my own compunctions."[28] Ironically, it may be precisely because Roth did not intend to "illustrate Jewish life *per se*" that the novel is, among other things, such an excellent illustration of Jewish life in the early years of this century. In other words, because he did not write under any pressure to present a "balanced" or "representative" view, Roth avoided the danger of writing about stock characters and stereotypical behavior.

Roth denies any profound knowledge of either Jewish mysticism or mysticism in general. He explains, "What may have happened was that sometime in early childhood some relative would spin a yarn about a rabbi or somebody with some powers or other. So that by the time I began to write, this would be a subconscious reserve or reservoir."[29] The fact that Roth wrote *Call It Sleep* to fulfill certain of his "own compunctions," tapping his "subconscious reserve or reservoir" or memories rather than deliberately trying to manipulate traditional Jewish mystical materials is no doubt largely responsible for his success with his basic theme.

Call It Sleep is a profoundly Jewish novel in its language, allusions, and narrative materials. As an illustration of immigrant Jewish life in the early years of this century, it is fascinating for both its historical and sociological insights into that crucial period of American Jewish life. But *Call It Sleep* is also a Jewish novel in another, more important sense: in his articulation of his central theme, his exploration of David Schearl's mystical quest, Roth manipulates Jewish material as the very "stuff" of the narrative and explores Judaism as "a state of mind."

By this conclusion I do not mean to imply that *Call It Sleep* is in any sense a parochial novel—its themes and scope are universal. In fact, *Call It Sleep* transcends any category more limiting than that of "novel."

NOTES

[1] Robert Alter, *After the Tradition: Essays on Modern Jewish Writing* (New York: Dutton, 1969), p. 116.

[2] Kenneth M. Nelson, "A Religious Metaphor," *Reconstructionist,* 31, No. 15 (1965), 7.

[3] Leslie A. Fiedler, *The Jew in the American Novel* (New York: Herzl Institute Pamphlet No. 10, 1959), p. 38.

[4] Leslie A. Fiedler, "Henry Roth's Neglected Masterpiece," *Commentary,* 30 (August 1960), 106.

[5] Irving Howe, "Life Never Let Up," *The New York Times Book Review,* 25 Oct. 1964, p. 61.

[6] Walter Allen, *The Modern Novel in Britain and the United States* (New York: Dutton, 1965), p. 172.

[7] Allen Guttmann, *The Jewish Writer in America: Assimilation and the Crisis of Identity* (New York: Oxford Univ. Press, 1971) p. 5.

[8] Guttmann, p. 7.

[9] Appendix, p. 295.

[10] Fiedler, *The Jew in the American Novel,* pp. 35-36.

[11] Fiedler, *The Jew in the American Novel,* p. 38.

[12] Guttmann, p. 13.

[13] Alter, p. 22.

[14] Nelson, p. 8.

[15] Charles Angoff and Meyer Levin, eds., *The Rise of American Jewish Literature: An Anthology of Selections from the Major Novels* (New York: Simon and Schuster, 1970), p. 7.

[16] See Chapter III of Part II above.

[17] Solomon Liptzin, *The Jew in American Literature* (New York: Bloch, 1966), p. 111.

[18] Liptzin, p. 112.

[19] Gershom G. Scholem, *Major Trends in Jewish Mysticism* (London: Thames and Hudson, 1955), p. 6.

[20] Isaac Broydé, "Isaiah," *The Jewish Encyclopedia,* 1904.

[21] See Chapter II of Part II above.

[22] Moses Buttenwieser, "Messiah," *The Jewish Encyclopedia,* 1904.

[23] Hayyim Schauss, *Guide to Jewish Holy Days: History and Observance,* trans. Samuel Jaffe (New York: Schocken, 1962), p. 44.

[24] Schauss, p. 44.

[25] Schauss, p. 56.

[26] "The Meaning of *Galut* in America Today: A Symposium," *Midstream,* 9 No. 1 (1963), 33.

[27] Philip Rahv, "Introduction" to *A Malamud Reader* (New York: Farrar, Straus and Giroux, 1967), p. vii.

[28] Appendix, p. 304.

[29] Appendix, p. 295.

PART IV

OTHER WORKS

Although Roth never published a second novel, he has not been artistically silent since *Call It Sleep*. His novel fragment "If We Had Bacon" appeared in *Signatures: Work in Progress* in 1936. During a thirty year period beginning in 1939, he has published seven other pieces of short fiction. Four appeared in *The New Yorker* ("Broker," November 19, 1939; "Somebody Always Grabs the Purple," March 23, 1940; "Petey and Yotsee and Mario," July 14, 1956; and "The Surveyor," August 6, 1966); two parables appeared in *Commentary* ("At Times in Flight," July, 1959, and "The Dun Dakotas," August, 1960); and one story, Roth's most recent, appeared in *The Atlantic* ("Final Dwarf," July, 1969). While not a prodigious output, the fragment and stories amply reveal Roth's continuing stylistic mastery. In addition to their intrinsic literary merit, they are of interest both in relation to *Call It Sleep* and to Roth's biography.

"If We Had Bacon" consists of three short chapters containing 7, 8, and 5 pages respectively. In the opening chapter, the protagonist, Walter Loem, an unemployed laborer, is carrying home a slab of bacon that he has stolen, when he is "attacked" by a flying hat thrown by an unknown assailant. Loem wrongly presumes that "three dapper, derbied young men"[1] lounging in a doorway threw the hat, but then he discovers that the real culprit is a young boy. After slyly persuading an old German cigar store owner to sell him tobacco on credit, Loem effectively deals with the hat-throwing culprit—by twisting his ear. Loem's character is thus swiftly revealed by the way he handles himself in each encounter and by the reactions of the other characters to him. Self-confident, contemptuous of the three "skinny birds in spats" (p. 140) who live off women, he is idealized by the street children as a fighter and a successful thief.

In the second chapter Loem is at home with this three children and his part-Cherokee, part-Dutch wife, Juno. Deftly characterizing the family members, Roth at the same time establishes the conflict between Loem and his wife, the basis of which is a chronic lack of money. Humoring his complaining wife and not revealing the bacon he has hidden under his jumper, Loem triumphantly pulls the slab out and throws it on the table, only to find that the bacon package contains a piece of white pine board: "The package didn't land at all with the flabby, fatly cushioned thump expected of it. It clacked glibly, bounced spryly" (pp. 153-154).

In the third chapter Loem belittles his wife's newly found interest in astrology and goes off to steal something to replace the bacon. The piece closes with Juno's dire astrological prediction: " 'Go ahead,' said Juno prophetically. 'Find out fer your own self what it means t' go buttin' your head into the stars!' " (p. 158). Thus by the end of chapter three, Roth has carefully established his characters and set in motion a plot line of considerable dramatic tension.

Since the second novel was never completed, it is impossible to say whether Roth would have provided an aesthetically satisfying ending, but on the basis of the extant fragment, it seems safe to say that he would not have had problems in characterization. As in *Call It Sleep,* which has such moving, believable characters that one critic admitted trying to telephone "Genya Roth,"[2] in "If We Had Bacon" Roth establishes the foundation for complex, ambiguous personalities. Loem, the protagonist, is no simple, one-dimensional figure. A hero to the streetboys, he is also a petty thief and a braggart who is outmaneuvered and cuckolded by his wife. A street fighter who relishes memories of former brawls and carries a wagonbolt in his pocket with which he can "brain a steer," Loem nonetheless marvels at a boy's face, "at the mobile, fragile enamel of the cheek bones, flesh of split almond" (p 144). Roth clearly differentiates between Loem's children and provides hints of their human complexity, and the characterization of Loem's wife is especially strong and convincing. Highly feminine and petit bourgeois in her aspirations, Juno keeps the front door locked lest her husband track mud on her clean carpets, and she dreams of educating their daughter to be a bookkeeper: " 'A bookkeepin' gal got the best chances these days. Settin' in offices an' lookin' neat' " (p. 150). Fiercely ambitious, she has prostituted herself, or in Loem's words, " 'just followed her instincts and made money at it' " (p. 148).

Roth's success at characterization is related to his ability to render dialogue convincingly. The author's ear for dialect, for the sound and texture of the human voice, is everywhere apparent in "If We Had Bacon." While much of the dialect in *Call It Sleep* is New York-Jewish, here the midwesterner's "Americanese" is rendered with the same expertness. The dialogue captures the biting sarcasm, humor, and pungent vocabulary of the characters. For example, Juno Loem silences her husband by saying:

" 'Ef talk wuz all I ladled onto your dish some night, you wouldn't ask fer an extree helpin' ' " (p. 150). Loem's sharply sarcastic "explanation" of the astrological signs Juno has taken to reading is highly comical:

> "This one means a big lump o' grub and two bits throwed in by a nice ol' maid an' no dog. But this little curlikew goes on to say, look out fer the town-clown, boys, meanin' the marshall. Because the one right nex' to it warns you—you'll git et alive in thet jail-house. Look again! There's a race goin' on up the wall b'tween the bedbugs an' the body-lice, with here an' yon a head louse takin' the bit in his mouth an' hightailin' it up the home stretch. The rest of them figgers on the side is the time they clocked 'em at." (p. 157)

Within its limitations, the fragment contains much of the richness and stylistic brilliance of *Call It Sleep*. The first paragraph of "If We Had Bacon" reveals Roth's acute visual perception as well as his ability to find the precise words to convey that vision with exactness—two of the most striking aspects of *Call It Sleep*. He begins by impressionistically evoking a flying object: "Hung in the sky, a cored and bronzed and shrunken sun, a pineapple-rind buzz-saw"; then he identifies the object in the final words of the paragraph: "the broken brim of a crownless straw hat" (p. 139).

Roth also uses the Whitmanesque catalogue which gives the reader a sense of the variety and amplitude of life surrounding the characters, and provides visual images which seem to "catch" these figures in their most revealing stances. For example, while looking around to find out who threw the hat at him, Loem sees "The bakery-wagon driver slipping the reins into the ring of the imitation sapling stump hitching-post; the old barfly watching a pair of husky teamsters in doormat-colored canvas aprons launch beer-kegs down the cellar ways" (p. 140). The "imitation sapling" and "doormat-colored" aprons provide exactly the touches that "fix" these figures.

Besides a rich and supple vocabulary, Roth uses highly metaphorical language to achieve concreteness and sharpness of focus. His description of how the hat-thrower's cohorts react to his capture by Loem is strikingly apt: "The others had darted off like minnows at the shred of panic; they returned like minnows, round-eyed and blank, and fed with quivering lips upon the scene" (p. 143).

Roth's seven published stories can best be studied by dividing them into three chronologically and thematically significant groups. The three earliest stories: "Broker," "Somebody Always Grabs the Purple," and "Petey and Yotsee and Mario," are suggestive sketches about New York City life in the early years of the century—the first dealing with a wryly humorous Negro, the others with children (who resemble Roth himself as a child). Each of these early stories deftly captures the rhythms of New York City speech and life styles, including the contrast of various ethnic groups. The second group of stories includes "At Times in Flight" and "The Dun Dakotas," neither of which is a traditional short story. Each contains a central parable and reflections upon its meanings. The two pieces are similar in that both reveal Roth's complex and ambiguous attitudes towards his life and work, especially during the Thirties after the publication of *Call It Sleep*. The final group, "The Surveyor," and "Final Dwarf," shows a return to the conventional short story form; in fact, they are the most fully achieved short stories Roth has published to date. The two recent stories are particularly noteworthy because they explore thematic concerns relative to *Call It Sleep* and Roth's life. "The Surveyor" focuses on the meaning of Jewish identification—a central concern in Roth's life and one which *Call It Sleep* treats at least obliquely. In "Final Dwarf" Roth brilliantly evokes the troubled relationship between a middle-aged man and his elderly father. As in *Call It Sleep* and Roth's life, the father-son relationship is full of unresolved tension and bitterness. Both "The Surveyor" and "Final Dwarf" contain characters who resemble Henry Roth himself and thus are of special interest in their revelation of the author's later life.

Roth's earliest published story, "Broker," is still generally unknown, perhaps because the story, though published in *The New Yorker* of November 18, 1939, was not included in *The Reader's Guide to Periodical Literature* for 1939.[3] Within its limited scope, it is a well-written, engaging story. It demonstrates one of the principal virtues of *Call It Sleep:* Roth's ability to depict various New York ethnic groups. While the central characters of *Call It Sleep* are Jewish, the main figure in "Broker" is a bemused, ironically passive Negro truck driver.

In the story, the Negro's old truck, loaded high with mason's and plasterer's equipment, has collided with the underside of the Elevated. The Negro, whose long-suffering patience is tinged with humor, is resigned to the irrationality of life, and delights ruefully in its craziness. This wry humor is revealed in the opening paragraphs of the story when the truck driver explains his situation to a sympathetic and amused Negro who has just driven up in a car:

"Man, tha's trouble!" [the second Negro says.]

"Man"—the owner threw his head back—"any kind of trouble is trouble enough. But that truck just keeps on bein' trouble. Don't pay no more attention to it!"

"What you mean, don't pay no more attention to it?" the other demanded. "I never seen that before. What you call that?"

"I call it broker."

"Broker?"

"Yeah," said the owner of the truck. "Every time somebody look at that truck, it gets broker." [4]

Roth concludes this exchange by saying, "They both laughed richly" (p. 45). The remainder of the story is proof of the truck owner's observation—the more people look at the truck, the "broker" it gets—and the result is the reader's rich laughter.

In "Broker," Roth swiftly and effectively dramatizes the plight of the Negro and his seemingly accursed truck. His primary human opponent is, naturally, a policeman "with a sour expression and eyes set close together" (p. 45).

All of the Negro's observations about his situation are perfectly reasonable, yet taken together they somehow lead him into conflict with the traffic laws of the city. For example, when an onlooker points out that the Negro should have measured his load, the truck owner observes that he *did* measure it "with the naked eye." Asked for his rough estimate of the load's height, the Negro reports, " 'Bout thirteen an' a quarter.' " But when the by-stander points out that the sign beneath the Elevated says "HEADROOM 12 FEET 2 INCHES," the Negro triumphantly observes that his truck was going in the opposite direction, and thus he could not see the sign (p. 45).

As the story continues, a series of disasters develops around this broken-down truck. Two passing cabs collide as their drivers gape at the vehicle. A cameraman for the *Mirror* appears out of nowhere, and a swarm of children in football helmets jump on the truck to get the cameraman to take their picture—as a result, the entire load collapses. The street then becomes completely blocked, and the policeman is "almost strangling with rage" (p. 48). The truck driver himself is awed by the destructive power of his truck: " 'Man! Man!' " the Negro marvels, in the story's concluding lines, " 'Every time somebody look at that truck, somethin' else go wrong' " (p. 48).

Based on an incident Roth actually witnessed and could "spin out, embroider," [5] "Broker" is a charming piece that reveals Roth's sharp sense of comedy and ethnic humor.

"Somebody always Grabs the Purple" is Roth's first piece after *Call It Sleep* to deal with a child. Unlike the novel, the moods and tones of which are highly complex and contain everything from absolute horror to religious ecstacy, "Somebody" is essentially light; its tone is gentle humor and nostalgia. The story opens with a description of the 123rd Street Branch Library in New York City into which Sammy Farber, "a thickset, alert boy, eleven or twelve years old" [6] enters in a search of the *Purple Fairy Book*. Sammy Farber is apparently very much like the young Henry Roth, who "started off with fairy tales at about age ten." In Roth's words, "I think the only reason I got off fairy tales was that I once picked up *Huckleberry Finn* by mistake." [7]

One of the central motifs of the story—the contrast between the real world and the sublime mythic world of fairy tales—is suggested obliquely in the first paragraph. In the branch library are "two boys in colored jerseys . . . whispering at one of the bookcases" while on the wall above their heads is "a frieze of Grecian urchins blowing trumpets" (p. 69).

Much of the humor of the story develops out of the contrast between the prim "graying and impassive" (p. 69) librarian with a pince-nez and Sammy Farber with his combined vulgarity and dreams. Naturally the librarian carefully inspects Sammy's hands before allowing him to touch the books and refers to him as Samuel. The dialogue between the librarian and the eager reader is humorous and seems absolutely "right" in the way it captures the librarian's stiff correctness and Sammy's contrasting Yiddish-American speech, which is vulgar but vital. Explaining his desire for the *Purple Fairy Book,* Sammy shyly admits that his mother, who considers fairy tales too childish for him, call them "stories with a bear" (p. 69). When the librarian does not understand this definition of fairy tales, Sammy's revealing comment is that " 'she don't know English good' " (p. 69). But while Sammy also obviously "don't know English good," his language has flavor of its own. For example, after he is unable to find the *Purple Fairy Book* on the shelves, he hesitantly agrees to the librarian's suggestion that he search on the table: " 'I'll look,' he said, 'but I know. Once they grab it, it's goodbye' " (p. 69).

What Sammy hopes to find in the *Purple Fairy Book* is apparent from the picture he sees in it while glancing over the shoulder of another youngster who is raptly reading it: "On one page there was print, on the other a colored illustration, a serene princeling, hand on the hilt of his sword, regarding a gnarled and glowering gnome" (p. 69). The would-be "serene princeling," Sammy Farber, then engages in two attempts to wrest the book from its reader—first with the librarian's help, then in direct confrontation with the boy.

Despite the fact that Sammy and the other youngster are avid readers of fairy tale books, both possess the earthy realism and shrewd psychological insight of city children. Sammy knows what librarians are like and slyly suggests to this one that he is more deserving of the book than its present reader because "his hands ain't as clean as mine" (p. 69). When the librarian tries to suggest other types of books to Sammy, his brief, pungent answers reveal his attitude to his entire life. His disdainful verdict on adventure books is that " 'If a man finds a treasure in an adventure book, so right away it's with dollars and cents. Who cares from dollars and cents? I get enough of that in my house' " (p. 69). Likewise his opinion of fiction is "brief and pitying" (p. 69). He once read a fiction book which had "a hero with eyeglasses" (p. 69). In Sammy's words, " 'How could heroes be with eyeglasses? That's like my father!' " (p. 69). Sammy's harsh appraisal of heroes with glasses naturally makes the librarian place "her pince-nez a little more securely on her nose" (p. 69).

Giving up on the librarian, Sammy then moves to the boy in possession of the *Purple Fairy Book*. Sammy's first words to him startle the absorbed reader "like one jarred out of sleep." (p. 69). Interestingly, the comparison of the absorption in an imaginative world—the trancelike state of imagination—with sleep is one of the central motifs of Roth's novel and is reflected in the title, *Call It Sleep*. As David Schearl is frequently "sleeping" in *Call It Sleep,* so Sammy Farber and the other unnamed reader of fairy stories in "Somebody Always Grabs the Purple" wish to enter the timeless, magical realm of imagination.

What fairy tales must have meant to the ghetto child caught in a world of stark, loveless realities has been suggested by Michael Gold in his autobiographical novel *Jews Without Money:*

> Once my sister sat on the tenement stoop, reading the Blue Fairy Tale Book. This book was her treasure. It was a big beautiful edition with colored pictures that Harry had given her. She had copied many of those pictures with her crayons, and knew every story by heart. But she loved to read them again and again, her lips moving dreamily, as if she were singing to herself. She was reading now on the stoop,

> while the New York sun burned out above the tenements in glorious purple, amber, and rose.
>
> Esther was in her own world. The street whirled and clashed around her, the gray old solemn Jews went by, and gobbling [sic] mommas, and pimps, pushcarts, and rattling wagons. A scabby dog rummaged with its front paws in a garbage can. Three tough guys lounged nearby, and quarreled, and spat tobacco juice. The saloon was busy, the prostitutes were busy, the slum wretchedness was huge and triumphant. But Esther had escaped from it all. She was reading her book. The twilight fell on the white pages and illuminated her face.
>
> She looked up as I approached. I can still see the flushed little face, with its Jewish cheekbones, ardent mouth, and large eyes. She looked at me and did not see me. She was lost in the land of fairies and giants, where children talked familiarly with swans and lions, and sought enchanted castles beyond the mountains of glass.[8]

While Sammy and the other boy are "dreamers," anxious to be lost in the fairy tale world of "wonder and beguilement" (p. 70), both are also worldly-wise street children. Thus the other boy sees through all of Sammy's plots to wrest the book from him. Sammy tries shaming him about reading fairy tales and interesting him in adventure books or other volumes of fairy tales—ploys which adults have tried on him to no avail.

A. Sidney Knowles observed that "The story ends with the suggestion that Sammy intends to follow the boy home and get 'the Purple' one way or another." [9] Knowles apparently reached this conclusion because Sammy waits "until the boy had had time to get out of the reading room and down the stairs before he put his worn library card in his pocket and made for the exit" (p. 70). Although it is perhaps a minor point, this interpretation seems to me to suggest that Knowles missed the tone of the ending. Sammy's waiting is not caused by a plan to obtain the book through physical abuse, but rather by his last lingering hope that something, somehow, will cause the fairy tale book miraculously to fall into his hands.

"Petey and Yotsee and Mario," the third of the early New York City sketches, is also about childhood. Unlike either of the other earlier stories, "Petey" is written in first person in the form of a nostalgic memoir. The setting is geographically close to that of "Somebody Always Grabs the Purple," for "Petey" takes place at "the Harlem River at about 130th Street." [10] The reader's intuition that "Petey" is autobiographical is reinforced by the fact that the narrator (like Roth in his youth) is called "Fat." Additionally, the presence in the story of a younger sister corresponds to the facts of Roth's life. Through characters' names, as well as themes, "Petey" has direct links to *Call It Sleep*. In the novel, David is accosted by three gentile boys while "daydreaming" at the river. These gentile boys, one of whom is named Pedey and another Weasel, cruelly force David to push a sheet-zinc sword into the trolley tracks. In *Call It Sleep* their anti-Semitism is apparent: "with ominous eagerness" they observe that David's street is " a sheeny block" (p. 250). In "Petey and Yotsee and Mario" Pedey (here spelled Petey) and Weasel reappear, but it is the gentile boys' lack of anti-Semitism (or transcendence of it) that provides the theme of the story.

The story consists of three "scenes"—first, "Fat," the narrator, who is swimming in the Harlem River, is saved from drowning by the three boys named in the story's title. Later, Fat's mother decides to bake the boys a cake as a way of thanking them, despite Fat's protests that they will not like a "Jewish cake." Finally, after Fat's mother gives the cake to the boys, who eat it with gusto, she triumphantly explains how she knew the boys would like a Jewish cake.

Simple in structure and limited in scope, the story nonetheless has charm because of its success with small details. The opening of the story is effective in evoking a sense of time and place. When his gentile friends save Fat, the story could have lapsed into sentimentality, but Roth saves it by underlining the street boys' sarcasm, toughness, and biting humor. To Fat's comment, " 'Gee, I must have been drowning,' " Yotsee retorts sarcastically, " 'You wasn't drownin'. You was just fetchin' way down' " and Mario adds, " 'He wasn't drownin'. . . . He was just tryin' to dive to the bottom and run like hell for the shore!' " (p. 72).

In the second section of the story when Fat returns home and tells his mother and sister about his near-mishap, their reactions are swiftly and realistically discriminated. His mother piously blesses his saviors, but his sister says, " 'You're a dope to go out so far' " (p. 72). The contrast between Jewish and American culture is also sharply defined with comic effectiveness. Fat is sure that the gentile boys will not like a Jewish spice cake, which is "embossed with walnuts, dark with crystallized honey, and full of raisins," because it is unlike those of "Ward's, Tip-Top, and Golden Queen"—names which nicely capture a bit of Americana.

In the third section of the story, the focus moves to Fat's mother. As with Genya in *Call It Sleep,* we hear her verbal limitation in English, which contrasts with her sensibility. Although her English is broken, she expresses her thanks by her gestures and "between the lines," as it were. It is she who has the last enigmatic words of the story; she triumphantly tells Fat: " 'You were afraid they wouldn't like Jewish cake. What kind of people would they be if they didn't like Jewish cake? Would they even have saved you?' " (p. 74). Her meaning seems to be that if the boys had not liked the cake, their dislike would mean that they rejected everything Jewish, a priori. And if they disliked everything Jewish, in other words, were anti-Semitic, they would not have reacted to Fat as a person when he was drowning—their anti-Semitism would have precluded their saving him.

Interestingly, the boys' explanation of their rescue of Fat is based on another group-identification that provides a substitute for the religious one that separates them. In Mario's words, " 'Fat's—I mean, he's from the block' " (p. 74). This is another touch that reveals Roth's deftness in evoking early twentieth-century New York City life with its fierce geographical and religious loyalties.

The publication of "Petey and Yotsee and Mario" in 1956 seems to have ended a period in Roth's writing; it is the last of his stories to deal with either New York City or childhood.

It is difficult to distinguish between memoir and fiction in the two middle pieces, "At Times in Flight" and "The Dun Dakotas." Both are written in the first person, and in both pieces the narrator recounts events that parallel Roth's real life. Both contain an opening section of suggestive comments about the atmosphere of the Thirties followed by a seemingly autobiographical story or parable which probes the causes of Roth's artistic collapse after *Call It Sleep*.

"At Times in Flight: A Parable," which Knowles called "an impressive piece,"[11] opens with a description of "Z, the artists' colony"[12] (in reality, Yaddo, where Roth was invited in the summer of 1938). The narrator describes the world situation and his own more immediate one. In the background are the Spanish Civil War, the threat of World War, and "the Marxist mood," while at Z the summer residents "loafed or spent a great deal of time in frivolity and idle chatter" (p. 51). The narrator is alienated from all the other residents at Z except for Martha (a portrait of Roth's wife, Muriel, who attended Yaddo as a composer and musician). The general atmosphere at Z is superficial, "ingrown," and clever—the word "clever" is repeated sarcastically three times in one sentence describing the place.

After the opening descriptive section, the narrator proceeds to the parable itself which has two related symbols—the bubbling waters of Saratoga Springs and the tragic horse race. The meaning (or meanings) of these two symbols is provocative and ambiguous. The narrator explains that "ever since childhood I have regarded carbonated water as something of a treat. . . . And here it was free, and not only free but salutary" (p. 52). The waters seem to represent childhood, health, and closeness to nature—things which the narrator appreciates in contrast to the other artists at Z. The narrator's description of the other artists' disdainful rejection of his invitation to visit the spring emphasizes his difference from them—his simplicity versus their cleverness and facile sophistication. The fact that only "one person did reply in the affirmative," Martha, sets the two apart from the Z group.

Knowles remarked that "the trips to Saratoga Springs to the bubbling fountain . . . suggest a continuing attempt to reuse the experiences of childhood. It is a kind of escape; it comes easy, the waters are now 'free.' "[13] Thus Knowles interpreted the bubbling waters as Roth's inability to move from childhood materials to materials closer to his adult reality. This interpretation seems to belie the narrator's positive tone about the water: "She [Martha] liked the water; it shortly became apparent that she liked it as much as I did" (p. 52). Rather than suggesting "a kind of escape," the water seems quite positive in implication; it appears to embody, like Martha herself, "the most wholesome traditions" (p. 51) as opposed to the cynicism, worldliness, and sophistication of the other artists.

In describing his trip with Martha to the horse race, the narrator again underlines his alienation from his surroundings by saying that "The path was one not frequently trodden" and that their view of the track was from "a peculiar angle, one might say, to the normal" (p. 52).

Watching the race far from the grandstand, he and Martha see the horses and their riders as "tiny and remote figures," or "as though it were a race track in an Easter egg" (p. 53). However, as the horses and riders come toward the couple, "they were no longer toy horses and toy riders. They were very real and growing in reality every [sic] second" (p. 53). The narrator now sees "the utter seriousness of the thing, the supreme effort," and "the fierce and bitter competition" (p. 53). Suddenly one of the beautiful horses, who while working out "seemed at times in flight," topples, breaking his leg (p. 52). In answer to Martha's question about how the fall happened, the narrator says only, " 'Jolted I imagine' " (p. 53).

Subsequently the horse is shot and the narrator comments: "So that was the end? *Ars brevis, vita longa*" (p. 54). As Knowles suggested, "The horse race is life; the fallen horse is Roth's art."[14] In the narrator's words, "At Times in Flight" describes "a horse destroyed when the race became real" (p. 54). What precisely is meant by the "reality" of the race is not altogether clear. Knowles interpreted the bubbling water as Roth's desire to escape into childhood materials and suggested that Roth was unable to deal with more recent material; in Knowles' words, "As long as he [Roth] wrote about childhood, there was a certain comfortable distance between Roth and his material. It was an art not quite grounded in reality, like the horses in training and 'seemed at times in flight.' "[15] A more general or sociological interpretation of the horse race, however, seems closer to Roth's own suggestion, made in a biographical note attached to the piece, that the story projected "the inadequacy of a man's art in the face of modern realities." Part of the "reality" which destroyed Roth's art may have been the current political situation in 1938— the desperate reality of the Spanish Civil War, for example, as opposed to the make-believe atmosphere of Yaddo. In any case, the exact cause of the horse's "jolt" remains ambiguous.

What is clearer is the narrator's subsequent decision to pursue a new path with Martha as his guide; in the closing paragraph of the parable, he asserts that Martha has "a better sense of direction" than he has (p. 54). While his art lies dead behind him, ahead "lay a glade with a measure of sunlight" (p. 54).

Like "At Times in Flight," "The Dun Dakotas" bears directly on Roth's life and his failure to publish another novel after *Call It Sleep*. The narrator begins the piece by asserting that "there was something ruinous about the time"[16]—thus seeming to suggest that whatever caused his failure was both external and general. Nine years after the publication of "The Dun Dakotas," Roth again stressed the impersonal aspect of his unproductiveness after *Call It Sleep;* in an interview in 1969, he remarked,

> For a long time I thought that I was afflicted by some peculiar curse. But I have come to believe that there was something deeper and less personal in my misfortune, that what had happened to me was common to a whole generation of writers in the Thirties. One author after another, whether he was Gentile or Jewish, stopped writing, became repetitive, ran out of anything new to say or just plain died artistically.[17]

The second portion of "The Dun Dakotas" is "a story, a yarn" which the narrator says "concerns an expedition into the Dakotas, and more particularly concerns a prologue that I was engaged in writing for the second novel" (p. 108). The yarn about the expedition into the Dakotas is enigmatic and ambiguous. The group "crossing from the Bad Lands to the Black Hills" seems to represent Roth and his generation, who "had been commissioned to do a topographical study of their part of the country" (p. 108). This "topographical study" or writing was to cover the "gnarled terrain," presumably the "waste land" of T. S. Eliot. In other words, Roth's generation was to find a way around or through the impasse of the waste land vision.

In the yarn, the captain and the scout of the expedition are stopped by an Indian chief and his braves, who represent either external, political forces or internal, subconscious opposition to the progress of the expedition. Knowing no sure way to deal successfully with the hostile forces, the Scout is forced to gamble with the Chief. After the Chief wins all the Scout's money, the Scout asks if now the expedition can continue. The Chief does not answer; he simply "folded his arms across his chest and dreamed a long dream or a long thought" (p. 109). The "dreaming" of the Chief may suggest that the Chief represents some part of Roth's psyche, his imagination or subconscious, which blocked his progress for many years.

The narrator asserts that he waited twenty years for the Chief "to decide what history was in the dun Dakotas, waiting for a sanction" (p. 109). He adds that "oddly enough it would have to be the victim who would provide it [the sanction], though none could say who was the victim, who the victor" (p. 109). If the hostile forces are assumed to represent something external to Roth, the political or social chaos of the Thirties and World War II, then Roth seems to imply here that only those who were victimized, who suffered personally, could plot a course out of the waste land. The Indian Chief may also represent destructive subconscious forces which Roth had to work against for years.

Unlike "At Times in Flight," which concludes on a note of resignation to artistic collapse, "The Dun Dakotas" appears to close with guarded but undeniable optimism. The narrator ends the piece by saying "And now I can tell you [the meaning of what happened in the Thirties], and perhaps it's a good sign . . . though perhaps it's too late" (p. 109). The difference in attitude in the two parables is no doubt related to the reappearance of *Call It Sleep* in 1960—the same year that "The Dun Dakotas" was published. The artistic promise implied at the end of "The

Dun Dakotas" is at least partially fulfilled by Roth's two latest published stories.

"The Surveyor" is a rather long story (approximately 7,300 words) about an American couple, very much like Henry Roth and his wife, who are visiting Seville. Aaron Stigman, a Jew, is a "slight, middle-aged man" with "unruly gray hair."[18] His Protestant wife, Mary, is "also middle-aged, but taller and more slender than the man, with a gentle face and a high forehead." The opening section of the story describes the couple's intent and harried efforts to survey a site on the *Avenida del Cid* in Seville. While the two rapidly count off paces and adjust their instruments, a crowd of curious Spaniards gathers. What the American couple is doing is clear neither to the Spanish bystanders nor to the reader.

After the rushed surveying job, the Americans hurry away in a taxi and discuss their enigmatic actions together. Aaron asks whether the surveying was foolish or not: " 'Was it my passion for accuracy, do you think? Or am I turning into an absurd old man?' " (p 24). Mary replies, " 'No, I just think it's Seville. . . . Too many cathedrals, too many *retablos,* stained-glass windows, saints, crucifixes, Virgins' " (p. 24). In short, Spain is too full of objects of Catholic veneration, and even Mary's "Protestant mind" "rebels at it" (p. 24). This conversation is the first oblique indication in the story that the surveying has something to do with religion, but why the couple is surveying continues to be unclear.

Several hours later, Aaron and Mary return to the *Avenida del Cid* and deposit a wreath on the spot they surveyed earlier. Stigman realizes the futility of the gesture, since a gardener will probably move the wreath to the statue of *El Cid,* and he concludes tellingly, " 'There's little one can do against oblivion, anyway' " (p. 24). While the couple is discussing where to go next, a Spanish policeman stops and questions them. Ascertaining that they are the same couple he saw surveying earlier that day, he asks them about the meaning of their actions, is dissatisfied by Stigman's vague answer that he "tried to locate a place of some sentimental value" (p. 25) to himself, and escorts the couple along with the wreath to the police station.

At the police station, two men question the couple: one is a seated man with "a blue sweater and large tinted glasses"; the other man is "unusually tall for a Spaniard and the way he stood, in a stooped, hollow fashion, was even more uncommon" (p. 27). Moreover, "wincing and unwincing, the tall man's difficult face seemed to belong at times to two different individuals" (p. 27).

Although Stigman continues to refuse to explain exactly why he placed the wreath, beyond saying that it was for personal, sentimental reasons, the wincing man has the case dismissed and asks to accompany the couple for a drink. The couple stops with him in a little cafe where he discusses their mission with them. The lawyer—he turns out to be a state attorney—says that Stigman intrigues him, " 'that any man would be so—I hesitate to use the word—so naive' " (p 29). The lawyer goes on to explain that he knows that Stigman wanted to place the wreath on the *quemadero,* because that was where "heretics found guilty by the Holy Inquisition were burned—among others, relapsed *conversos,* those Catholics who secretly clung to their old Judaic faith" (p. 29).

Now it is Stigman's turn to question the Spaniard—how did he know where the *quemadero* stood, since it no longer even appears on maps of the city? The Spaniard says that his grandfather told him "that his father when he became very old, would light a candle on Friday nights" (p. 29)—in other words, would observe the Jewish Sabbath. This Jewish background is apparently what distinguishes the lawyer, with his wincing and unwincing face that "seemed to belong at times to two different individuals" from the "Spaniards with placid faces" (p. 29).

The Spanish lawyer sees the martyred heretics as "Spaniards who were also Jews" (p. 29), while Stigman objects that "it was the heroic constancy of Jews who were also Spaniards" (p. 29).

Ironically the two men are similar in their Jewish ancestors and interest in the Jewish past—and also in their non-observance. The lawyer lights only "a candle in consciousness" on Friday nights, while Stigman remarks that he "left the faith of my ancestors many years ago" (p. 30). In another ironic touch, it is Stigman's Protestant wife who offers the Jewish toast of *l'chaim* as the three drink cognac together before separating.

The final irony is that the Stigmans must find their way out of the Spanish *barrio* using "the Giralda, *la Fe,* the weathervane" (p. 30) for a guide. The Giralda or Faith "stood on her high pinnacle above the Cathedral, pointing at every wind with her palm branch of triumph" (p. 30). Despite being guided by Faith, Stigman finds when he reaches his hotel that he has forgotten the wreath in the cafe.

"The Surveyor," captivating as a story in itself, is made more so by its apparent revelation of Roth as a man, especially his continuing concern with what it means to be a Jew. The ironic combinations in "The Surveyor" of steadfastness and non-observance, faith and disbelief, memory and forgetfulness, reveal a man still puzzling over his multifaceted, ambiguous relationship to his religion. Written during the Roths' trip to Spain in 1965, "The Surveyor" reflects the rebirth of interest in Judaism Roth felt during this period. In his words, "Essentially what I was interested in, as I look back on it now, was trying to find my way back into something related to Judaism. It's like a blind force looking for an outlet." [19]

Like "The Surveyor," which has thematic connections with *Call It Sleep* and Roth's life, "Final Dwarf" is also noteworthy in these regards. But unlike "The Surveyor," which is generally mild and ironic in tone, Roth's latest published story is a savagely bitter account about the hostility between a middle-aged man and his aging father. The entire story takes place during a shopping trip, but during this brief period, subtly hostile action and retaliations between the two men reach an almost murderous level.

The story opens with the middle-aged man, Kestrel, completing his purchase in Sears of a pair of reading glasses he has ordered from a catalogue. Kestrel thinks, "At least fifteen bucks to the good . . . that's how much more the unholy alliance of opticians and the American Optical Society would have soaked him." [20] Delighted with his saving, he gives the clerk his new glasses to try on, but she returns them "with a rather bewildered expression" looking "as if she had been disturbed by what she had seen" (p. 57).

Kestrel returns happily to his car nonetheless and asks his father what his errands in town are, while thinking "it was always necessary to shield Pop from the idea that the trip to town was being made on his behalf. Otherwise he would balk at going, and then sulk" (p. 58).

In a "whimsical, placating drawl," (p. 58) Pop announces that he wants to go to two grocery stores—to one for his general marketing, and to the A&P for coffee. Sensing "an old ruse," (p. 58) Kestrel asks why Pop does not buy coffee in the first store; Kestrel knows that the reason is that the A&P "coffee was a cent cheaper than any other brand in town" (p. 58). One of the most biting aspects of "Final Dwarf" is that while Kestrel triumphantly gloats over saving money by purchasing mail-order glasses, he is continually enraged by his father's cheapness.

Pop reluctantly decides to do all his shopping at the A&P, and Kestrel seems to relent from his unpleasant thoughts about his father's "usual guile" (p. 58). Kestrel drops his father off at the A&P, saying " 'I've got plenty of time. So shop for everything you need.' " (p. 58). Just then Kestrel remembers that he needs a freezer lock, and the hardware store where he wishes to look for one is in the shopping plaza right next to "the

First National where Pop had wanted to stop" (p. 58). Kestrel runs to the hardware store and rushes back, so that Pop will not observe "his son's breach of faith" (p. 58). After a few snide remarks to Kestrel about the A&P trading stamps, Pop announces that he wants to go to Arlene's for "a few day-old cookies" (p. 58) which are sold for half-price and then to Russell's Hardware Store. As Kestrel drives off, Pop notices that the A&P had a special on hamburger he missed; Pop tells Kestrel he missed the special because he did not have enough time to look around. Kestrel becomes enraged at the accusation that he rushed his father, and his anger is heightened by his father's speech about the price of chicken "in your state" as opposed to New York.

With his rage rising, Kestrel tries unsuccessfully to get Pop to fasten his seat belt, and then drives to Arlene's. When Kestrel passes up a tight parking space in front of the store, saying " 'Too many cars behind me. I didn't want to hold up traffic,' " Pop bitterly mutters " 'For them you got consideration' " (p. 59). Furiously, Kestrel thinks that since childhood, "he could never do anything to please his father" (p. 59). But then he is able to control his temper with the self-satisfied, patronizing thought that "It was ridiculous to bear a grudge against the old guy. There was nothing left of him. A little dwarf in a baggy pair of pants. *The final dwarf*" (p. 59). At this thought, Kestrel smiles.

Pop retaliates for Kestrel's parking by returning empty-handed and saying that there was only one salesgirl and many customers, again implying that Kestrel is impatient. When his son reacts against this unspoken accusation, Pop remarks with "disabling mockery," " 'So you'll be home a few minutes later to your wife. She won't miss you' " (p. 59).

The bitter rancor and sly innuendos about saving time and money continue throughout the shopping trip. Finally, enroute home, Pop begins a new and more savage attack. He announces that he is glad about the assassination of the Kennedys, because " 'There's where the mugging and the robbing started. Only Kennedys. *Noo,* sure, they [the blacks] know a President is their friend. So whatever they do, he'll say: Nebich! It's a pity! So they rape . . . so they rob, so they mug, so they loot' " (p. 60).

Again Kestrel's fury rises; it shows itself in his futile insistence that his father put on his seat belt. Thinking of deliberately having a wreck to kill his father, Kestrel peers in the rear view mirror and finds his own face there, "forbidding and ominous against the empty highway" (p. 61).

Pop dismisses Kestrel's remark that " 'Nobody is the cause. . . . Nobody in particular. All of us,' " with a sarcastic " 'You and the other *philosophes'* " (p. 61). Finally Pop reaches his most wildly infuriating point by asserting to Kestrel " 'You'll be just like me in a few years. Just wait. All I'm saying you'll say' " (p. 61). That is, Kestrel too will become the final dwarf his father is. Having made his last and most painful verbal attack, Pop asks to see Kestrel's new glasses. Looking through them, Pop recoils, saying " 'You're going right into the stone wall' " (p. 61). The story ends with Kestrel feeling "shriveled," (p. 61) already one step closer perhaps to being "a little dwarf in baggy pants." And with his son's glasses on, Pop (like the salesgirl in the opening scene) has seen something of Kestrel's vision: the last thing Pop does is to grope "beside him for the seat-belt buckles" (p. 61).

The brilliance of this savage story depends largely on the complex connections between the images of the final dwarf and Kestrel's glasses. The final dwarf image first appears in the story's epigraph from Wallace Stevens: " '. . . the final dwarf of you/That is woven and woven and waiting to be worn. . . .' " Kestrel's primary defense against his father's insinuations and accusations is to attempt to feel superior to him by picturing the old man as "a little old dwarf in a baggy pair of pants." Thus when his father assures Kestrel that only a few years separate them, that in time Kestrel will come to see things his father's way, Kestrel is forced to see himself as "shriveled" into a pathetic dwarf.

The Stevens quotation is particularly interesting in that it uses a "weaving" image Roth himself frequently uses. For example, in *Call It Sleep,* Roth writes that Luter's questions to David intrude "like a false weave into the fabric and pattern of his thought" (p. 30). Similarly, Roth describes David's awakening the morning after his sexual initiation with Annie: "One by one the shuttles stirred, awoke, knit morning to night, night to evening" (p. 56). In "The Dun Dakotas" Roth again uses this evocative image to describe the movement of the mind and life itself: "The mind shuttles and rewinds. We go this way only once; and shuttles again and rejoins; once is enough" (p. 108).

As the final dwarf image involves the transposition of selves, so do the glasses. Wearing Kestrel's glasses, the old man sees through Kestrel's eyes. What he sees is an image of Kestrel's murderous fantasy, the magnified approach of the stone wall. The double transformation of father to son and son to father achieved by the two central images is extremely effective. The successful employment of these organizing devices serves as proof of Roth's skill in the short story.

Asked whether the murderously hostile relationship between Kestrel and Pop reflected his adult relationship with his own father, Roth observed, "This is a relationship that could not be resolved—and will not be resolved in my lifetime." Although "not very" autobiographical, "Final Dwarf," in Roth's words, "seems to me sort of prophetic, because to me it meant the shrinking of the liberal. The retreat of the liberal from his own position. Oddly enough what Pop was seeing was what he then saw." [21]

Although none of Roth's short pieces are of the same caliber as *Call It Sleep,* they are of literary interest. All are well written and effective minor works. Moreover, they have considerable variety in subject matter, themes, and tone. The three early New York sketches demonstrate Roth's ability to capture the precise flavor of life in the city—the sounds and styles of its inhabitants. The two middle pieces probe aspects of Roth's life in the Thirties and remain suggestive and provocative even while they "explain." The latest stories, which focus on two of the author's lifelong concerns—his relationships to Judaism and to his father—show Roth once again successfully transmuting his life into significant art.

NOTES

[1] "If We Had Bacon," *Signatures: Work in Progress,* 1, No. 2 (1936), 140. Subsequent references are noted in the text by page number.

[2] William Freedman, "Henry Roth and the Redemptive Imagination," in *The Thirties: Fiction, Poetry, Drama,* ed. Warren French (Deland, Florida: Everett/Edwards, 1967), p. 108.

[3] I learned of the existence of "Broker" through correspondence with Dr. Howard B. Gotlieb, Chief of Special Collections at the Mugar Memorial Library.

[4] Henry Roth, "Broker," *The New Yorker,* 15 (18 Nov. 1939), 45. Subsequent references to the story are noted in the text by page number.

[5] Appendix, p. 306.

[6] Henry Roth, "Somebody Always Grabs the Purple," *The New Yorker,* 16 (23 March 1940), 69. Subsequent references to the story are noted in the text by page number.

[7] Appendix, p. 293.

[8] Michael Gold, *Jews Without Money* (New York: Horace Liveright, 1930), pp. 375-76.

[9] A. Sidney Knowles, Jr., "The Fiction of Henry Roth," *MFS,* 11 (Winter 1965-66), 400.

[10] Henry Roth, "Petey and Yotsee and Mario," *The New Yorker,* 32 (14 July 1956), 70. Subsequent references to the story are noted in the text by page number.

[11] Knowles, p. 401.

[12] Henry Roth, "At Times in Flight," *Commentary,* 29 (July 1959), 51. Subsequent references to the story are noted in the text by page number.

[13] Knowles, p. 402.

[14] Knowles, p. 402.

[15] Knowles, p. 402.

[16] Henry Roth, "The Dun Dakotas," *Commentary,* 30 (August, 1960), 107. Subsequent references to the story are noted in the text by page number.

[17] David Bronsen, "A Conversation with Henry Roth," *Partisan Review,* 36 (1969), 274.

[18] Henry Roth, "The Surveyor," *The New Yorker,* 42 (6 Aug. 1966), 22. Subsequent references to the story are noted in the text by page number.

[19] Appendix, p. 308.

[20] Henry Roth, "The Final Dwarf," *The Atlantic,* 224 (July 1969), 57. Subsequent references to the story are noted in the text by page number.

[21] Appendix, p. 307.

CONCLUSION

Henry Roth is a writer of striking interest. The extraordinary twists and turns of his life, his many careers—precision tool grinder, teacher, state hospital attendant, waterfowl farmer—and his equally bumpy publishing history—an overlooked first short story, an unknown novel fragment, a novel reissued with remarkable acclaim after twenty-six years of virtual neglect—arouse curiosity like an unpaved country road.

This interest in the man and his career is, fortunately, a good path into his work. Roth's life—his experiences and reflections—is the raw material of his fiction. He is like a painter who repeatedly draws the scenes around his home, not because they are the most beautiful, but because he knows them best. Paradoxically, Roth handles this subjective material with such artistic detachment that he creates an impression of stark objectivity.

It is difficult to assess the value of Roth's total production. While it is undeniable that so far Roth is a one-novel writer, that novel is an extraordinary achievement. It is also true that he has shown considerable literary ability in other work. His seven published short stories and his novel fragment, "If We Had Bacon," reveal some of Roth's most characteristic talents: his ability to evoke a precise scene, to establish characters, to capture the sound and texture of the speaking voice.

In the afterword of the paperback edition, Walter Allen remarked that "to have written *Call It Sleep* is itself enough to make any man's reputation."[1] Clearly Roth's reputation (at least to date) must rest on this major work. The beauty and intricacy of the novel establish Roth's claim to a more central position in modern American literature than he has thus far been accorded. While some of the most influential contemporary critics have called the novel a "neglected masterpiece," a "classic," and "one of the few genuinely distinguished novels written by a 20th-century Ameri-

[1] Walter Allen, "Afterword," *Call It Sleep* (New York: Avon Books, 1964), p. 447.

can," *Call It Sleep* has yet to receive the *close* scrutiny and praise it deserves.

The central theme, the search for redemption or mystical transfiguration, is universal, and the delicacy and artistry with which Roth develops his material grow ever more apparent the more the novel is studied. The intricate symbolic structure, complex motifs, wide variety of narrative techniques, and archetypal initiation patterns combine with realistic detail, rounded characters, convincing dialect, and exciting plot to produce a novel with the compression and intensity of poetry: *Call It Sleep* is still an underrated modern American classic.

APPENDIX

An Interview with Henry Roth

The following interview was conducted on October 17 and 18, 1972, in a charming adobe motel near the Roths' home in Albuquerque. Self-deprecating and ironic, Roth says that this will be his last interview, since he wants neither to be a legend in his own time nor to repeat himself.

Interviewer: How would you describe your relationship to your parents and sister in early life?

Roth: My sister almost doesn't come into the picture for a number of reasons. Primarily because I was that much of an egotist as a child or young man. I so continually monopolized my mother's affection that I regarded myself as the one and only child around—with the exception of my father. My sister was his favorite. That I would say is a thumbnail sketch—with all its Freudian meanings.

Interviewer: Can you describe the process that goes into making a real person into a fictional character?

Roth: In my own case, I try to hold the real person in front of myself as clearly as I can and then abstract the necessary actions and qualities in a given situation which I pose. I try to think what this person has said in a similar situation—and if I can't use it, then I have to make it up. I hate to do that—and I have to most of the time.

Interviewer: Did your own mother form the basis of Genya, David Schearl's mother, in *Call It Sleep?*

Roth: In that case, I decided my mother had two sides: one was the sensitive, noble person, Genya. The other was like Aunt Bertha in the novel. All I had to do was remember Mom in her contemplative moments and she was Genya; in her irritation, anxieties, and angers she was Bertha.

Interviewer: Is David Schearl a self-portrait of you as a child?

Roth: At the time I wrote *Call It Sleep* I thought I was honestly portraying my childhood—I think this is one of the things which gives the novel its strength. Now I think I wasn't really portraying myself at all: the child is much too innocent, almost completely victimized, passive. It was simply an idealization based on the notion that I was a much finer sensibility than what was around me—so fine that I was being persecuted and victimized. With my own maturing, I've come to see the child as much more active, not victimized but on the contrary doing his own share of victimizing, having admirable traits, but some faults. This attitude is undoubtedly one of the things that prevented me from writing anything else, because I had to disentangle, to uproot attitudes I had to myself.

Interviewer: How about the picture of Albert, David's father? Was your father like that?

Roth: Albert originally started off as my father. But in order to maintain the integrity of this idealized child, to focus the novel, I had to change the father just as I had to eliminate the sister. I had to increase his magnitude and dimension; I had to fictionalize a character not based on the petty, little man my real father was. Actually, coming back to your question about developing characters out of real people, I don't know who the hell I thought of when I wrote about Albert!

Interviewer: What was your relationship to Eda Lou Walton like?

Roth: I lived with Eda Lou from about my senior year in college until 1938, a ten year period. I came to know her through a friend with whom I went to high school. He was a very, very handsome middle class boy—polished, worldly, well-groomed—why he latched on to *me* is still a bit of a mystery. Anyhow, he was a predental student at NYU, where Eda Lou was a professor of English. She was his freshman English teacher and had just formed a club for aspiring writers; I met her at one of these meetings. He became the club secretary, and they had an affair. Now this says something about this woman: she was thirty and an instructor and he was a freshman of eighteen—what her insecurity and neurosis were, I found out in time, in terms of my living with her. During their relationship, I would tag along. I would be invited—and while they spooned, I read. God, I just felt like a toad! Their affair was very shortlived, and her insecurity led her to any number of affairs, almost promiscuity, but not quite.

Meanwhile, one peculiar thing happened my freshman year at City College. I was given this assignment in English to write about some experiment or how to construct something. The previous summer, 1924, I had been a plumber's helper, installing pipes in new buildings in the Bronx. So I decided to write on how to install piping. And suddenly it turned into an impressionistic piece. Toward the end of the semester, the instructor announced that one of our themes was so good that he would recommend it for publication in the City College *Lavender*. When he mentioned my name, I almost died—and yet again, I wasn't *too* surprised. It was printed in the *Lavender,* and was the first intimation that I had something special. And I got a D in the course.

Interviewer: On what basis did you get a D?

Roth: I didn't do what I was supposed to do: an expositional piece of work. I can't blame the instructor. So I got a D in English my first semester; the next term I got an A. My whole college career was like that, full of these incredible see-saws. And having known this friend and Eda Lou, my original aim or vector to become a biology teacher, or maybe a zoologist, shifted to becoming a writer.

Interviewer: Was Eda Lou politically active in these years?

Roth: After the 30s. I graduated in '28 and started writing in '29. At that time we were all under the influence of the critics and writers of the late 20s: art for art's sake, apolitical, in fact antipolitical. And that had its momentum—or inertia—into the 30s, the mid-30s for her. It was not until '35 or '36 that she became really active politically. Up 'til then, she bitterly opposed my premature politicalization, oh yes! When I became a member of the Communist Party in about '33, she thought it was my finish as a writer. And in some ways she was right. It was a serious shift for which I was not prepared emotionally or mentally. You might say it was a sentimental thing. As far as my whole artistic or creative way of thinking, it didn't go in patterns of class or class struggle. What I was trying to do was Procrustean, trying to force life into this class polarity, and it didn't work.

Interviewer: Did your relationship with Eda Lou—and the fact that she was older and non-Jewish—estrange you from your family?

Roth: The estrangement took place first. Like so many first generation American Jewish youth, I had already come to dissociate from family, Judaism, the whole thing—and to embrace the American scene, the new American attitudes. My mother knew about our relationship, and I think she approved. She wanted *somebody* to take care of me!

Interviewer: What kind of circle did you and Eda Lou move in? Were you in some sort of literary group?

Roth: Well, there were a number of people who had distinction in

American letters, and some from other fields. Eda Lou's Ph.D. was in anthropology; her dissertation was about Navajo dance rhythms and poetic forms. As an anthropologist, she came in contact with Margaret Mead, Ruth Benedict, Constance Rourke. They'd drop in around once a month. While studying at Berkeley, Eda Lou had been writing verse and was in Witter Bynner's poetry writing class. Later she published some free translations of Navajo poetry as well as her own poetry. Besides the anthropologists, people like Hart Crane and Léonie Adams would appear from time to time.

Interviewer: Do you feel that you gained from any of your contemporaries or shared any literary experiences?

Roth: No, that was the problem. I was very hermetic, I mean hermitic. Part of it was the nature of my material. I didn't make the intellectual transition or connection; I couldn't bridge my background. I was able to speak glibly enough at the cocktail party level, but as far as *digesting* what was going on, especially in the literary world, it just did not sink in. My whole orientation was to try to understand my own childhood, my own background. Had I gone on after *Call It Sleep* to write about the transition of the youth into the world of American literature, into the literary, intellectual world, I might have made the transition.

Interviewer: Can you describe what happened after *Call It Sleep?*

Roth: I finished *Call It Sleep* in the winter of '33 when I was exactly 27 years old. The main reason I think I didn't go on was that I didn't mature. In *Call It Sleep* I stuck with the child, so I didn't have to mature. And I was being supported by Eda Lou, so I didn't have to mature. I think I just failed at maturity, at adulthood.

Interviewer: Can you describe your break-up with Eda Lou?

Roth: When I left, it was a real rupture. I really felt that in writing I wasn't getting anywhere—but I really don't think that had anything to do with it—so much as that I felt this kind of decay going on in myself. I was a dependent person; it was a real continuation of infancy to be supported by a woman so long. More and more I felt that I was collapsing inside myself. I probably would have gone on indefinitely, except that in the summer of 1938 I went to Yaddo, where I met Muriel [Roth's wife], who had been invited as a composer. It was hardly a romantic love affair. I feel that Muriel just retrieved me in time. I don't think I would have lived very long; I just didn't feel like it. I think that one of the reasons I joined the Communist Party was to feel that I was doing something to redeem myself, but I wasn't—because it was not the kind of thing I could function in. I'm just not built to be a revolutionary.

Interviewer: Do you think that in joining the Communist Party you tried to replace the communal sense you felt as a child on the East Side?

Roth: Yes, but that's a bankruptcy. I think that's the reason why so many of us—especially so many Jews—in the 30s headed that way—because we lacked the larger thing with which to identify. We were all seeking for a re-entry into the people as a whole. And for a while we thought we could do it irrespective of Judaism. It was a much larger re-integration—a wonderful idea—but it doesn't work that way. It seems to work via some national identification first as stage one, if you wish, in the total unification of the human race. But we thought you could storm the heavens—we thought you could walk right into paradise. But like Dante you have to go around and around in these terrible circles, through purgatories, before you can get to the rest of it.

Interviewer: There seems to have been a simultaneity about the break with Eda Lou, the break with the Communist Party, and your artistic problems after *Call It Sleep*. In retrospect, do you now see any order, or pattern, or cause and effect to these things?

Roth: One could almost put the break with Eda Lou and the artistic problem either in parallel or tandem. I can't really say. I know the two things did go together in some kind of simultaneous fashion. They were very intimately linked: my literary frustration and this feeling of just rotting away in dependency upon her—although she herself was as generous as it's possible for anybody to be. I had anything I wanted. And that probably was exactly wrong. So I don't know if I can answer that question.

Interviewer: But the split with Communism preceded both these things?

Roth: Oh, yes, that happened earlier. Incidentally, the break was not an ideological break, it was a party break: I didn't have the courage to maintain myself as a member of the Communist Party. That's how it seemed to me: that I was cravenly ducking out. In my own self-defense I might say that I just didn't see how I could fit into this dynamic, objective, antimeditative, activist business. But ideologically I still felt that the proletarian revolution was the necessary step for establishing a just society. I felt a great deal of suspicion of Stalin; in fact, I wrote in my diary that if the revolution ever came to power, I was finished. I knew that with all my sensibilities and subjectivities I would just never survive, yet I wanted it to come to power.

Interviewer: Do you have any other thoughts or ideas about what happened after *Call It Sleep?*

Roth: This is one of the things I've pondered on since about 1938 or '39—since I first realized I was completely frustrated, about the time of my separation from Eda Lou. She probably represented the opportunity to be creative, and I could not exploit the opportunity. By 1939 I felt that I was finished as a literary person. I was certain that the divorce was permanent—as permanent as my divorce from Eda Lou. I interpret it as a matter of maturity; I had not grown up enough to be able to deal with adult problems in a creative way. I apparently belong to that category of writers who has to write about the stages of his own development. And then when he does it he is ready to go on to the next stage. There was probably a point there at which I should have dealt with adolescent problems. Since I didn't go on after *Call It Sleep,* it apparently would indicate that I didn't develop.

It's only now that I'm past 60 that I feel mature. I'll tell you a peculiar thing: at least until I was 50, if you asked me who was the identity that I called to mind, who represented me, I would have said the youth—although the mirror told me quite otherwise.

Interviewer: How did Eda Lou react to your break-up?

Roth: She was very, very seriously upset when we separated, and she was very bitter.

Interviewer: Did you have a single break or did you go back and forth?

Roth: It was a single break. I went back for clothes and things like that. And I went back to try to explain. It didn't do much good—at least with her. Some people try to maintain a little more rationality. Eda Lou was extremely generous but also extremely possessive. There *is* that combination. In fact, some people are generous in order to *be* possessive. On the other hand, I should stress the fact that I could not have written *Call It Sleep* without her generosity. Most of *Call It Sleep* was written in the early '30s—during a period of profound economic depression. This country was in the midst of the most violent, profound depression this country or any country has ever experienced—there were breadlines without end, soup lines, people living in hovels, shacks made out of tin and cardboard, and literally scrounging out an existence from garbage cans. And my being comfortably situated during all that period—I've been talking about guilt and anxiety—you can see how this would accentuate it. I was so well taken care of, even to the extent of having a studio and having all the time at my disposal for writing, rewriting, experimenting, wiping out experiments. None of that would have been possible without Eda Lou Walton's assistance. And that's just one phase of it. I could go on and say that *Call It Sleep* is the result of a number of very favorable circumstances: for example, I could not have written it at a later stage because my own development would have canceled or negated my conviction—as later developments show. Also I would have started to forget. So that everything had to be more or less at that particular time. And I needed that kind of encouragement and steady affection because I didn't show the novel to anybody until it was done—I wasn't sure of it.

Interviewer: Did you have any trouble selling *Call It Sleep* after you finished it?

Roth: It was sent to several publishers and some of the more important people. I remember Harcourt, Brace kept it for quite awhile and then said regretfully they didn't think this type of material would have much market or audience at this particular time—and they were right. This was 1934, and people were very much interested in novels or studies having to do with society; everyone was now searching and groping for some new way of attacking this problem or some new solution for our ills. This is what people wanted to know—and *Call It Sleep* was anything but that. The publishing question brings up another coincidence or intersection of circumstances. David Mandel, who later married Eda Lou, was her lover simultaneously when I was living with her. I knew about it, and so it became a kind of *ménage à trois*. This probably didn't help my ego either, even though I said "What else can I do" at the moment. It also seems to me an indication of a moral breakdown—not in the sense of puritanism—but of moral fiber, character. Now to come back: Mandel bought into Ballou Publishing Company. He and Eda Lou had already begun this liaison, and she influenced him to get *Call It Sleep* published.

Interviewer: How would you describe Eda Lou's character?

Roth: Eda Lou mothered, initiated, and otherwise befriended young writers, poets, and artists. You might say that she would take on these people who needed strong maternal affection, because she herself had a strong maternal urge. Now that's all very well up to a certain stage, but to continue beyond that stage becomes very bad. And I continued too long. I remember that in 1932, when I was living in Maine and was almost 2/3 of the way through with *Call It Sleep,* Eda Lou wrote and said that she had met this interesting man in New York. I remember writing back that if she had finally found an adult who would take care of her, she ought to go ahead and marry him. I *thought* I was being very self-abnegating. But actually what I was doing was blindly trying to rescue myself. I was near to finishing the novel—it was the time to turn me loose, on my own, to experience the world around me. You can see that with someone protecting me while I'm writing about childhood on the East Side, I really don't need to experience much more. I've got enough material. But when that's done, I should be turned loose—but I wasn't. And I didn't have the character to turn myself loose.

Interviewer: Was Eda Lou a healthy person?

Roth: From the '30s on and even perhaps in the late '20s she was beginning to get increasing pain, discomfort from her whole intestinal tract. I think she developed bad colitis, all of which would indicate a highly nervous person. I don't think she had any other health problems, except her intestinal problems which kept getting steadily worse. On the other hand, she consumed more and more alcohol as time went on. Maybe again this was counteractive to the neuroticism which expressed itself in her extreme intestinal discomfort.

Interviewer: Did you see or hear from her after your separation?

Roth: I last saw her in 1943 or so, before leaving New York. The meeting was relaxed and friendly. I never saw her again. She wrote and I made no effort. Well, there's no justification for it—just simply a complete collapse of the whole literary impulse and the desire to eliminate everything connected with it.

Interviewer: During the time you were associated with the Communist Party did you think of "art as a weapon" or any of those other slogans?

Roth: I tried to, but I couldn't see it.

Interviewer: Some critics have discussed *Call It Sleep* as a proletarian novel. Do you feel it has any connection?

Roth: I never felt that way—life never illuminated itself to me in terms of class struggle. It was just some sort of blob that went in all directions at once. *Call It Sleep* did not illustrate or reflect the massive class struggle that was going on at the time. If the novel exalted anything, it exalted human beings, not the proletariat. The Party itself panned the novel when it was published, not knowing that I had just joined.

Interviewer: *Call It Sleep* seems too excellent to be a first novel. Had you written anything previously?

Roth: Just that little essay that was published in the *Lavender,* which I mentioned before. I started the novel in the summer of '29. Eda Lou had been invited to this art colony, Peterborough. She took me along. I was deposited in this inn nearby and started writing *Call It Sleep.* The opening chapters were straight autobiographical first person. I suppose I had some gift for writing already, but my God! The novel was actually the product of its own process. I learned to write a novel by writing it. As I went along, I would see what it needed and what I was doing wrong.

Interviewer: Did you have any method of construction?

Roth: I started out in the first person and slavishly kept to the facts for about 75 pages. In the meantime, other fancies, ideas, and notions were taking hold of me—but they weren't true. Finally the conflict between my fantasizing or fictionalizing and actuality became so strong that I had to stop. The victory was ultimately won by my fabricating side, because I stopped right there and spent the next two weeks outlining what I suppose the novel became. I outlined all kinds of things; for example, that's when I split Mama into two people and Pa had to take on much greater magnitude. I outlined in little blue examination booklets; in fact, I wrote the whole novel by hand in them—that was one thing there was in great plenty in Eda Lou's apartment. Besides being plentiful, the blue booklets were good because after you finish one of these eight page jobs you have a feeling of accomplishment!

Interviewer: Did you have the whole plot outlined in the blue booklets?

Roth: I began by outlining what the chapters would be about; then as time went on, I elaborated on them, and wrote in between the pages. And then I elaborated on *that,* and wrote in between. In the end, it was some sort of graphology—I had written in every conceivable space. Sometimes I just wanted to replace one word with another. Essentially I outlined the entire plot, adding variations that came up in time. But I never dreamed I was going to finish still in the childhood of the character. In fact in the back of my mind I sometimes even think of myself as having done part of the adolescence already. The ending of *Call It Sleep* came as sort of an artistic accession or an assumption into artistry. The whole process of development of the writer took place in *Call It Sleep*—starting from just an autobiography to a self-conscious literary person.

Interviewer: Did the four book structure, "The Cellar," "The Picture," "The Coal," and "The Rail" develop as you were writing, or was that part of the original plot outline?

Roth: I'm not sure whether I had already envisaged the four basic sections or whether that was part of the whole process of development. As I developed into a conscious literary artist *that* reflected back on the structure: the development of the person led to the restructuring of the material. I think that if a person with any kind of gift for reflection concentrates on a problem long enough, the problem is bound to yield certain illuminations about itself. One of my main virtues is tenaciousness; I will not give up a problem.

Interviewer: Did you have any ideas about the novel as a form or vehicle when you started out?

Roth: I'd read uncritically but voluminously. Anything that had a narrative had immediate appeal. Any kind of damn yarn immediately affected me. I started off with fairy tales at about age ten. I think the only reason I got off fairy tales was that I once picked up *Huckleberry Finn* by mistake. I remember that as one of my great transitions, from fairy tales to more realistic fiction. "The Ancient Mariner" was another wonderful formative influence and a revelation. My reading went all the way from fairy tales to people like Twain and Jack London, to playwrights and Hugo, all the way to Eliot and Joyce.

Interviewer: Several critics have talked about the poetic qualities of *Call It Sleep* and consider it almost in terms of being a poem. Could you comment?

Roth: It's not a novel in the sense of various ideas coming into conflict. I was probably playing to my own strength. In sticking to the child and patterning the world around him, I was able to use all my lyrical impulses. And therefore the whole texture of the novel is like that of a long poem or metaphor. At the same time I had all the freedom of prose. When I think of novelists like Bellow or Philip Roth, social commentary seems to be the most important aspect of their books. In *Call It Sleep,* social commentary was anything *but.* What *was* important was the sensuous world that kind of flowed and the subjective reaction to this sensuous world.

Interviewer: You've mentioned elsewhere that you had read *Ulysses* as a freshman and that you thought it had a great influence on you. Can you elaborate on what exactly you think you gained from Joyce?

Roth: What I gained was this awed realization that you didn't have to go anywhere at all except around the corner to flesh out a literary work of art—given some kind of vision, of course. In stream of consciousness I recognized that my own continual dialogue with myself could be made into literature. It was a tremendous impetus toward writing.

Interviewer: Some critics have mentioned that the "Nighttown" episode seems to have influenced the electrocution scene of *Call It Sleep* in the exploration of the unconscious mind and the counterpointing of voices.

Roth: Well, it's hard to point to any special place in *Ulysses* that had a particular influence. Certain people—and I'm one of them—make extensions and applications to themselves almost unconsciously.

Interviewer: At the time you were writing *Call It Sleep,* how conscious were you of Freud and psychology?

Roth: I was aware only in a diffuse, general cultural way. I heard about these ideas and terms in my literary, intellectual group but never went to the discipline of studying it myself.

Interviewer: Had you read any Jewish mysticism or anything about mysticism in general?

Roth: The only particularly Jewish things I read were all read in translation in English—novelists and playwrights like Sholem Asch. What may have happened was that sometime in early childhood some relative would spin a yarn about a rabbi or somebody with some powers or other. So that by the time I began to write, this would be a subconscious reserve or reservoir. *Consciously,* I was already faced in opposition to things Jewish.

Interviewer: How about mythology?

Roth: Mythology itself I read as part of the whole fairy tale sequence. Later on I read both Eliot's *Waste Land* and *The Golden Bough*—I don't remember which came first.

Interviewer: How much of the mythological material of *Call It Sleep* was consciously developed?

Roth: I did very little of it consciously. What would happen is that while writing I would think of some particular point I could make that would heighten the novel's effect. In the process, I would sometimes get an insight into the fact that this had a mythological overtone. And that was very satisfying. But if the addition did not contribute to the general flow of the narrative, whether it had mythological overtones or not, I wouldn't have included it. I will say that this is a cardinal rule or guide: the primary thing had to be its potential for heightening the narrative flow.

Interviewer: How about the motifs in *Call It Sleep* that seem to come to a climax when David is knocked unconscious?

Roth: I think the motifs were conscious—I think I felt the *need* of them. When you speak about the evolution of the form and the recognition of the individual—how to achieve form in the course of a long work like that—this is one of the things that I recognized that I needed. Really it gives added interior structure. Again that's a Joycean thing. During the time I was writing, especially toward the end, the whole novel was in my consciousness at once. I thought of it musically—that's how I really felt about it. My attitude was what a musician must feel about his composition.

Interviewer: Chapter xxi, the climactic chapter, seems to be the most experimental in form. Besides the fact that this chapter is an effective climax to the novel, do you think that the experimental writing in it indicates the direction your work was moving in?

Roth: I had the feeling that this was going to be my forte: that by using a kaleidoscopic or montage effect I could build up a picture of any society or city. *Now* it seems to me that up until that point I had written a fairly cohesive, formally recognizable novel. And then I ruptured the whole envelope of the novel—because I left the child and wandered all over the city. It's as though I tired of the tight, compact structure of the novel and burst the envelope—take it for what it's worth.

Interviewer: Elsewhere you've said, "The impressionable boy living in hostile surroundings adopts as his own a destructive act to which he is instigated by outsiders to whom he has no personal relationship." My question is: doesn't David transform that destructive act into a positive act?

Roth: He's applying it, but I don't know just in what sense he applies it. The first time he's a victim of a destructive force, then he uses it. I don't know how you interpret *his* doing it within the context of the novel, but for the *novelist* it has a peculiar meaning—and maybe only in retrospect. The meaning it has for the novelist is a short circuit. It seems too farfetched that he should have already intuitively realized that his own career was going to suffer this kind of short circuit. And yet how well the fable speaks of the rest of the man's history—it did become the metaphor of himself. But how did one know at the time what was going to follow—now there's really something worth pondering. At the time I thought this was a beautiful symbol of power destroying—what? The child was symbolically destroyed although he lived on. Something was destroyed in him, I don't know exactly what—perhaps his flights of fancy, the artist in him, perhaps it was childhood.

Interviewer: But the vision was positive.

Roth: Well, in the process apocalyptic, yes, okay. But in the process something went and something was gained, true. He does feel a sense of triumph. I don't know what he feels triumphant about. At this stage of the game, if you ask me, I can't tell you. The only thing that I think he feels triumphant about (aside from the fact that *I* felt triumphant that I was finishing the novel!) was that for one brief second he was able to summon something up that unified the world. But the same time, in the process of doing that, he couldn't do it scot-free. He paid a price. And maybe the unification attained that way is again a storming of the heavens. It is not the way a true unification is attained. By a slow laborious development one gets there, but not all at once in mortal splendor.

Interviewer: Leslie Fiedler has said that David's gesture is a "failed sacrifice," and that "his intended sacrifice redeems no one. The boy does not die, the world is not made clean." Although the world is not purified, doesn't David have a private, internal transformation?

Roth: Well, I think so.

Interviewer: Even though he has to return to the "fallen world"?

Roth: I think that accounts for his triumph. Perhaps the triumph is really in the intent. The sense of triumph he feels in the end was that he made the attempt, even though it is a failure. Everybody goes back to his mundane and sordid and squalid life. But there is something even in a wrong attempt of this kind, an attempt to purify or better the world. Even if it does not succeed, the martyr cannot be deprived of the feeling that he made the attempt—even if he shows that this is wrong, that this is not the way to do it. Somebody has actually got to do it, so that the next guy who comes along knows that this is the wrong way to go about it. I'm trying to say why the child feels some sort of triumph at the end. He's obviously established that his way is not the right way. Great satisfaction. Now he stirred something up for a moment, that's the way it is psychologically for the child. I mean it's valid psychologically. He did stir up an entire community for one second. I think that probably accounts for a good deal of modern vandalism—you want to stir something up for one minute.

Interviewer: In the "street voices" of chapter xxi there are many echoes of Christian motifs. Did you include this material to widen the focus or to give a more general focus?

Roth: I think it all had to do with this streak of mysticism I felt. You know how people have floating anxiety? Well, I had floating mysticism. Probably to assuage my anxieties. I picked here, there, and everywhere. Somebody says something about a whore-master—well, actually what I was thinking of was ahura mazdah, who is the god of light in Persian religion or Zoroastrianism. I punned away. Having had someone like Joyce do it, it's more than even a stimulation, it's a permissiveness.

Interviewer: Your relationship to Judaism seems to have gone through a number of stages. Could you discuss these changing attitudes?

Roth: One crucial event was that in 1914 my family moved from the East Side to Harlem. My grandparents had come to America and settled in Harlem and my mother wanted to be near her family, so the transference took place. Now in cheder I was just on the verge of entering the stage of translation when my family moved. But when we moved, I wanted to adapt to this gentile Irish neighborhood in the shortest time possible; and one of the conditions for adapting was to get away from Judaism. Now had I taken the step of learning to translate, this would have riveted me to Judaism much more strongly at this sensitive hinge place. After the break, the mystical urge was still there, but it could no longer fix on Judaism and it developed into a sort of pantheism.

Interviewer: In a 1963 colloquium in *Midstream* about Judaism and the American Jew, you said that the best thing that Jews could do at this time was "orienting themselves toward ceasing to be Jews." Would you maintain that position now?

Roth: I've thought about that statement many times because it shows how definitely one can be in a certain phase or stage. I'm glad I made it though I probably wouldn't make that kind of statement again the rest of my life. At that time, I thought that assimilation was the only way out for the Jews; I couldn't conceive of any other solution. The Six-Day War changed my whole way of thinking. I still don't have any great attachment to Diaspora Judaism. And I don't think of myself as a Zionist exactly—but I think of myself as a partisan of a country. It's like a regeneration process when a person like me can think of patriotism and valor.

Interviewer: Do you have any feelings of connection with the Jewish people historically?

Roth: I really know very little about Jewish history, and it is no great passion, whereas the Israeli state *is* a passion with me: a real profound identification with a people in the making, in the process of becoming a people again from the shadows we were.

Interviewer: Can you talk a bit about the two other novels you began after *Call It Sleep?*

Roth: About mid-1935 after the trauma of *Call It Sleep* had worn off, I began to get the itch to write again. Now here is where the Party must have had its influence—because I now felt that I wanted to break away from an extension of the immigrant East Side Jewish child and do somebody from the American middle west. Now suppose I hadn't known anything about the Party—I probably would have done the adolescent years, perhaps taking it as far as meeting Eda Lou or consciousness of artistic abilities. Instead, I broke away and was going to do the proletariat, right out of the American scene. I did know such an individual who provided me with material and a kind of model—this ties in with what I said about how I develop characters. I wrote about 100 or 125 pages and submitted them to Scribner's. The famous Maxwell Perkins paid an advance to David Mandel, who was a partner in Ballou [the publishers of *Call It Sleep*]. So it was all set. This is the irony: as soon as they accepted the first section, I didn't want to write any more. Here again there are delicate problems all interwoven. There was no necessity upon me to do any more; I was being supported. If they hadn't accepted it or if I had been a poor guy and they said: "Finish another section and you get another $1000," I probably would have knuckled down. But with no necessity, I just fooled around. Then, having failed to finish *that* novel, I tried to do the adolescence. But this failure was crucial—my will was gone, broken by this first failure.

Interviewer: You actually destroyed what you had done?

Roth: Yes, when I went to Maine in 1946. I was convinced that my whole literary career was over. After all I was a nonentity—*Call It Sleep* just disappeared. I felt my whole literary past no longer had any bearing on *me*. So why keep the stuff. And also the '50s were approaching and the terror was beginning to fall on all. [At this point Roth looked nervously around the room and out the window.] You see my reaction? I still look around.

Interviewer: And the third novel—the one that was to deal with your adolescence?

Roth: I finished around 40 or 50 pages—I destroyed that as well. And it's too bad because I can remember some of it vividly, which means that it had something. I destroyed them both in Maine—it seemed like I was just carrying around a lot of baggage. During the war I had been a precision metal grinder and then in 1946, when the war was over, we moved to Maine—which was probably a mistake. It was partly for the kids' sake; I had two boys, and one of them developed a very bad stammer. It seemed that going to the country was a good idea. Besides I wanted to get away—away from a world I had completely failed in.

Interviewer: Was the move a conscious rejection of that kind of world or more a practical decision?

Roth: I think as much consciousness as I was capable of existed in the rejection of that world. You can only go on feeling failure so long—it's a very destructive thing. So you try to put a term to this destruction by—what do the kids call it?—copping out. I had no idea that that's what I was doing—but that's what it comes down to. When you say *consciously*

—I was consciously trying to get out away from a terrific failure, a terrific frustration.

Interviewer: Do you consider *Call It Sleep* a Jewish novel?

Roth: No, because I just used whatever background or material was available to me, and this was it. I did not use a Jewish background to illustrate Jewish life *per se.* I used it to fulfill certain of my own compulsions.

Interviewer: Do you have any explanation of why *Call It Sleep* has re-emerged with such success?

Roth: It costs 95 cents! Seriously, I think it's something about the time—it seems to have an affinity for the apocalyptic—and there is something apocalyptic about *Call It Sleep.* It may also have something to do with the disappearance of a pattern in American life: there's no more East Side, no more Jewish ghetto. Then I suppose, one can flatter oneself and say that the novel has real artistic stature.

Interviewer: Did you read the Bible after you became an atheist at fourteen?

Roth: Yes, I read it in college—I enjoyed it tremendously as a piece of literature.

Interviewer: How did you choose the story about Isaiah's purification with God's coal that is so central to *Call It Sleep?*

Roth: Well, that's a very peculiar thing—it's almost unaccountable. I left cheder at eight and I wasn't yet translating—so I didn't know what portions were read when. But like Picasso—I knew what I needed. I wanted this purification, it was a necessary symbol—so I put it in. Then having done so, I went to the Hebrew Theological Institute and asked the rabbi when they would read this. Well, he told me that this would be the selection for the week—isn't that amazing? For that very week, that's what they would be reading. So by some kind of divine inspiration I chose exactly the right thing, the right passage. I really feel foolish, because this sounds kind of crazy. You've heard people disavow their own ingenuity or talent? Well, this is the way I feel at this particular moment. I'm disavowing something to show how genuinely inspired I was—now let's drop all the rest of it. I picked it because it was what I wanted for "The Coal" section.

Interviewer: I'd like to ask a few questions about the short stories. Your first published story, "Broker" [*The New Yorker,* November 18, 1939] has a Negro for a main character. Is there any special significance to the unautobiographical focus?

Roth: I wrote the story when my relationship with Eda Lou was over. I was now independent, *alas*. I had to find a way of making a living and this was the only thing I knew how to do. I probably could have made it as a short story writer if I had just persisted. But again, this didn't have anything to do with my own development. And this apparently was the only thing that mattered. Anyhow I happened to see an incident like the one in the story and I could spin it out, embroider.

Interviewer: In "Petey and Yotsee and Mario" [*The New Yorker,* July 14, 1956] the three boys appear to be the same boys as the gentile boys in *Call It Sleep* who force David to put the sword into the trolley tracks. Does the fact that the boys are anti-Semitic in the novel and not in the story reflect any change in your attitude?

Roth: Yes, I'm sure it does. Because in the interim, my soul had been scrubbed by Marxism-Leninism and the new look about the proletariat. And I think justifiably, after all. I had lots wrong with me to justify antagonism, if not anti-Semitism—kids like everybody else just look for the first handle they can grab. The attitude that I changed—and this was the most difficult one to transform—was from the feeling of being victimized to one where I saw that I was as much to blame, as much an active agent as a passive agent.

Interviewer: In "Final Dwarf" [*The Atlantic,* July, 1969] the relationship between Kestrel and his father seems murderously hostile. Do you think that reflects your adult relationship with your father?

Roth: This was a relationship that could not be resolved—and will not be resolved in my lifetime. And that's all there is to it.

Interviewer: How autobiographical is the story?

Roth: Not very, but I'll tell you a funny thing. It seems to me sort of prophetic, because to me it meant the shrinking of the liberal. The retreat of the liberal from his own position without his knowing it. Oddly enough, what Pop was seeing was what he then saw.

Interviewer: After the initial success of the paperback edition of *Call It Sleep* you said that you thought you would use some of the money for travel and that your travel would be connected with your work. Has it worked out that way?

Roth: This is interesting—how peculiarly, how concealed, how obscure the individual's drives are from himself. In other words, how hidden they are from himself. This identification I now have for Israel—it didn't develop in a straight line. In 1965 when I was in Seville I felt this strong urge to do something about the Inquisition. What I finally got out of it was "The Surveyor" [*The New Yorker,* August 6, 1966]. But essentially what I was interested in, as I look back on it now, was trying to find my way back into something related to Judaism. It's like a blind force looking for an outlet.

Interviewer: About your present life: do you prefer the Southwest to Maine?

Roth: I just wish I'd come sooner—you can get out more and it's cheerier. In New England, those long, long winters really aid and abet depression. You know, the New Englander and his dour ways.

Interviewer: Can you talk a little about your recent work and plans?

Roth: Until about a year and a half ago, I was writing a kind of "continuum" journal—what someone called "awarenesses." These "awarenesses" were reminiscences and observations about my surroundings—and I had written a pile of them, notebooks at least a foot high. Then about a year and a half ago, I began to write something that was a continuity, also in the past, and with this I became more and more curious. First I tried to write it as a play—then I thought it's about time that you acknowledged that one goes on in an art. You don't just break away into a different form—you use the techniques you have developed even if they are a bit rusty. And that's what I'm doing now. It's essentially an account of the entrance of the young man into consciousness of a literary impulse, a desire to create great art. It brings to bear the peculiar, separate, and yet distinctly related world of the Jews in Harlem—that's the parental, Jewish world—and the world of Greenwich Village and the literary intellectuals. The individual about whom I'm writing is a young man who slowly becomes conscious of his literary tendencies. He is the nexus between the two worlds that never met. He simply carries it back and forth like a shuttle. Quite recently, I think that I've stumbled on this remarkable kind of an idea, a remarkable point of view or attitude. I hope the whole thing can live up to the point of view or attitude. So I shall finish this particular draft and then go back to it. And God knows what will happen.

BIBLIOGRAPHY

WORKS BY HENRY ROTH

Roth, Henry. "At Times in Flight: A Parable." *Commentary*, 29 (July 1959), 51-54.

———. "After *Call It Sleep*." *American Literature*, 45 (Jan. 1974), 610–612.

———. "'Broker': An Overlooked Story by Henry Roth." *SSF*, 10 (Winter 1973), 97–98.

———. "Broker." *The New Yorker*, 15 (18 Nov. 1939), 45-48.

———. *Call It Sleep*. Paterson, N. J.: Pageant Books, 1960. This edition contains the essays by Harold U. Ribalow, Maxwell Geismar, and Meyer Levin cited in the footnotes.

———. *Call It Sleep*. New York: Avon Books, 1964. This edition contains the afterword by Walter Allen cited in the footnotes.

———. "The Dun Dakotas." *Commentary*, 30 (Aug. 1960), 107-109.

———. "Equipment for Pennies." *The Magazine for Ducks and Geese*, Fall 1954, pp. 15-16.

———. "Final Dwarf." *The Atlantic*, 224 (July 1969), 57-61.

———. "An Interview with Henry Roth." *Shenandoah*, 25 (Fall 1973), 48–71.

———. "Impressions of a Plumber." *The Lavender*, May 1925, pp. 5-9.

———. "If We Had Bacon." *Signatures: Work in Progress*, 1, No. 2 (1936), 139-158.

———. "The Meaning of *Galut* in America Today: A Symposium." *Midstream*, 19 (March 1963), 32-33.

———. "Petey and Yotsee and Mario." *The New Yorker*, 32 (14 July 1956), 70-74.

———. "Somebody Always Grabs the Purple." *The New Yorker*, 16 (23 March 1940), 69-70.

———. "The Surveyor." *The New Yorker*, 42 (6 Aug. 1966), 22-30.

———. Unpublished and Miscellaneous Writings. Henry Roth Collection, Mugar Memorial Library of Boston University. The Collection contains the letters, postcards, papers, and a tape recording of the WFAU interview cited in the footnotes.

———. "Roth's *Call It Sleep*." *The Explicator,* 33 (Oct. 1974), item 10.

———. "The Symbolic Structure of Henry Roth's *Call It Sleep*." *Contemporary Literature,* 13 (Spring 1972), 186–203.

OTHER WORKS CONSULTED

Aaron, Daniel. *Writers on the Left: Episodes in American Literary Communism.* New York: Harcourt, Brace and World, 1961.

Allen, Walter. *The Modern Novel in Britain and the United States.* New York: Dutton, 1965.

———. "Two Neglected American Novelists," *The London Magazine* 2 (May 1962), 77-84.

Alter, Robert. *After the Tradition: Essays on Modern Jewish Writing.* New York: Dutton, 1969.

Angoff, Charles and Levin, Meyer, eds. *The Rise of American Jewish Literature: An Anthology of Selections from the Major Novels.* New York: Simon and Schuster, 1970.

Belitt, Ben. "E. L. W.: A Homage." *New Mexico Quarterly,* 33 (Autumn 1963), 266-271.

Bodkin, Maud. *Archetypal Patterns in Poetry.* London: Oxford Univ. Press, 1934.

Booth, Wayne C. *The Rhetoric of Fiction.* Chicago: Univ. of Chicago Press, 1961.

Bowling, Lawrence Edward. "What Is the Stream of Consciousness Technique?" *PMLA,* 65 (June 1950), 333-345.

Boynton, H. W. "The Story of a Ghetto Boyhood." *The New York Times Book Review,* 17 Feb. 1935, p. 7.

Bronsen, David. "A Conversation with Henry Roth." *Partisan Review,* 36, (1969), 265-280.

"Brief Review." *New Masses,* 14 (12 Feb. 1935), 27.

Brother, Alvah C. "Bourgeois-Critical Exploitation." *New Masses,* 14 (26 Feb. 1935), 21.

Brown, E. K. *Rhythm in the Novel.* Toronto: Univ. of Toronto Press, 1950.

Broydé, Isaac. "Isaiah." The Jewish Encyclopedia, 1904.

Burke, Kenneth. "More About Roth's *Call It Sleep*." *New Masses,* 14 (26 Feb. 1935), 21.

Buttenwieser, Moses. "Messiah." *The Jewish Encyclopedia,* 1904.

Cahan, Abraham. *The Rise of David Levinsky.* New York: Harper and Brothers, 1917.

Cantwell, Robert. *The Land of Plenty.* Carbondale and Edwardsville: Southern Illinois Univ. Press, 1971.

Crane, R[onald] S. "The Concept of Plot and the Plot of *Tom Jones*." *Critics and Criticism: Ancient and Modern.* Ed. R. S. Crane. Chicago: Univ. of Chicago Press, 1952.

Dahlberg, Edward. *Bottom Dogs.* London: G. P. Putnam's Sons, 1929.

Deutsch, Gotthard. "Haggadah Shel Pesah." *The Jewish Encyclopedia.* 1904.
Dos Passos, John. *U.S.A.* New York: The Modern Library, 1937.
Edel, Leon. *The Modern Psychological Novel.* New York: Grosset and Dunlap, 1955.
Eliade, Mircea. *Rites and Symbols of Initiation: The Mysteries of Birth and Rebirth.* Trans. Willard R. Trask. New York: Harper & Row, 1965.
Eliot, T. S. *"Ulysses,* Order, and Myth." *The Dial,* 75 (1923), 480-483.
Farrell, James T. *Studs Lonigan: A Trilogy.* New York: Vanguard Press, 1935.
Fiedler, Leslie A. "Because I Am a Man of Unclean Lips." *The Griffin.* Oct. 1960, pp. 10-16.
———. "Henry Roth's Neglected Masterpiece." *Commentary,* 30 (August 1960), 102-107.
———. *The Jew in the American Novel.* New York: Herzl Institute Pamphlet No. 10, 1959.
———. "Neglected Books." *The American Scholar,* 25 (Autumn 1956), 486.
Frankel, Haskel. "Awake at Last." *Saturday Review,* 47 (21 Nov. 1964), 29.
Freedman, William. "Henry Roth and the Redemptive Imagination." *The Thirties: Fiction, Poetry, Drama.* Ed. Warren French. Deland, Fla.: Everett/Edwards, 1967, 107-114.
———. "The Literary Motif: A Definition and Evaluation." *Novel,* 4 (Winter 1971), 123-131.
Friedman, Alan. "The Stream of Conscience [sic] as a Form in Fiction." *Hudson Review,* 17 (Winter 1964-65), 537-546.
Friedman, Melvin. *Stream of Consciousness: A Study in Literary Method.* New Haven: Yale Univ. Press, 1955.
Frye, Northrop. "The Archetypes of Literature." *Myth and Literature: Contemporary Theory and Practice.* Ed. John B. Vickery. Lincoln: Univ. of Nebraska Press, 1966, 87-97.
Fuchs, Daniel. *Homage to Blenholt.* New York: Vanguard Press, 1936.
———. *Low Company.* New York: Vanguard Press, 1937.
———. *Summer In Williamsburg.* New York: Vanguard Press, 1934.
Geismar, Maxwell. "Critical Introduction." *Call It Sleep,* Paterson, N. J.: Pageant Books, 1960, xxxvi-xlv.
Gold, Michael. *Jews without Money.* New York: Horace Liveright, 1930.
Greenhood, David. "Eda Lou Walton's Use of Her Native Scene." *New Mexico Quarterly,* 33 (Autumn 1963), 253-265.
———. "Another View of *Call It Sleep.*" *New Masses,* 14 (19 Feb. 1935), 20.
Gross, John. *Jame Joyce.* New York: The Viking Press, 1970.
Guttmann, Allen. *The Jewish Writer in America: Assimilation and the Crisis of Identity.* New York: Oxford Univ. Press, 1971.
Harrington, Michael. *The Other America: Poverty in the United States.* Baltimore: Penguin, 1962.
Heilman, Robert B. "The Possessed Artist and the Ailing Soul." *Canadian Literature,* No. 8 (Spring 1961), pp. 7-16.

Hicks, Granville, et. al., eds. *Proletarian Literature in the United States: An Anthology*. New York: International Publishers, 1935.

Hoffman, Frederick J. *Freudianism and the Literary Mind*. Baton Rouge: Louisiana State Univ. Press. 1957.

Hoffman, Frederick J., et al. *The Little Magazine: A History and Bibliography*. Princeton: Princeton Univ. Press, 1947.

Howard, Jane. "The Belated Success of Henry Roth." *Life*, 53 (8 Jan. 1965) 75-76.

Howe, Irving. "Life Never Let Up." *The New York Times Book Review*, 25 Oct. 1964, pp. 1, 60-61.

Humphrey, Robert. *Stream of Consciousness in the Modern Novel*. Berkeley and Los Angeles: Univ. of California Press, 1954.

Kazin, Alfred. *On Native Grounds: An Interpretation of Modern American Prose Literature*. Garden City, N. J.: Doubleday, 1956.

———. "Neglected Books." *The American Scholar*, 25 (Autumn 1956), 478.

Kempton, Murray. *Part of Our Time*. New York: Simon and Schuster, 1955.

Klein, Marcus. *After Alienation: American Novels at Mid-Century*. Cleveland and New York: World Publishing Co., 1962.

Knowles, A. Sidney Jr. "The Fiction of Henry Roth." *MFS*, 11 (Winter 1965-1966), 393-404.

Kohut, George Alexander. "Had Gadya." *The Jewish Encyclopedia*, 1904.

Kumar, Shiv K. *Bergson and the Stream of Consciousness Novel*. Glasgow and London: Blackie and Son, 1962.

Langer, Suzanne K. *Philosophic Sketches*. Baltimore: Johns Hopkins Univ. Press, 1962.

Ledbetter, Kenneth. "Henry Roth's *Call It Sleep:* The Revival of a Proletarian Novel." *TCL*, 12 (Oct. 1966), 123-130.

Lesser, Simon O. *Fiction and the Unconscious*. Boston: Beacon Press, 1957.

Levin, Harry. *James Joyce: A Critical Introduction*. Norfolk: New Directions, 1941.

———. *Symbolism and Fiction*. Charlottesville: Univ. of Virginia Press, 1956.

Liptzin, Solomon. *The Jew in American Literature*. New York: Bloch, 1966.

Lyons, Bonnie. " 'Broker': An Overlooked Story by Henry Roth." *SSF*, 10 (Winter 1973), 97–98.

———. "The Symbolic Structure of Henry Roth's *Call It Sleep*." *Contemporary Literature*, 13 (Spring 1972), 186–203.

MacGregor, Martha. "The Week in Books." *New York Post*, 8 Nov. 1964, p. 47.

Mack, Maynard. "Introduction." *Joseph Andrews*. New York: Holt, Rinehart, and Winston, 1961, vii-xvi.

Malin, Irving. *Jews and Americans*. Carbondale and Edwardsville: Southern Illinois Univ. Press, 1965.

Marsh, Fred T. "A Great Novel about Manhattan Boyhood." *New York Herald Tribune Books*, 17 Feb. 1935, p. 6.

Matthiessen, F. O. *American Renaissance: Art and Expression in the Age of Emerson and Whitman*. London, Oxford, and New York: Oxford Univ. Press, 1961.

Mudrick, Marvin. "Character and Event in Fiction." *Yale Review,* 50 (Dec. 1960), 202-218.

Murray, Henry A. *Myth and Mythmaking.* New York: George Braziller, 1960.

Nelson, Kenneth. "A Religious Metaphor." *Reconstructionist,* 31, No. 15 (1965), 7-17.

Ornitz, S. B. *Haunch Paunch and Jowl: An Anonymous Autobiography.* New York: Boni and Liveright, 1923.

Peter, John. "Joyce and the Novel." *Kenyon Review,* 18 (Autumn 1956), 619-632.

Pinsker, Sanford. "The Re-Awakening of Henry Roth's *Call It Sleep.*" *Jewish Social Studies,* 28 (July 1966), 148-158.

———. *The Schlemiel as Metaphor: Studies in the Yiddish and American Jewish Novel.* Carbondale and Edwardsville: Southern Illinois Univ. Press, 1971.

Pugh, David G. "Reading the Proletarians—Thirty Years Later." *The Thirties: Fiction, Poetry, Drama.* Ed. Warren French. Deland, Fla.: Everett/Edwards, 1967, 89-95.

Rahv, Philip. "Proletarian Literature: A Political Autopsy." *Southern Review,* 4 (1939), 616-628.

———. "Introduction." *A Malamud Reader.* New York: Farrar, Straus and Giroux, 1967, 7-14.

Ribalow, Harold U. "The History of Henry Roth and *Call It Sleep.*" *Call It Sleep.* Paterson, N. J.: Pageant Books, 1960, xi-xxxv.

———. "Henry Roth and His Novel *Call It Sleep.*" WSCL, 3 (Fall 1962), 5-14.

Rideout, Walter B. " 'O Workers' Revolution . . . The True Messiah': The Jew as Author and Subject in the American Jewish Novel." *American Jewish Archives,* 11 (Oct. 1959), 157-75.

———. *The Radical Novel in the United States 1900-1954.* Cambridge: Harvard Univ. Press, 1956.

Rosten, Leo. *The Joys of Yiddish.* New York: Pocket Books, 1970.

Schauss, Hayyim. *Guide to Jewish Holy Days: History and Observance.* Trans. Samuel Jaffe. New York: Schocken, 1962.

Scholem, Gershom G. *Major Trends in Jewish Mysticism.* London: Thames and Hudson, 1955.

Scholes, Robert, ed. *Approaches to the Novel: Materials for a Poetics.* San Francisco: Chandler Publishing Co., 1961.

Seaver, Edwin. "Caesar or Nothing." *New Masses,* 14 (5 March 1935), 21.

Slote, Bernice, ed. *Myth and Symbol: Critical Approaches and Applications.* Lincoln: Univ. of Nebraska Press, 1963.

Swados, Harvey, ed. *The American Writer and the Great Depression.* Indianapolis: Bobbs-Merrill, 1966.

Syrkin, Marie. "Revival of a Classic." *Midstream,* 7 (Winter 1961), 89-93.

Tindall, William York. *The Literary Symbol.* Bloomington: Indiana Univ. Press, 1955.

Tonnelat, E. "Teutonic Mythology—Germany and Scandanavia." *New Larousse Encyclopedia of Mythology,* 1968.

Trilling, Lionel. "Manners, Morals, and the Novel." *Approaches to the Novel: Materials for a Poetics.* Ed. Robert Scholes. San Francisco: Chandler Publishing Co., 1961, 231-246.

Vickery, John B., ed. *Myth and Literature: Contemporary Theory and Practice.* Lincoln, Univ. of Nebraska Press, 1966.

Walton, Eda Lou. "The Scene in Books Today." *Signatures: Work in Progress,* 1, No. 1 (1936), n. pag.

———. Unpublished Writings. Eda Lou Walton Collection, Bancroft Library, Univ. of California, Berkeley.

West, Nathanael. *Complete Works.* New York: Farrar, Straus and Cudahy, 1957.

Wheelwright, Philip. *The Burning Fountain: A Study in the Language of Symbolism.* Bloomington: Indiana Univ. Press, 1954.

Wisse, Ruth. *The Schlemiel as Modern Hero.* Chicago: Univ. of Chicago Press, 1971.

Wren, Paul. "Boy in the Ghetto." *The New Republic,* 82 (27 Feb. 1935), 82.